*Sponsored by*
The Consortium for Policy Research
in Education

Rutgers, the State University of New Jersey
University of Southern California
Harvard University
Michigan State University
Stanford University
University of Wisconsin, Madison

*Funded by*

The Office of Educational Research and Improvement, U.S. Department of Education, under cooperative agreement numbers R117G10007 and R117G10039

# DECENTRALIZATION AND SCHOOL IMPROVEMENT

Jane Hannaway
Martin Carnoy
Editors

# DECENTRALIZATION AND SCHOOL IMPROVEMENT

## CAN WE FULFILL the PROMISE?

Jossey-Bass Publishers · San Francisco

Substantial discounts on bulk quantities of Jossey-Bass books are available to corporations, professional associations, and other organizations. For details and discount information, contact the special sales department at Jossey-Bass Inc., Publishers. (415) 433-1740; Fax (415) 433-0499.

For sales outside the United States, contact Maxwell Macmillan International Publishing Group, 866 Third Avenue, New York, New York 10022.

Manufactured in the United States of America

10% POST CONSUMER WASTE

The paper used in this book is acid-free and meets the State of California requirements for recycled paper (50 percent recycled waste, including 10 percent postconsumer waste), which are the strictest guidelines for recycled paper currently in use in the United States.

The ink in this book is either soy- or vegetable-based and during the printing process emits fewer than half the volatile organic compounds (VOCs) emitted by petroleum-based ink.

---

**Library of Congress Cataloging-in-Publication Data**

Decentralization and school improvement : can we fulfill the promise? / Jane Hannaway, Martin Carnoy, editors. — 1st ed.
p. cm.—(The Jossey-Bass education series)
Papers based on a seminar sponsored by the Consortium for Policy Research in Education.
Includes bibliographical references and index.
ISBN 1-55542-505-4 (alk. paper)
1. Schools—United States-Decentralization. 2. School management and organization—United States. 3. Educational change—United States. I. Hannaway, Jane. II. Carnoy, Martin. III. Series.
LB2862.D427 1993
371.2'009773—dc20 92-29938
CIP

---

FIRST EDITION
*HB Printing* 10 9 8 7 6 5 4 3 2 1 *Code 9309*

The Jossey-Bass Education Series

# Contents

# Preface

Many analysts now argue that a structural overhaul—typically, some form of decentralization—is necessary to improve education in the United States. A decade of tinkering with the current system has produced only disappointing results, and business as usual is just not good enough. In this book we consider the possible merits and limitations associated with decentralization reforms in American education.

We began our analysis by organizing a Forum on Decentralization in Education under the sponsorship of the Consortium for Policy Research in Education (CPRE). We invited twenty scholars and practitioners from industry and education to spend two days with us at Stanford University, where we posed several key questions: Do decentralization reforms hold real promise for American education? Is there a relationship between the structure of the system and its performance? What can we learn from history? from other industries? from other public sectors? from other countries? What risks do decentralization reforms entail? From this discussion we identified topics and authors, and CPRE sponsored a smaller seminar in Washington, D.C., where the contributors to this book presented draft papers. Our discussions considered theoretical models, case studies, and comparative analyses of other sectors and other countries. Our central concern throughout was the likely effects of decentralizing school governance (that is, shifting decision making to lower levels in the system) on educational practice. The chapters in *Decentralization and School Improvement* reflect that concern. We consider system-level decentralization (decentralizing decision making from national to local jurisdictions), organization-level decentralization (decentralizing decision making from central authorities to school-level actors), and market decentralization (decentralizing decision making to parents).

Two major themes emerge in the book. The first (Chapters One through Four) is that governance reforms in education may have little to do with what actually happens in schools but have much to do with external political conditions. A number of the contributors to this book argue that centralization-decentralization debates reflect inevitable, cyclical, unresolvable tensions and contradictions in society and that the connection between these tensions and school performance is weak at best. The second (Chapters Five through Eight) is that decentralized decision making may indeed have important effects on schools but that standard theoretical arguments are not very helpful in explaining why. Extensions and modifications of these arguments are necessary for understanding decentralization effects, and only with this fuller understanding can we develop effective educational systems.

## Overview of Contents

The first chapter, by David Tyack, takes a historical look at governance reforms in the United States and suggests that the outlook for improving classroom practice with decentralization reforms is bleak. Tyack describes the cycles of centralization and decentralization debates from the days of the one-room schoolhouse until now. Noting a number of anomalies, he observes that arguments for greater centralization in one period of reform turn out to be the same arguments for greater decentralization in the next period. The reformers of the Progressive Era, for example, argued for greater central administrative control in order to enhance efficiency; reformers today seek greater school-level control, and less administrative control, for the very same reason. As Tyack puts it, "One period's common sense becomes a delusion in the next." No matter how education has been governed, Tyack contends, little has changed in the classroom. A second observation that Tyack makes is often overlooked by policy analysts: nongovernmental forces affect education in significant ways. For example, textbook publishers and ideologies about teaching practice may produce more homogeneity across classrooms in the United States than central directives could ever hope to yield. Thus, the system may behave as if it were highly centralized even with decentralization reforms in governance.

Chapter Two, by Richard F. Elmore, develops reasoning similar to that of Tyack. Elmore argues that decentralization debates are cyclical and reactionary and that governance structures have little effect on the efficiency, accountability, or effectiveness of school systems. Elmore argues that governance debates are about "*who* should have access to and influence over decisions, not about *what* the content and practice of teaching and learning should be or *how* to change those things." The political nature of the debate results in administrative outcomes that embody contradictions and ambiguities concerning the intended beneficiaries, the identification of the responsible parties, and the bases on which the system is to be evaluated. Largely as a consequence of these ambiguities, governance in education is not tightly coupled to educational practice.

Chapter Three, by Hans N. Weiler, is written from the point of view of the state and attempts to explain why centralization-decentralization governance debates are endemic to modern societies. Weiler argues that the modern state has two basic but contradictory interests: maintaining control and sustaining its own legitimacy. The persistent tension between these interests is evident in debates about centralization and decentralization, especially under conditions of conflict. Centralization promotes control; decentralization promotes legitimacy. Under conditions of conflict, decentralization is an attractive instrument of both conflict management and "compensatory legitimation," but it also results in some loss of control for the state. As a consequence, Weiler argues, "policies of decentralizing the governance of educational systems carry the seeds of their own contradictions." Rhetoric about decentralization is to be expected, but the state's interest in control is likely to limit the extent of any real decentralization.

In contrast to Weiler, Dan A. Lewis, in Chapter Four, sees decentralization, particularly forms of decentralization that rely on market mechanisms, as undermining the legitimacy of the state by legitimizing the privatization of services. Lewis claims that justification for reforms is typically advanced in terms of the *problem* being addressed—in the case of decentralization, the problem is defined as an institutional one—and not in terms of the *effects* that the reform itself is likely to produce. He analyzes current decentralization debates in education through the lens of deinstitutionalization reforms in mental health. Lewis concludes that if decentralization reforms in education are similar, they will have devastating effects for the poor.

Donald R. Winkler, in Chapter Five, lays out the expected advantages and disadvantages associated with *ideal* models of fiscal decentralization. He then compares those models with existing practice in developing and developed countries. He concentrates his analysis on four countries—Australia, the United States, Brazil, and Chile—that have distinctly different organizational arrangements. Most arguments for decentralization assume that its benefits derive largely from the nature of the accountability pressures it produces; Winkler's analysis suggests that the connection between decentralization and accountability is often problematic and depends on a number of other conditions. Thus, the advantages that decentralization is typically expected to yield are also problematic.

Jane Hannaway's analysis, in Chapter Six, questions the appropriateness of standard arguments for organizational decentralization in education. The standard arguments claim that organizational efficiency is enhanced when the actors with the best information about a particular area have the discretion to act on that information. These arguments certainly make sense, and many reformers use this reasoning to argue for more decision-making authority for teachers. Hannaway contends that teachers already have very high levels of discretion. Using the results of two case studies of reputedly successful decentralized school districts, she concludes that the behavior of teachers in successful decentralized districts is in fact more controlled than that of teachers in traditionally organized educational settings. Teachers have less, not more discretion. The controls, however, are social controls, rather than bureaucratic ones. The controls are also infused with technical demands that direct teachers' attention to well-defined areas directly concerned with issues of teaching and learning. Both conditions—

social controls and technical demands—may be necessary for effective decentralization in education, given the unclear nature of the teaching-learning process and the absence of clear performance indicators.

In Chapter Seven, Martin Carnoy also focuses on demands. He argues that "the most logical and consistent empirical explanation for higher-quality education, whether public or private, lies primarily in differential demand" for quality. Using data on differences in the achievement of various types of students in various situations, at various times in the United States, Carnoy argues that choice plans, either public or private, that decentralize decision making to parents are likely to improve the performance of only high-demand, low-middle-income families. A large fraction of students, particularly those from low-demand families, are likely to be worse off. According to this argument, the primary consequence of choice is likely to be an increase in the variance in students' achievement: some students may be better off, but others will be decidedly worse off. Carnoy also argues that students' performance can be promoted if central authorities set higher curriculum standards and thereby increase the schools' demand for higher achievement by students.

In Chapter Eight, Clair Brown describes decentralized management arrangements in industry and then considers the lessons for public schools. She cautions against making inferences about the effects of decentralization in education on the basis of experiences in industry. Differences between schools and industry are large and important. For example, the "production process in education is vastly more complicated than in the private sector, because of the large number of intervening social, political, and economic variables that are outside the control of schools." Evaluating changes that result from new decision-making arrangements is therefore problematic. Agency and monitoring costs are also different, largely because the employment security of teachers is not dependent on organizational performance. In general, experience in industry has shown that employee involvement in decision making may have marginal effects on organizational performance, but it cannot solve deeply rooted problems. Experience in education will probably show the same.

In Chapter Nine, we summarize the findings of the book and argue that decentralization reforms cannot be understood in isolation: they must be seen within the context of educational standards that society sets for itself.

This book as a whole suggests that decentralization reforms are unlikely to be the solution to education problems; simple solutions seldom solve complex problems. Similar reforms did not solve the problems of the past, current decentralization reforms are unlikely alone to solve the problems of today, and they certainly will not solve the problems of the poor. Nevertheless, decentralization reforms—accompanied by higher performance demands, more directed technical demands, and clearer accountability systems—may make important contributions to improving educational performance.

## Audience

This book is intended for education policy analysts and practitioners and for scholars of administration. Some of the chapters are primarily theoretical, but we feel that those chapters are just as relevant for practitioners as they are for scholars. Without a clear understanding of the conditions under which, and the ways in which, structural reforms affect educational practice and performance, policy initiatives have only a hit-or-miss chance of success.

## Acknowledgments

Many people contributed in different ways to making this book possible. Susan Fuhrman, director of the Consortium for Policy Research in Education, provided the initial impetus, encouragement, and support for the project. The beginning discussions at Stanford that shaped our thinking included G. Carl Ball, Eugene Bardach, William Clune, Norman Deets, Fritz Edelstein, Susan Fuhrman, Hakan Hakansson, Estelle James, James Jucker, Michael Kirst, Henry Levin, Marlaine Lockheed, James March, Terry Moe, Donald Moore, Carlos Ornelas, William Ouchi, Marshall Smith, and Priscilla Wohlstetter, in addition to the authors whose work appears in this volume. The chapters benefited from comments at the Washington, D.C., seminar by Norman Deets, Fritz Edelstein,

Allan Odden, and Carol Weiss, and especially by Susan Fuhrman and Estelle James, who served as formal discussants. We also want to acknowledge the able assistance of Brian Goldsmith and Shari Seider in putting this book together.

*Stanford, California*
*January 1993*

Jane Hannaway
Martin Carnoy

# The Editors

Jane Hannaway is associate professor in the School of Education at Stanford University, where she also directs the master's program in policy analysis. She has taught at Teachers College, Columbia University, and at the Woodrow Wilson School of Public and International Affairs, Princeton University. She is the author of *Managers Managing: The Working of an Administrative System* (1989) and has co-edited two books, *The Politics of Reforming School Administration* (1988, with R. Crowson) and *The Contributions of the Social Sciences to Educational Policy and Practice* (1986, with M. Lockheed). She is currently completing a book on structural reforms in education. Hannaway is past vice president of the American Educational Research Association. She received her B.A. degree (1967) from Newton College of the Sacred Heart in political science, an M.A.T. degree (1968) from Manhattanville College, and an M.A. degree (1978) in sociology and a Ph.D. degree (1978) in education from Stanford University.

Martin Carnoy is professor of education and economics in the School of Education at Stanford University, where he also has headed the International Development Education program. He received his B.S. degree (1960) from the California Institute of Technology in electrical engineering and his A.M. degree (1961) and Ph.D. degree (1964) from the University of Chicago in economics. He is the author of *Economic Democracy* (1980, with D. Shearer), *Theories of the State* (1984), *Schooling and Work in the Democratic State* (1985, with H. Levin), and *Education and Social Transition in the Third World* (1989, with J. Samoff).

# The Contributors

Clair Brown is professor of economics at the University of California, Berkeley. She is also director of the Institute of Industrial Relations, University of California, Berkeley, and former editor of *Industrial Relations.* She received her B.A. degree (1968) from Wellesley College in mathematics and her Ph.D. degree (1973) from the University of Maryland in economics.

Richard F. Elmore is professor in the Graduate School of Education, Harvard University, and senior research fellow with the Consortium for Policy Research in Education. He has taught at the College of Education, Michigan State University, and at the Graduate School of Public Affairs, University of Washington, where he also served as associate dean. He is past president of the American Association for Public Policy and Management. He received his B.A. degree (1966) from Whitman College in political science, his M.A. degree (1969) from the Claremont Graduate School in government, and his Ed.D. degree (1976) from Harvard University.

Dan A. Lewis is professor of education in the School of Education and Social Policy, Northwestern University, where he has served as associate dean. He is also former associate director of the Center for Urban Affairs and Policy Research, Northwestern University, where he is on the research faculty. He received his B.A. degree (1968) from Stanford University in political science and his Ph.D. degree (1980) from the University of California, Santa Cruz, in history of consciousness.

David Tyack is the Vida Jacks Professor of Education and professor of history at Stanford University. He is past president of the History of Education Society, past vice president of the American Educational Research Association, and a member of the National Academy of Education. During the 1991-92 academic year, he was a fellow at the Stanford Humanities Center. The American Educational Research Association awarded Tyack both its Outstanding Book Award (for *Learning Together*, 1990, with E. Hansot) and its Distinguished Research Career Award in 1992. He received his B.A. degree (1952), his A.M.T. degree (1953), and his Ph.D. degree (1958) from Harvard University in history of education.

Hans N. Weiler is professor of education and political science at Stanford University and chair of the International Education Development Program. He is former associate dean of the Stanford School of Education and past director of UNESCO's International Institute for Educational Planning in Paris. His recent research has focused mainly on comparative analyses of educational reform in Europe. Weiler studied philosophy and political science at the University of Freiburg, Germany, and at the University of London. He received his Dr.Phil. degree (1965) from the University of Freiburg in political science.

Donald R. Winkler is senior economist in the Public Sector Management Division for Latin America and the Caribbean at the World Bank. He was formerly a professor and associate dean at the School of Public Administration, University of Southern California. He received his B.A. degree (1966) and his M.A. degree (1967) from the University of Wisconsin in Latin American Studies and his Ph.D. degree (1972) from the University of California, Berkeley, in economics.

# 1

# School Governance in the United States: Historical Puzzles and Anomalies

**David Tyack**

When Americans grow dissatisfied with public schools, they tend to blame the way they are governed. There is too much democracy or too little, critics insist, too much centralization or too little, too many actors in policy formation or too few. Although Americans have recurrently demonstrated a profound distrust of government (Farnham, 1963), they have also asserted a utopian faith that once Americans found the right pattern of school governance, education would thrive. Policy talk today about "restructuring" and "choice" and "national standards" is a recent rhetorical episode in a long series going back a century and a half (U.S. Department of Education, 1991; National Governors' Association, 1991). Despite this faith in reform through changes in governance, we know little about how different forms of governance might affect the heart of education—classroom practice. The answer may be "not much." As Richard F. Elmore says in Chapter Two, governance reforms have been mostly disconnected from what students learn. Moreover, no matter how schools have been run, basic patterns of instruction appear to have changed remarkably little over long periods of time (Cuban, 1984; Cohen, 1990).

Rhetoric about centralization and decentralization has promised much, for reformers have not been shy in their claims. Much of this policy talk is based on different ideologies and interests, either explicitly stated or taken for granted. One period's common sense becomes a delusion in the next. Reformers have been fond of arguing by analogy, and copying business has periodically been fashionable. In the Progressive Era, for example, business leaders wanted to centralize control of schools, emulating the consolidation of vast corporations; today they urge "restructuring" or decentralization, citing business practice in each case as a guide to reform in schooling.

This does not mean that the debate over governance should be dismissed as mere rhetoric, as opposed to some observable reality. Shared belief systems do matter: they build common cultural meanings that in turn shape schools and form public expectations about them (Meyer and Rowan, 1977; Thomas, Meyer, Ramirez, and Boli, 1987). Policy talk about control is a rich tapestry of symbols and cultural assumptions, even when it fails to map organizational practice or the distribution of political power accurately (Cohen and Rosenberg, 1977; Popkewitz, 1988).

This discourse, which often occurs in cycles (Downs, 1972), needs to be juxtaposed, however, to long-term institutional trends and to what little we know about life in classrooms (Cuban, 1990; Tyack, forthcoming). Some trend lines suggest that the advocates of centralization have won, hands down. In broad-brush terms, one can argue that there has been a steady march from decentralization to centralization. In nineteenth-century America—a mostly rural nation—local lay trustees vastly outnumbered teachers and had powers unmatched in any other system of public education in the world. Even in cities, large lay boards actively participated in all phases of decision making and delegated many powers to ward school committees. The federal office of education had minimal powers and staff, and state departments of education were tiny and had meager means of enforcing regulations. Local control seemed to be the paradigm of democratic education (Kaestle, 1983; Cremin, 1980; Warren, 1974; Tyack and Hansot, 1982).

Much of this changed in the twentieth century, however. Hundreds of thousands of school districts were collapsed to about sixteen thousand, and one-room schools nearly disappeared. City school systems became large, differentiated bureaucracies in which small school boards delegated policy formation to administrators. State departments of education—and, in more recent years, courts and the federal government—assumed an increasingly activist role in setting policies and imposing regulations (Firestone, Fuhrman, and Kirst, 1989; Tyack, 1990).

Observers with different ideologies have disagreed about how to evaluate these changes. Some have portrayed the past as a golden age of democratic participation. When schools were decentralized in rural America, they argue, parents and patrons called the shots, teachers were part of the community and met its needs, and bureaucracy and regulations were unnecessary. Schooling was cheap, effective, and responsive to parental concerns about morality and useful learning. Local people were right in resisting consolidation and state regulation, for they already had the kinds of schools that served them (Sher, 1977; Fuller, 1982).

Others tell a different story. According to this version, local control resulted in schools that were grossly unequal in resources, reproduced the "dull parochialism and attenuated totalitarianism" of village life (Lieberman, 1960, pp. 34–36), repressed the discretion and expertise of professional educators, and stirred petty politics. The cure was to consolidate country districts and to take city schools out of ward politics (Cubberley, 1914).

In urging centralization of control, educational reformers of the Progressive Era argued that concentrating authority in experts would bring a kind of accountability that was absent in a more fragmented and dispersed system. Regulation, bureaucratization, and centralization would equalize education by standardizing it, delegate decision making to experts, and "Americanize" a diverse population (Cubberley, 1934; Strayer, 1930).

In recent years, critics have argued that the reforms of the Progressive Era produced bureaucratic arteriosclerosis, insulation from parents and patrons, and the low productivity of a declining industry protected as a quasi monopoly. Some call for decentralized decision making, coupled with accountability for "high performance"; others argue that the whole system of political and bureaucratic control is so ineffective that there should be an open market of schooling in which competition would guarantee results (Chubb and Moe, 1990; Clune and Witte, 1990; U.S. Department of Education, 1991).

## Muddying the Waters of an Imagined Past

Beneath the different evaluations and the apparently triumphant transition from decentralization to centralized governance, however, lie puzzles that complicate any simple, linear logic. Patterns of governance, and especially the relation of systems of control to contrasting ideologies and educational practice, have been more nuanced and complex than the conventional terms of debate would suggest. Organizational charts and organizational behavior often diverged. Anomalies appear at every turn:

- Even though control of rural schools in the nineteenth century appeared to be highly decentralized and responsive to grassroots demands, what happened in classrooms in these one-room schools seemed surprisingly alike (Adams, 1875; Tyack and Hansot, 1982).
- Key actors in standardizing schooling during the nineteenth century—such as the American Book Company or the Women's Christian Temperance Union (WCTU)—don't even appear in most accounts of public school governance, for they were private corporations or voluntary groups, not public agencies (Bordin, 1981; "Confessions of Three Superintendents," 1896).
- The governance of urban schools in the nineteenth century was often chaotic and pluralistic—resembling one of Rube Goldberg's comic machines—but in many cities curriculum and instruction were models of tight coupling (Philbrick, 1885).
- Streamlined modern forms of "apolitical" administrative control in the Progressive Era promised efficient coordination of school systems but have often become only loosely coupled with practice in classrooms (Weick, 1976).
- Broad-based social movements of the 1960s, such as the civil rights movement, struggled to make schools more responsive to their needs, but legal and organizational responses tended to produce increased bureaucracy and fragmented what centralization existed at the local level (Meyer, 1980).
- Today, the label of "restructuring" is plastered on an astonishing variety of practices, while people seem to call at the same time for greater national uniformity and more local autonomy (Elmore and Associates, 1990).

Recent scholarship in organizational studies and in the history of education helps to interpret such apparent anomalies or puzzles about governance. Historians and organizational sociologists are coming increasingly to appreciate, for example, the force of common cultural beliefs—what one might call "the invisible hand of ideology"—in shaping institutions. This is a key, for example, to the remarkable uniformity found in schools during the nineteenth century, even in apparently autonomous and isolated rural communities. One misses this standardizing and centralizing influence of ideology if one looks only at the formal powers of officials and at organizational charts (Adams, 1875; Mansfield, 1851).

The "new institutionalists" help to explain continuities in schools once established within this ideological framework. As March and Olsen (1984) remind us, institutions are neither simply arenas for individuals to pursue their own agendas nor creatures of outside forces, ever permeable to the winds of change; they may show continuity over long periods of time and an ability to resist or co-opt outside demands for reform. Institutionalized schools (Meyer and Rowan, 1977) gained a kind of autonomy and momentum that deflected deliberate efforts to change organizational structure and behavior. Schools also have shown great resilience in the face of social upheavals. Even the Great Depression, a major economic catastrophe, had surprisingly little impact on public schools (Tyack, Lowe, and Hansot, 1984).

Continuity in classroom practice illustrates an observation of Stinchcombe's (1965): that many organizations continue to bear the imprint of their time of origin. Even in the case of bureaucratized city schools, one might argue, the isolated individual classroom in the "egg-crate" structure of the graded school system, each with its own teacher and twenty to thirty pupils, retained some key features of the original one-room school.

A striking example of institutional continuity is the new prototype for the schools that New York plans to build in the 1990s ("Jolt," 1991, pp. 23–24). The architects decided that "the classroom is the cell of the school system." They rejected the large open classroom as a design "predicated on infinite optimism" because it failed to consider fractious student behavior and pedagogical custom. Their innovation consisted of giving a "jolt" to the standard square of the self-contained room to provide more light and flexible space. But conservatism asserted itself when they decided that "the teacher would remain the real focus of the room." Despite spaces for computers, one architect said, the center of activity "is still the blackboard. A teacher up there with a piece of slate and a lump of chalk." This episode offers confirmation of Cuban's argument (1984) that even after major changes in the organizational size and complexity of schools, older patterns of teacher-centered instruction changed very little at the secondary level, while in elementary schools "hybrid" adaptations of certain progressive practices appeared here and there, but rarely did they occasion fundamental transformation in instruction.

Research on "loose coupling" in schools has demonstrated that the relationships among centralization, bureaucratization, and systems of organizational control are more complicated than reformers (Cubberley, 1934) had expected. The architects of differentiated school bureaucracies in the Progressive Era, like Cubberley, thought that specialized structures would produce accountability; one could tell which expert was in charge of which domain (whether traditional, such as the teaching of mathematics, or new, such as special education). But specialization also produced the classic bureaucratic response: "That's not my department." Furthermore, the connections between line administrators and classroom teachers have proved tenuous. Organizational theorists such as Weick (1976) declare that schools are classic examples of "loosely coupled" systems. Meyer, Scott, Strang, and Creighton (1985) have suggested that recent federal and state categorical programs and centralized mandates have produced bureaucratization but not centralization. Because the directors of the new programs often owe more loyalty to their specialized domains than to school districts as a whole, and because they report to bureaucrats at state or federal levels, the fragmented governance that results may destabilize normal lines of command and turn accountability into accounting.

Cohen (1978) has observed that some of the most powerful standardizing agencies rarely appear on organizational charts of school governance. A number of the more influential organizations—textbook publishers, test companies, and accreditation agencies, for example—are private groups whose accountability to the public is slight. One could add to this list scores of powerful voluntary special-interest groups. The Women's Christian Temperance

Union (Bordin, 1981), for example, managed by 1900 to install the one subject required in all school districts (on the evils of alcohol); fundamentalist creationists succeeded for many years in stifling, if not preventing, the teaching of evolutionary biology (Nelkin, 1982).

In this chapter, in light of this new scholarship on cultural values, institutionalization, and nongovernmental influences on public education, I will explore further some of the historical puzzles concerning school governance. Despite statistical trends that track an apparent shift from autonomous and decentralized schools to centralized state systems, reform rhetoric about governance has often obscured more than it revealed about actual practice in classrooms. This is still the case, and I shall conclude by pointing out some anomalies in current efforts to reform education by changing governance.

## The Invisible Hand of Ideology

In the nineteenth century, public schools—called "common schools"—were largely grass-roots affairs, especially in rural America: local in support and control. There were differences between schools, of course, according to community wealth, ethnicity, and region (the South, for example, was late in adopting the common school and had an impoverished and racially segregated system). As settlers moved across the continent, however, they built schools that were remarkably similar in institutional character and that taught similar lessons (Kaestle, 1983; Adams, 1875).

How can one explain these similarities, in the absence of centralized formal control? They resulted in part from the new communities' emulation of the older, but there was a less obvious and deeper source of standardization as well: a common Protestant-republican ideology, adapted to the common-school crusade in the 1840s by people such as Horace Mann and repeated by countless other leaders in later decades. Common culture, more than common political command, was a source of standardization. The crusaders who spread public education generally shared a set of beliefs: that public education's purpose was to train upright citizens by inculcating a common denominator of nonsectarian morality and nonpartisan civic instruction and that the common school should be free, open to all children, and public in support and control (Wiebe, 1969; Higham, 1974).

In 1860, four out of five Americans lived in rural areas. Dotting the nineteenth-century countryside were the one-room public schools that were the sole form of schooling for most children. Small and sparsely equipped, but often with a bell tower resembling a church steeple, the school was closely linked to two other local institutions: the family and the church. Local trustees and parents selected the teachers, supervised their work, and sometimes boarded them in their homes. Brothers, sisters, and cousins went to school together and, with their classmates, gave "exhibitions" of their knowledge to the members of the community at public assemblies (Fuller, 1982; Tyack and Hansot, 1990).

The school, like the church, was expected to be, in Waller's phrase (1965), a "museum of virtue." Ministers were key leaders in persuading local citizens to build common schools, and they often held church services in school buildings (Smith, 1967). Although officially nonsectarian in religion and nonpartisan in politics, the school was expected to be religious and moral in tone and republican in doctrine. No one better represented the common denominator of civic virtue than the Reverend William Holmes McGuffey, whose textbooks were read and reread by generations of schoolchildren.

There were, of course, dissenters from the sort of public culture desired by the majority of school reformers. The attempts of nativist and Protestant educational leaders to incorporate this ideology into the schools produced conflict as well as consensus: Catholics might protest the use of the King James Bible, and immigrant groups might want their languages and cultures included and honored in the schools. Just what was to be a common public culture, like what is to be the canon today, might be contested in communities. More often, however, citizens agreed with Mann's model of moral and civic instruction (James, 1991; Perko, 1988; Troen, 1975).

Legally, the local public ("common") schools were part of the state system. Some states were more aggressive than others in trying to impose state standards on local districts, but few during the nineteenth century had the power or staff to coerce local trustees. As late as 1890, the average size of a state department of education was two. This was no accident: most citizens did not want active state government (Bryce, 1888).

When they wrote or revised their state constitutions, citizens of states and territories over and over again showed their disdain for strong government by limiting their legislatures and weakening the executive branch. In 1879, a delegate to the convention to revise the California constitution proposed the following resolution: "There shall be no Legislature convened from and after the adoption of this Constitution . . . and any person who shall be guilty of suggesting that a Legislature shall be held, shall be punished as a felon without benefit of clergy" (Sargent, 1917, p. 12).

Despite their fear of centralized government, the writers of state constitutions, like most leaders in public education, shared a powerful ideology that linked the survival of the republic to the education of all its citizens. Key members of the U.S. Congress subscribed to a similar ideology and gave large grants of land to create what might be called "land-grant common schools." After the Civil War, Congress actually required all new states to provide a free, nonsectarian system of public schools (Tyack, James, and Benavot, 1987).

During most of the nineteenth century, however, neither the federal government (Warren, 1974) nor the states had the capacity to control the process of schooling or even to require communities to build schools or enforce attendance (Tyack, 1976). The resulting decentralization of control was quite compatible with the similarity of aspirations and practices in public schooling. A common ideology provided a blueprint that coordinated the efforts of scattered local communities. In like fashion, churches founded on successive frontiers by local citizens might reproduce common rituals, church architecture, and catechisms (Smith, 1967).

Grass-roots organizations such as schools and churches also linked up with nonpublic national agencies to promote uniformity of doctrine by providing the books that constituted the core of learning. One of the most centralized and bureaucratized organizations in the United States before the Civil War was the American Sunday School Union, which supplied millions of its approved texts to pupils across the nation (Rice, 1917). A parallel in public school bookselling was the American Book Company, which sold over

120,000,000 copies of the McGuffey Readers, most of them used in one-room rural schools, and which accomplished distinctly non-McGuffeyesque feats of corruption as it sought to build a monopoly in the textbook business ("Confessions of Three Superintendents," 1896).

Today, the creation of Christian day schools illustrates a similar connection between a pervasive national ideology and local institution building. Christian day schools appear to be paradigm cases of grass-roots institutions, for it is usually local church members who create them. The sponsors of these schools often want no truck with government in any form, state or national (they often refuse even to submit reports to government agencies). But Christian fundamentalists are also inspired to create such schools by nationally televised evangelists. In supermarkets, they buy the best-selling fundamentalist guide for parents by James Dobson (1977). Fundamentalist educators often belong to the Association of Christian Schools International and use national textbooks and curricula produced by fundamentalist publishers. Thus an ideology expressed by national leaders and coordinated by centralized agencies inspires and reinforces local uniformity of ideals and practice today, just as in the nineteenth-century rural common school (Lewis, 1991; Kienel, 1985).

## Tight Coupling

Many of the city school systems of the period from 1870 to 1900 present an apparent anomaly: patterns of governance were extremely heterogeneous, not to say chaotic, but instruction was tightly coupled to the course of study established by administrators. Ideological agreement among most citizens concerning the general purpose and nature of schooling encouraged school leaders to organize instruction more efficiently, even where politicians contested over the spoils of office or engaged in ethnocultural disputes. In many places, city councils created school boards when they found that they could not discharge all their duties and hence needed subsidiary agencies. These councils, however, often divided up responsibility for schools among different governing bodies. In Nashville, for example, the board of public works controlled buildings, so that "while the board of education had authority to purchase chalk, brooms, pens, and soap, it could not supply furniture, stoves, or curtains" (Reller, 1935, pp. 150, 156). In Buffalo, janitors were appointed by the mayor, teachers by the superintendent; the city council chose school sites; and the department of public works erected buildings. One reason why authority was so splintered was that each domain offered opportunities for political patronage and graft. Powerful machines sometimes coordinated school politics behind the scenes, as in New York, where Tammany Hall ran the show and raked in the profit (Reller, 1935; Cronin, 1973).

Another source of conflict was the division of power between the central boards of education and the local ward boards. In Pittsburgh, the thirty-nine local boards raised their own taxes and made all educational decisions except about paying teachers, selecting textbooks, and running the high school. In both central and ward boards, laypeople took an active part in what today would seem administrative matters, such as methods of teaching reading, choosing a grammar text, visiting schools on a cold day to make sure that the furnaces were working, or buying blackboards and desks. People argued that large central and ward boards were necessary because there were so many tasks for committeemen to perform. Philadelphia had 42 members on the central board and 504 on the ward committees (Tyack, 1974).

Reformers vigorously complained that so many cooks spoiled the broth of urban education, even when they were not after lucrative contracts. Having so many bosses certainly complicated the task of superintendents who were determined to create what John Philbrick of Boston called a "uniformity of excellence" in urban schools. But superintendents persisted in that task. Believing that there was "one best way" of educating children, Philbrick (1885, pp. 58–59) and his professional peers were intent on "the perfecting of the system itself . . . the devising of a more rational program and a more rational system of school examinations."

Despite the obstacles of chaotic governance, a large number of urban superintendents did succeed in systematizing schooling. They divided pupils into grades by academic proficiency. They installed a uniform curriculum and calibrated teaching and testing to that system. In the process, they devised the most tightly coupled form of instruction that the United States has produced. They were so successful, in fact, that much of "progressive education" was a reaction to the rigidity of this top-down percolation of what was called "positive knowledge." Teachers as well as students were expected to "toe the line"—a literal phrase at the time, meaning that toes were to line up to the edge of the floorboard when a child recited (Rice, 1893). The measure of accountability for pupils was the passing of tests, presumably the *product* of their labors; teachers were held accountable for following the approved *process* of instruction.

Superintendents and principals used three main devices to ensure that all pupils learned the same thing. First, they wrote out the required curriculum in detail, grade by grade, with textbooks aligned (urban educators sometimes wrote the textbooks themselves). Second, principals supervised the teachers to make sure that they were following the course of study exactly (the model of supervision many of them proposed was that of inspector general). Third, they wrote tests that were taken by all the pupils. Promotion from grade to grade and entrance into high school (for a meritocratic few) depended on passing these tests. The examinations were so demanding that large numbers of pupils failed at each grade, especially the first three grades, which caused a disproportionate distribution of children in the primary grades (Philbrick, 1885; Ayres, 1909).

Some cities went beyond these three devices that produced tight coupling by creating special normal (or teacher-training) classes to prepare young women specifically to teach the course of study in the approved manner. In Washington, D.C., the "normalites" actually practiced the proper way to "yawn and stretch," a prescribed midmorning ritual (Tyack and Hansot, 1990). Strict control of classroom teaching—an ideal of some reformers today, who want teachers to toe the line of "accountability"—coexisted with nonsystems of "governance" that seemed a nightmare to reformers of the time.

## A Corporate Model of Schooling

At the turn of the twentieth century, the administrative progressives in education sought to accomplish two major aims: to depoliticize schooling and to differentiate it. They regarded the pattern of lay governance as chaotic and intrusive when it was not also corrupt. They considered the uniform curriculum of the nineteenth century school to be rigid, bookish, and ill adapted to the variety of pupils flooding the nation's classrooms. They turned to business for inspiration and support, and businesspeople proved to be useful allies. By emulating patterns of control found in corporations, school leaders thought, they could take the schools out of politics. By copying the functional specialization and methods of coordination of centralized firms, they believed, they could make school systems efficient, differentiated by function, and accountable (Callahan, 1962; Spring, 1972; Tyack, 1974).

In the process, they sought to define what was a standard school system. A school became standard because it conformed to a professional model, often written into state law and local policies and eventually engraved on the public mind as essential to the institution (Meyer and Rowan, 1977). A teacher, for example, was a person who was certified to instruct at a particular level or in a particular subject. A high school was a separate building where teenaged students could take a variety of different subjects ranging from the academic to the vocational.

In an era of massive consolidation of industrial and commercial organizations, the administrative progressives and their allies in business and the professions saw central state and district planning, not the invisible hand of the market, as the key to reforming education (Chandler, 1977). For Cubberley (1934), the board of a bank was a good model for city school trustees. Admiring the functional differentiation of large firms, Cubberley described the school as a factory turning children (raw materials) into products desired by society. The school should resemble the advanced corporate sector in governance and in internal operation; that was one way to break down the walls between school and society.

Educational leaders and their business allies believed that progress was possible because science had given the experts the necessary tools to plan the course of social and economic evolution. In Delaware, for example, Pierre S. DuPont sought to apply to schools the principles he had used in consolidating and reorganizing giant corporations such as General Motors and the Du Pont

Company. Convinced that Delaware needed to improve its schools if it was to hold its own in economic competition with other states, he formed and subsidized an elite organization called Service Citizens of Delaware (much like today's Business Roundtables). DuPont and this group promoted studies, experiments, and media and legislative campaigns to modernize public education. If there was "one best way"—and these reformers believed that there was—then centralized authority and expert administration were necessary to its implementation. Decentralization of control was anachronistic, a drag on progress; centralization promised more choices, as well as greater efficiency (Taggart, 1988).

There were many reformers of the time, of course, who dissented from this corporate model (Cremin, 1964). John Dewey believed that the family, not the firm, should be the prototype of the school: "What the best and wisest parent wants for his own child," he wrote, "that must the community want for all its children" (Dewey, 1899, p. 43). Dewey wanted much more democracy in education, not less, both in governance and in the classroom. But the administrative progressives were remarkably successful in changing the size and functioning of school boards, consolidating schools, and bureaucratizing urban systems. Such changes probably made it more difficult for the followers of Dewey to carry out his social philosophy and pedagogical reforms.

Urban schools of the nineteenth century had many school board members but few professional administrators other than principals. That changed in the decades from 1890 to 1920. In those years, city after city abolished ward boards, and the average number of central board members in cities of more than 100,000 dropped from about twenty-one to about seven. According to the new ideal of corporate management, these smaller boards were expected not to busy themselves with the details of running the system, as in the nineteenth century, but to decide "policy" and to delegate "administration" to the superintendent and the specialists. As new state charters altered the form of governance of city schools, the boards were increasingly composed of business and professional elites. All this, of course, did not mean that schools were taken "out of" politics, but simply that political structures and participants changed. One result of the new style of "progressive" politics was that in the early decades of the twentieth century the percentage of the population who voted declined drastically (Tyack, 1974).

In 1889, the average city had only four employees who spent most of their time in supervision; by 1920, the large cities counted them in the hundreds (New York had 1,310). Lynd and Lynd (1929, p. 210) found that in 1890, in Middletown, the only person who did not teach was the superintendent; in the 1920s, there appeared "a whole galaxy of principals, assistant principals, supervisors of special subjects, directors of vocational education and home economics, deans, attendance officers, and clerks, who [did] no teaching but [were] concerned in one way or another with keeping the system going." Specialization and new functions of schooling greatly expanded school bureaucracies.

Underlying this new notion of "keeping the system going" was a concept of accountability different from that of the nineteenth century and from that now advanced by many advocates of the "restructuring" of schools. Both in the nineteenth century and today, accountability often has referred to the results of instruction, usually measured by testing pupils' knowledge. The administrative progressives used tests for a variety of bureaucratic purposes, such as tracking children, but they generally did not release the results to the public. They meant several things by accountability: having a specialized hierarchy, so that individuals (such as a chief attendance officer or a vocational supervisor) could be identified as responsible for segments of the program; keeping close track of costs (they could calculate the expense of an English lesson down to the last penny); and showing that the structure of the system was in accord with the latest "scientific" practice, the correct institutional grammar of the modern school (Callahan, 1962; Caswell, 1929). In short, this was an internal bureaucratic accountability of structure and process more than of results.

In this process of standardization, states played a prominent part through legislation and regulations that decreed what a modern school district should include. Scorecard in hand, educational experts went out to evaluate individual schools and check how well they matched the new model. Professional teams surveyed districts and whole states according to a template of approved practice, and they told elected officials what was needed to bring schools up to modern standards (Strayer, 1930; Caswell, 1929).

Private organizations not directly responsible to the public also played a prominent part in reorganizing the educational system. Accrediting agencies gave the stamp of approval to systems that included up-to-date practices. Standardized tests of "intelligence" and "achievement" were largely products of the private sector. Foundations subsidized surveys and financed pilot projects. Business lobbies such as the National Association of Manufacturers pressed for reforms such as vocational training. Private professional groups, such as the National Education Association and an invitational group of elite educators called the Cleveland Conference, became forums for deciding what changes should be adopted. All these agencies worked to produce a national consensus, even though formal decision making in education remained mostly at the local level (Tyack and Hansot, 1982; Cohen, 1978).

Under the corporate model of schooling, in theory, these new pieces fit together into coherent state and local systems organized from the top down. Specialists, coordinated by managers above them in the hierarchy, could be held responsible for distinct parts of the program of education. In practice, however, as so often happens in bureaucracies, the splintering of responsibility left gaps and made integration of efforts difficult. Differentiation also created many functional interest groups within the schools, each with its own agenda, its own professional organization, and its own ideas about what constituted personal and educational advancement. At best, then, the schools were imperfectly centralized.

Perhaps more important, amid all the functional differentiation of the structure of urban schooling, the classroom in many ways remained self-contained, isolated, and cellular, still reflecting some prototypical characteristics of its origins. Many people—supervisors, curriculum directors, counselors, principals, clerks—might have claims on teachers' attention, people eager to plan or monitor some part of their work; but behind the classroom doors, teachers found a kind of autonomy that led to "loose coupling" of a sort that had been harder to achieve in the tightly coupled urban system of the nineteenth century. No longer was there one undifferentiated curriculum; instead, the very variety of programs, bosses, and expectations gave teachers some room to maneuver, some freedom between the cracks in the bureaucracy.

Familiar habits of pedagogy played a part in shaping the continuity of instruction. Teachers taught courses with new titles, used new textbooks, and were expected to care for "the whole child." From supervisors and in curriculum workshops, they heard about new ways to teach. Many teachers, especially in the elementary grades, selectively adopted some of the new practices. As Cuban (1984) has found, however, teachers by and large continued to teach in the same old ways, despite the elaboration of school systems and abundant rhetoric about "the new education."

Even though reforming instruction proved to be far more difficult than altering the scope and structure of the system, the corporate model of governance persisted. It became so durable a feature of American school districts that political scientists of the 1950s sometimes referred to local public education as a "closed system." That was to change rapidly as social movements of "outsiders" challenged this system (Tyack, Kirst, and Hansot, 1980).

## The Old Order Changes

A number of groups stood outside the arena of educational politics in the years from 1900 to 1950. During the generation following the *Brown* school desegregation decision in 1954, many of these groups entered school politics at the grass-roots level, as state and national protest groups, and in the courts (Mosher, Hastings, and Wagoner, 1979).

These social protest movements of the 1960s and early 1970s shook the old order of school governance, but the response of the establishment to their demands did not produce a coherent new order. Activists sought change at all levels of school politics—local, state, and national. One way in which school districts and state and federal agencies responded to dissent was to bureaucratize it. New problems became identified, and new district administrators were appointed to deal with them and to coordinate outside funding and accounting for new programs. As Meyer (1980) has noted, this produced a fragmented form of centralization. In addition, the establishment sometimes responded to the demand for community control by adding new layers of decentralized governance (Ornstein, 1989) or new forms of "community participation." The result of all of this, more often than not, was a more elaborate and less coordinated bureaucracy—more the appearance than the reality of democracy.

African-Americans organized the most powerful social protest movement yet to appear in educational history: the campaign for civil rights. Eloquent leaders such as Martin Luther King, Jr., mobilized black and white citizens by appealing to the values of equality and social justice. In translating such an ideology into political demands, however, black leaders were typically flexible and pragmatic, tailoring remedies for injustice to the particular circumstances they faced. What they wanted was more power over their lives and better education for their children, and accomplishing these aims varied with the context. In the South, where racial segregation of pupils reflected the general denial of full citizenship, these leaders courageously demonstrated in local communities and used the federal courts to overthrow the racial caste system. In northern ghettoes, by contrast, when school boards dragged their feet on desegregation, black activists pressed instead for radical decentralization and community control (Kluger, 1977; Levin, 1970; Newby and Tyack, 1971).

Other groups that had little voice under the old order—Hispanics, Native Americans, women, parents of children with special needs, and others—studied and emulated the strategies of black leaders. On one point most activists in social movements agreed: local school boards and bureaucracies were often unresponsive. Under the corporate model that allegedly took schools out of politics, administrators were in fact supposed to be unresponsive to "pressure groups" that wanted them to engage in "social engineering," although social engineering by educational experts was another matter (Cuban, 1976).

When local officials were deaf to their demands, activists pursued a variety of tactics. They took to the streets to protest, sought media coverage, lobbied Congress and state legislatures for new laws, and litigated in federal and state courts (Kirp, 1982). They found allies in the administrations of Presidents Kennedy and Johnson and in some state capitols. Through judges' decrees, legislation, and administrative regulations, they sought to secure rights and win entitlements long denied at the local level (Rist and Anson, 1977; Ravitch, 1983).

Law offered a centralized lever for educational change. Federal courts in both the South and the North required laggard districts to desegregate the schools by race; feminists used Title IX, passed by Congress in 1972, to desegregate schools by sex and eliminate institutional sexism. Public Law 94-142 mandated services for the handicapped. In the *Lau* decision, the Supreme Court required educators to assist non-English-speaking students; through legislation and regulations, the federal government and many states translated that mandate into programs for bilingual education. Activists in the War on Poverty targeted funds in categorical programs to students from low-income families and devised regulations to make sure that they reached poor children (Sadker and Sadker, 1982; Kirp, 1977).

These programs and others enlarged and complicated the role of the federal government and the states in the governance of education. Some strategies promoted centralization. At the same time, however, some protest groups wanted radical decentralization. Militant blacks in cities, who were fed up with the glacial pace of desegregation and eager to run local schools, called for community control of ghetto schools. Responding to such demands for local participation in school decision making, federal and state lawmakers sometimes mandated school-community councils to administer the new categorical programs, thereby sometimes strengthening the influence and participation of parents in individual schools but rarely altering the overall distribution of power (Levin, 1970).

The result of the new politics of education in the 1960s was a blending of different forms of governance—Meyer's "fragmented centralization" (1980). To put the matter another way, everybody and nobody was in charge of public schooling in that tumultuous decade. School district leaders lost their sense of control over schooling, but the influence of outsiders was patchy and incomplete (Tyack and Hansot, 1982).

The fragmentation arose in part from the character of the new categorical programs created by the federal and state governments. Like vocational education (which since 1918 had developed its own bureaucratic apparatus at the federal, state, and local levels), many of the new programs produced new specialists at each level, whose responsibility it was to seek and disburse funds and oversee the new programs. These new categorical programs were often uncoordinated, and sometimes they conflicted with one another (Kaestle and Smith, 1982).

One result of such fragmented centralization, as already mentioned, was that accountability often became accounting. New middle managers became accountants for new categorical programs, compartmentalized domains that linked local bureaucrats more to state and federal officials than to local districts. Meyer (1980) suggests that, in the face of possibly contradictory mandates and requirements, a sensible strategy for school superintendents was calculated ignorance or incompetence, rather than the masterful planning that had been the aim of their predecessors.

The older faith in a science of education and in universal solutions to educational problems did not disappear in the 1960s, however. Indeed, educational research was a growth industry during that decade. In particular, the number of evaluators expanded rapidly as government agencies demanded that someone assess the success of reforms. In the new version of accountability, much early evaluation was based on a rational model of planning and implementation—calibration of how well reforms matched, in practice, the intent of legislation. But sophisticated evaluators soon concluded that reform is a complex social and political process fraught with assumptions and interests that are ignored in the rational model of top-down reform. It was difficult if not impossible to separate the effects of centralized programs from the influences permeating the local context (McLaughlin, 1987).

The responses of the educational system to the demands of protest groups in the 1960s and early 1970s produced a patchwork of centralized and decentralized governance. "Accountability" became a cloak of many colors. One concept of accountability was responsiveness to the many protest groups that demanded attention to their agendas. Such responsiveness might take the form of introducing black history in the curriculum, for example, or appointing a Title IX coordinator to correct gender injustices. Accountability also became compliance with the legal mandates that resulted from the expansion of litigation in education (districts had to respond to court-ordered racial desegregation, elimination of sex discrimination, and protection of procedural rights for students and teachers). Still another kind of accountability consisted of offering students more choices, as in electives or alternative schools—creating minimarkets within the educational system in which the student became the consumer and the high school a shopping mall (Powell, Farrar, and Cohen, 1985).

In the 1980s, the pendulum of policy swung to state-level centralization (Firestone, Fuhrman, and Kirst, 1989). States passed legislation to "make the little buggers work harder" (Kirst, 1988, 1989), prescribing more courses, requiring more time in classes, and seeking to rachet up the system to world-class standards. Attention shifted away from the older forms of educational accountability (being responsive to outsider groups, measuring the effectiveness of reform programs, complying with equity legislation, or providing students with choices within the public system). The compelling measure of effectiveness—the major form of accountability—became performance on standardized tests. In the 1990s, while national and state leaders portray the United States as embroiled in a bleak economic competition with other nations, test scores on wall charts dominate discourse about what is wrong with American education. Once again, people are seeking to perfect the schools through changes in governance.

## Governance in Current Reforms

Imagine that the shapers of educational policy in the past were to wake up in 1991 as modern-day Rip Van Winkles, unaware of what has been happening, and observe the present moment in the reform of educational governance:

> Horace Mann discovers that many key policy makers, including the president of the United States, think that schooling should be part of an open market where parents, as consumers, choose where to send their children. What happened, asks the evangelist for the common school ideal, to the notion that public

education is a common good? Do not all citizens have a stake in the civic and moral instruction of the next generation? Has education become merely a consumer good in 1991 (Messerli, 1972)?

A board member of a one-room school of the 1890s, one of almost a half million lay trustees of American schools, the most numerous class of public officials in the world, awakens to find that there are fewer than one thousand one-room schools and that districts have been consolidated until there are fewer than sixteen thousand. The ranks of school trustees have been decimated. He discovers that few lament the loss of this traditional form of democratic governance. In fact, he notes that in policy talk about reforming education, people discuss roles for the nation, the states, and the individual school staff and parents—but rarely for school trustees (National Center for Education Statistics, 1988; U.S. Department of Education, 1991).

Ellwood P. Cubberley wakes up to find that the Chicago of 1991 has outdone the Philadelphia of 1904 in participatory democracy, having eleven school board members for each of its schools and a complex network of central, middling, and ancillary authorities. Good grief, he might exclaim, how can the wise and expert leader avert chaos and corruption (Cubberley, 1934)?

Pierre S. DuPont awakens to discover that businessmen today denounce centralization as bureaucracy gone mad and call for "restructuring" in education as in business—by which they usually mean decentralization of decision making to the school site. Do they know nothing about the value of scientific management, economies of scale, consolidation, and coordination (Taggart, 1988)?

> A U.S. senator who fought federal aid to education for thirty years, from 1932 to 1962—because control, he believed, followed the dollar—is startled to learn that the president and all fifty governors are now advocating a national curriculum and national standards, all to be policed by national examinations. They had the gall to call this idea "A Jeffersonian Compact"—an insult to that great advocate of states' rights. Have the Russians taken over the government, in the guise of the Charlottesville 51? Does no one recall that one hundred congressmen were so bothered by federal control that they voted to name the U.S. Commissioner of Education the Commissar of Education (Tyack, 1990)?

> John Dewey, who encouraged children and teachers to create a distinctively democratic form of social learning and who believed that education had no goals beyond itself—surely no targets of achievement imposed from the top down—is alarmed. Now national leaders assume—they do not have to prove—that the central purpose of education is to make the United States economically competitive. In a Darwinian world of survival by test score, autocratic Korea becomes a country to beat and centralized Japan a nation to emulate (Dewey, 1899; Hlebowitsh, 1990).

From the perspective of the long history of school governance, anomalies abound in present-day proposals for reform as people advocate change from opposite directions. Some believe that there should be a national curriculum and "restructured" individual schools where professionals decide how but not what to teach. Some advocate subsidized choice of schools—public or private—but want a highly prescribed curriculum to eliminate a traditional form of choice: elective subjects in a diversified curriculum. Solutions suitable for bumper stickers appear: small is beautiful; choice is the answer; blame the bureaucrats; too much "democracy." These replace older ones: take the schools out of politics; big is better; experts know best (Olson, 1988).

Underlying much current policy talk about school governance is a set of assumptions: that ineffective schools are to blame for the perceived lack of competitiveness of the U.S. economy (Kaplan, 1991); that faulty governance produces faulty education (Chubb and Moe, 1990); that there is "one best way" to govern schools, and it can be learned from business. Each of these assumptions, it seems to me, is questionable, whether one looks at the past or at the present. To paraphrase an aphorism, there are simple solutions to difficult problems, and they are wrong.

What themes, what cautions, might one draw from this brief account of historical puzzles and anomalies in school governance? One theme is that most changes in governance, whether touted as centralization or as decentralization, have generally left institutional deposits that made school structures more rather than less complex (Cohen, 1990). A typical response to outside demands for change has been to add a new department, a new layer of government, or an agency. Such accretions rarely disappear. This fact prompts a caution: do not assume that through the reform of governance, even in the name of decentralization, the old will evaporate; it seems more likely that accommodating to new demands will complicate, not simplify.

A second theme is that private agencies not subject to direct public control have exerted great influence over public education. Consider the power of textbook publishers over the curriculum or of test companies over the destiny of individual students (especially in the current rage for more high-stakes testing). President Bush's current proposals (U.S. Department of Education, 1991) to define accountability in terms of test results, to turn over the design of new schools to a privately funded and privately managed agency, and to develop a basic national curriculum prompt another caution: What happens to democratic control of education? Who will balance conflicting purposes? How can conflicts of interest or indoctrination be avoided when huge corporations that sell to an educational market also take a central role in designing schools and in providing instructional technology and materials for them? Is business to be considered the disinterested broker of the interest, or is it one among many voices to be heard (Putka, 1991)?

A third theme, drawn from considerable evidence, is that changes in governance have generally failed to alter basic patterns of instruction. One reason may be that teachers are rarely consulted when leaders seek to change schooling. In its list of "Who Does What," *America 2000* (U.S. Department of Education, 1991) mentions the president, Congress, the governors, and the business community, finally remembering teachers as one of eleven groups "at the community level." The caution here is obvious: Why should teachers buy into reform when they are an afterthought or are blamed as mossbacks, the source of the problem (McLaughlin, 1991)? Educational reform, as Elmore and McLaughlin (1988) say, is "steady work." A key way to improve schooling is to start with the classroom and to attend to the teachers who do that steady work. By moving from the inside out, and not from the top down, one may gain a better sense of how to improve instruction.

A fourth theme is the persistent importance of ideology in school reform. In many ways, common belief systems have proved at least as important as formal patterns of governance in shaping American education. The history of American public schools is rich in visions of possibility, beginning with the evangelists of Horace Mann's generation. Leaders such as John Dewey and Martin Luther King, Jr., expressed a powerful commitment to social justice that energized their contemporaries. A comparison of the ideas of such cultural leaders with those of reform advocates today prompts a final caution: we must attend to what is being left out of discussions of educational purpose today, and in the process we must develop a vision of a decent future for all citizens.

The belief systems underlying much of current American educational reform seem impoverished and incomplete in comparison with earlier ideologies. As Mann, Dewey, and King would have perceived, such statements as *A Nation at Risk* (National Commission on Excellence in Education, 1983) and *America 2000* (U.S. Department of Education, 1991) narrow both the sense of purpose and the measure of success in U.S. education. These recent manifestos have moved away from the tradition of a broad-based conception of democratic citizenship, revealed in action. They substitute the aim of economic competitiveness, to be certified by higher test scores. Such a narrowing of purpose omits much that is of value from the discussion of educational policy and constricts the historical vision of the common school. The ideology of competition may resonate among current opinion shapers and may create a temporary sense of public urgency, but is it a lasting and generous conception of educational purpose?

## References

Adams, F. *The Free School System of the United States.* London: Chapman and Hall, 1875.

Ayres, L. P. *Laggards in Our Schools: A Study of Retardation and Elimination in City School Systems.* New York: Charities Publication Committee, 1909.

Bordin, R. *Woman and Temperance: The Quest for Power and Liberty, 1973–1900.* Philadelphia: Temple University Press, 1981.

Bryce, J. *The American Commonwealth.* 2 vols. New York: Macmillan, 1888.

Callahan, R. *Education and the Cult of Efficiency.* Chicago: University of Chicago Press, 1962.

Caswell, H. L. *City School Surveys: An Interpretation and Appraisal.* New York: Teachers College, 1929.

Chandler, A. *The Visible Hand: The Managerial Revolution in American Business.* Cambridge, Mass.: Harvard University Press, 1977.

Chubb, J. E., and Moe, T. M. *Politics, Markets, & America's Schools.* Washington, D.C.: Brookings Institution, 1990.

Clune, W. H., and Witte, J. F. (eds.). *Choice and Control in American Education.* 2 vols. New York: Falmer Press, 1990.

Cohen, D. K. "Reforming School Politics." *Harvard Educational Review,* 1978, *48,* 429–447.

Cohen, D. K. "Governance and Instruction: The Promise of Decentralization and Choice." In W. H. Clune and J. F. Witte (eds.), *Choice and Control in American Education.* New York: Falmer Press, 1990.

Cohen, D. K., and Rosenberg, B. H. "Functions and Fantasies: Understanding Schools in Capitalist America." *History of Education Quarterly,* 1977, *17,* 130–137.

"Confessions of Three Superintendents." *Atlantic Monthly,* 1896, *82,* 644–653.

Cremin, L. A. *The Transformation of the School: Progressivism in American Education, 1876–1957.* New York: Vintage, 1964.

Cremin, L. A. *American Education: The National Experience, 1783–1876.* New York: HarperCollins, 1980.

Cronin, J. M. *The Control of Urban Schools: Perspectives on the Power of Educational Reformers.* New York: Free Press, 1973.

Cuban, L. *Urban School Chiefs Under Fire.* Chicago: University of Chicago Press, 1976.

Cuban, L. *How Teachers Taught: Constancy and Change in American Classrooms, 1890–1980.* New York: Longman, 1984.

Cuban, L. "Reforming Again, Again, and Again." *Educational Researcher,* 1990, *19,* 3–13.

Cubberley, E. P. *Rural Life and Education: A Study of the Rural-School Problem as a Phase of the Rural-Life Problem.* Boston: Houghton Mifflin, 1914.

Cubberley, E. P. *Public Education in the United States.* Boston: Houghton Mifflin, 1934.

Dewey, J. *The School and Society.* Chicago: University of Chicago Press, 1899.

Dobson, J. *Dare to Discipline.* New York: Bantam Books, 1977.

Downs, A. "Up and Down with Ecology—The Issue-Attention Cycle." *Public Interest,* 1972, *28,* 38–50.

Elmore, R. F., and McLaughlin, M. W. *Steady Work: Policy, Practice, and the Reform of American Education.* Santa Monica, Calif.: Rand Corporation, 1988.

Elmore, R. F., and Associates. *Restructuring Schools: The Next Generation of Educational Reform.* San Francisco: Jossey-Bass, 1990.

Farnham, W. D. "The Weakened Spring of Government: A Study in Nineteenth Century American History." *American Historical Review,* 1963, *68,* 662–680.

Firestone, W. A., Fuhrman, S. H., and Kirst, M. W. *The Progress of Reform: An Appraisal of State Education Initiatives.* New Brunswick, N. J.: Center for Policy Research in Education, 1989.

Fuller, E. *The Old Country School: The Story of Rural Education in the Middle West.* Chicago: University of Chicago Press, 1982.

Higham, J. "Hanging Together: Divergent Unities in American History." *Journal of American History,* 1974, *61,* 5–28.

Hlebowitsh, P. S. "Playing Power Politics: How *A Nation at Risk* Achieved Its National Stature." *Journal of Research and Development in Education,* 1990, *23,* 82–88.

James, T. "Rights of Conscience and State School Systems in Nineteenth-Century America." In P. Finkelman and S. E. Gottlieb (eds.), *Toward a Usable Past: Liberty Under State Constitutions.* Athens: University of Georgia Press, 1991.

"Jolt." *The New Yorker,* Aug. 12, 1991, pp. 23–24.

Kaestle, C. *Pillars of the Republic: Common Schools and American Society, 1780–1860.* New York: Hill and Wang, 1983.

Kaestle, C., and Smith, M. "The Federal Role in Elementary and Secondary Education, 1940–1980." *Harvard Educational Review,* 1982, *52,* 384–408.

Kaplan, G. "Scapegoating the Schools." In William T. Grant Foundation, *Voices from the Field: 30 Expert Opinions on America 2000, the Bush Administration Strategy to "Reinvent" America's Schools.* Washington, D. C.: Commission on Work, Family and Citizenship, William T. Grant Foundation, 1991.

Kienel, P. A. *Why Christian Schools Are Good for America.* Whittier, Calif.: Association of Christian Schools International, 1985.

Kirp, D. L. "Law, Politics, and Equal Educational Opportunity: The Limits of Judicial Involvement." *Harvard Educational Review,* 1977, *47,* 117–136.

Kirp, D. L. *Just Schools: The Idea of Racial Equality in American Education.* Berkeley: University of California Press, 1982.

Kirst, M. W. "Recent State Education Reform in the United States: Looking Backward and Forward." *Educational Administration Quarterly,* 1988, *24,* 319–328.

Kirst, M. W. *The Progress of Reform: An Appraisal of State Education Initiatives.* New Brunswick, N. J.: Center for Policy Research in Education, 1989.

Kluger, R. *Simple Jusice: The History of Brown v. Board of Education and Black America's Struggle for Equality.* New York: Knopf, 1977.

Levin, H. *Community Control of Schools.* Washington, D.C.: Brookings Institution, 1970.

Lewis, P. S. "Private Education and the Subcultures of Dissent: Alternative/Free Schools (1965-1975) and Christian Fundamentalist Schools (1965-1990)." Unpublished doctoral dissertation, School of Education, Stanford University, 1991.

Lieberman, M. *The Future of Public Education.* Chicago: University of Chicago Press, 1960.

Lynd, R. S., and Lynd, H. M. *Middletown: A Study in Contemporary American Culture.* New York: Harcourt Brace Jovanovich, 1929.

McLaughlin, M. W. "Learning from Experience: Lessons from Policy Implementation." *Educational Evaluation and Policy Analysis,* 1987, *9,* 171-178.

McLaughlin, M. W. "Where's the Community in *America 2000*?" In William T. Grant Foundation, *Voices from the Field: 30 Expert Opinions on America 2000, the Bush Administration Strategy to "Reinvent" America's Schools.* Washington, D.C.: Commission on Work, Family, and Citizenship, William T. Grant Foundation, 1991.

Mansfield, E. D. *American Education, Its Principles and Elements.* New York: Barnes, 1851.

March, J. G., and Olsen, J. P. "The New Institutionalism: Organizational Factors in Political Life." *American Political Science Review,* 1984, *78,* 734-749.

Messerli, J. *Horace Mann: A Biography.* New York: Knopf, 1972.

Meyer, J. W. *The Impact of the Centralization of Educational Funding and Control of State and Local Educational Governance.* Stanford, Calif.: Institute for Research on Educational Finance and Governance, Stanford University, 1980.

Meyer, J. W., and Rowan, B. "Institutionalized Organizations: Formal Structure as Myth and Ceremony." *American Journal of Sociology,* 1977, *83,* 340-363.

Meyer, J. W., Scott, W. R., Strang, D., and Creighton, A. *Bureaucratization Without Centralization: Changes in the Organizational System of American Public Education, 1940-1980.* Project Report No. 85-A11. Stanford, Calif.: Institute for Finance and Governance, Stanford University, 1985.

Mosher, E., Hastings, A. H., and Wagoner, J., Jr. *Pursuing Equal Educational Opportunity: The New Activists.* New York: ERIC Clearing House on Urban Education, 1979.

National Center for Education Statistics. *Digest of Education Statistics, 1988.* Washington, D.C.: National Center for Education Statistics, 1988.

National Commission on Excellence in Education. *A Nation at Risk.* Washington, D.C.: U.S. Government Printing Office, 1983.

National Governors' Association. *From Rhetoric to Action: State Progress in Restructuring the Educational System.* Washington, D.C.: National Governors' Association, 1991.

Nelkin, D. *The Creation Controversy: Science and Scripture in the Schools.* New York: Norton, 1982.

Newby, R., and Tyack, D. "Victims Without 'Crimes': Some Historical Perspectives on Black Education." *Journal of Negro Education,* 1971, *40,* 192–206.

Olson, L. "The 'Restructuring' Puzzle: Ideas for Revamping 'Egg-Crate' Schools Abound, But to What Ends?" *Education Week,* Nov. 2, 1988, pp. 7, 7–11.

Ornstein, A. C. "Centralization and Decentralization of Large Public School Systems." *Urban Education,* 1989, *24,* 233–235.

Perko, F. M. *A Time to Favor Zion: The Ecology of Religious and School Developments on the Urban Frontier, Cincinnati, 1830–1870.* Chicago: Educational Studies Press, 1988.

Philbrick, J. D. *City School Systems in the United States.* Washington, D.C.: U.S. Government Printing Office, 1885.

Popkewitz, T. S. "Educational Reform: Rhetoric, Ritual, and Social Interest." *Educational Theory,* 1988, *38,* 77–93.

Powell, A. G., Farrar, E., and Cohen, D. K. *The Shopping Mall High School: Winners and Losers in the Educational Market Place.* Boston: Houghton Mifflin, 1985.

Putka, G. "Foundation Encourages Firms to Devise a New Class of Schools." *Wall Street Journal,* Aug. 26, 1991, pp. B1–B2.

Ravitch, D. *The Uncertain Crusade.* New York: Basic Books, 1983.

Reller, T. L. *The Development of the City Superintendency of Schools in the United States.* Philadelphia: T. L. Reller, 1935.

Rice, E. *The Sunday-School Movement 1780–1917 and the Ameri-*

*can Sunday-School Union 1817-1917.* Philadelphia: American Sunday School Union, 1917.

Rice, J. M. *The Public School System of the United States.* New York: Century, 1893.

Rist, R., and Anson, D. *Education, Social Science, and the Judicial Process.* New York: Teachers College Press, 1977.

Sadker, M. P., and Sadker, D. M. *Sex Equity Handbook for Schools.* New York: Longman, 1982.

Sargent, N. "The California Constitutional Convention of 1878–79." *California Law Review,* 1917, *6,* 10–35.

Sher, J. (ed.). *Education in Rural America: A Reassessment of Conventional Wisdom.* Boulder, Colo.: Westview Press, 1977.

Smith, T. "Protestant Schooling and American Nationality, 1800–1850." *Journal of American History,* 1967, *53,* 679–695.

Spring, J. H. *Education and the Rise of the Corporate State.* Boston: Beacon Press, 1972.

Stinchcombe, A. L. "Social Structure and Organizations." In J. G. March (ed.), *Handbook of Organizations.* Chicago: Rand McNally, 1965.

Strayer, G. D. "Progress in City School Administration During the Past Twenty-Five Years." *School and Society,* 1930, *32,* 325–345.

Taggart, R. J. *Private Philanthropy and Public Education: Pierre S. DuPont and the Delaware Schools 1890–1940.* Newark: University of Delaware Press, 1988.

Thomas, G. M., Meyer, J. W., Ramirez, F. O., and Boli, J. *Institutional Structure: Constituting State, Society, and the Individual.* Newbury Park, Calif.: Sage, 1987.

Troen, S. *The Public and the Schools: Shaping the St. Louis System, 1838–1920.* Columbus: University of Missouri Press, 1975.

Tyack, D. B. *The One Best System: A History of American Urban Education.* Cambridge, Mass.: Harvard University Press, 1974.

Tyack, D. "Ways of Seeing: An Essay on the History of Compulsory Schooling." *Harvard Educational Review,* 1976, *46,* 355–389.

Tyack, D. "'Restructuring' in Historical Perspective: Tinkering Toward Utopia." *Teachers College Record,* 1990, *92,* 170–191.

Tyack, D. "Public School Reform: Reflections on Policy and Practice." *American Journal of Education,* forthcoming.

Tyack, D., and Hansot, E. *Managers of Virtue: Public School Leadership in America, 1820–1980.* New York: Basic Books, 1982.

Tyack, D., and Hansot, E. *Learning Together: A History of Coeducation in American Public Schools.* New Haven, Conn.: Yale University Press and Russell Sage Foundation, 1990.

Tyack, D., James, T., and Benavot, A. *Law and the Shaping of Public Education, 1785–1954.* Madison: University of Wisconsin Press, 1987.

Tyack, D., Kirst, M. W., and Hansot, E. "Educational Reform: Retrospect and Prospect." *Teachers College Record,* 1980, *81,* 253–269.

Tyack, D., Lowe, R., and Hansot, E. *Public Schools in Hard Times: The Great Depression and Recent Years.* Cambridge, Mass.: Harvard University Press, 1984.

U.S. Department of Education. *America 2000: An Education Strategy.* Washington, D.C.: U.S. Government Printing Office, 1991.

Waller, W. *The Sociology of Teaching.* New York: Wiley, 1932.

Warren, D. R. *To Enforce Education: A History of the Founding Years of the United States Office of Education.* Detroit, Mich: Wayne State University Press, 1974.

Weick, K. "Educational Organizations as Loosely Coupled Systems." *Administrative Science Quarterly,* 1976, *21,* 1–19.

Wiebe, R. "The Social Functions of Public Education." *American Quarterly,* 1969, *21,* 147–164.

# 2

# School Decentralization: Who Gains? Who Loses?

**Richard F. Elmore**

Debates about centralized and decentralized governance structures in education have much in common with the egg dispute reported by Jonathan Swift in *Gulliver's Travels,* book 1, chapter 4:

> It is allowed on all hands, that the primitive way of breaking eggs before we eat them, was upon the larger end: But his present Majesty's grandfather, while he was a boy, going to eat an egg, and breaking it according to the ancient practice, happened to cut one of his fingers. Whereupon the Emperor, his father, published an edict commanding all his subjects, upon great penalties, to break the smaller end of their eggs. The people have so highly resented this law, that our histories tell us, there have been six rebellions raised on that account; wherein one emperor lost his life, and another his crown. . . . It is computed that eleven thousand persons have, at several times, suffered death, rather than submit to break their eggs at the smaller end. Many hundred large volumes have been published upon this controversy: But the books of the Big-Endians have been long forbidden, and the whole party rendred [sic] incapable by law of holding employments [Swift, 1947, p. 231].

## Decentralization and the Democratic Wish

American education is once again in the throes of decentralization. As in past periods, the doctrinal lines are firmly drawn. Public school bureaucracy, school reformers widely agree, has become too large, too inefficient, and too unresponsive, especially in the nation's cities. As a consequence of the growth of centralized school bureaucracies, schools have become mired in rules and cut off from their clients—students, parents, and community members. Ambitious, if not radical, reforms are required to rectify this situation. Central bureaucracy must be substantially reduced; schools must be given more autonomy and more responsibility on such matters as personnel, budget, and curriculum; new governance structures must be designed that hold schools accountable to their clients, rather than to their bureaucratic superiors. Reformers yearn for a simpler, more direct link between the schools and "the people." In this link, according to reformers, lies the solution to a variety of ills of American education, including the inefficiencies of centralized administration, the isolation of public schools from the political support of the communities in which they operate, and the poor performance and lax standards that have made American education mediocre by international standards.

In any specific case, decentralizing reforms seem, at least on the surface, to provide very plausible answers to the ills of public education. In general, however, repeated cycles of centralizing and decentralizing reforms in education have had little discernible effect on the efficiency, accountability, or effectiveness of public schools. From this broader vantage point, the cycles of centralization and decentralization in public education bear a striking similarity to Jonathan Swift's account of the dispute between the Big-Endians and the Little-Endians. An event triggers the formation of a doctrine about whether administrative or political responsibility should be centralized or decentralized. A debate ensues about the merits of centralization and decentralization. At any given point in the debate, the "correct" or "enlightened" position is usually clear: it is the opposite of whatever was previously correct. Each doctrine is well developed, to the point where it can be recited more or less as a mantra by reformers and practitioners. Although those who subscribe to the old "incorrect" or "unenlightened" doctrine are not usually treated with the harshness of Swift's Big-Endians, they are consigned, albeit temporarily, to a sort of intellectual bullpen, on the periphery of play, where they try to keep their doctrine warm for the next inning. Swift's account captures the fervor with which these orthodoxies are established and argued, usually in isolation from any serious analysis of their practical consequences. What practical difference, after all, is there between breaking the egg on the big end and breaking it on the little end? One might as well ask what practical consequences follow from the centralization or decentralization of administrative or political responsibility in American education.

Indeed, research on centralization and decentralization in American education is characterized by the virtually complete disconnection between structural reform and anything having to do with classroom instruction or the learning of students. Whatever the politics of centralization and decentralization is "about" in American education—and it is about many things, as we shall see—it is not fundamentally or directly about teaching and learning. This disconnection between structural reform and the core technology of schooling means that major reforms can wash over the educational system, consuming large amounts of scarce resources—money; time; the energy of parents, teachers, and administrators; the political capital of elected officials—without having any discernible effect on what students actually learn in school. Furthermore, because the process of centralization and decentralization is cyclical, and because each cycle leaves behind some vestige of its reforms, the cumulative effect of several cycles of reform is to make the educational system more complex, less accessible to its clients, less comprehensible to those who work in it, and therefore less manageable, even though each reform, taken by itself, is predicated on the assumption that it alone will make the system simpler, more comprehensible, and more manageable (see Cohen, 1990).

America's fascination with centralization and decentralization in education is an example of what Morone (1990) has called the "democratic wish." American political culture is based on two fundamental convictions: faith in government, based on direct, communal democracy; and the fear that concentrations of power in governmental institutions are dangerous to individual liberty. As a protection against concentrations of power, we construct political institutions in ways that institutionalize conflict and disperse responsibility. These institutions are vulnerable to stalemate; they are especially good at blocking and frustrating attempts at change. Periodically, reformers act on the democratic wish to return power to "the people," through reforms that push decision making out into smaller, simpler, more directly accountable institutions. These new reforms almost never displace existing institutions, which are the products of earlier, similar reforms and of attempts to disperse and fragment power. The new institutional forms, born of the democratic wish, emerge and become routinized. Concern for maintenance of these new institutions displaces the fervor of the reforms that spawned them. Soon this concern for maintenance provokes opposition and results in the mobilization of new groups bent on reform. Political opposition mobilizes, and these institutions lose their legitimacy as truly representative of "the people." The institutions in turn become the subjects of the next generation of protest and reform, which in turn spawns yet another set of institutions, this time truly responsive to "the people" in the eyes of the reformers. And so it goes.

The first reformers in American education, during the early nineteenth century, saw the formation of the common school as a way of putting education in the hands of the people. As Tyack and Hansot have argued, this period of reform had the character of a highly decentralized social movement. It was held together by voluntary networks and consciously modeled on the missionary model. It produced an atomized structure of individual schools, each one tied closely to its immediate constituency (Tyack and Hansot, 1982). This approach was an ingenious way to spread public education in a vast country with major regional differences, but it also contained the seeds of its own demise.

The reformers of the Progressive Era saw the old system as parochial and, at its worst, corrupt. The very closeness of schools to their communities meant that they had become places where relatives and political cronies could be employed, rather than places where good education (defined by the Progressives as enlightened professional practice) would occur. Public schools should be accountable to a broader community, the reformers argued, which usually meant to business and social elites. The administrative progressives created the locally centralized structure that forms the basic organizational template of American education today: locally elected boards, central administrative staffs, and building-level administrators, all overseeing teachers who work, for the most part, in isolated classrooms. From the 1920s through the 1950s, this structure proved durable.

In the 1960s, growing consciousness of racial injustice spawned a reaction to the centralized systems constructed by the administrative progressives, which resulted in several ambitious attempts at decentralization and in a general loosening of central administrative control, even in local school systems that underwent no formal decentralization. These reforms were designed to bring schools closer to people who had traditionally been excluded from active participation in the governance of public education. By the late 1970s, critics were observing that loosening central control, particularly in large urban systems, had resulted in substantial variation among schools in curriculum and students' performance.

In the early 1980s, the crisis of confidence in public education generated by the so-called excellence movement resulted in states' introducing clearer standards for teachers and students and in districts' introducing greater consistency among schools in curriculum and teaching. These reforms were based on the assumption that schools had lost sight of their accountability to the broader community.

No sooner were these reforms under way than another set of reforms emerged, in the mid 1980s, all predicated on a strong doubt that school bureaucracies, as currently constituted, could ever manage to provide high-quality education. These reformers are split at least three ways: among advocates of administrative decentralization, now called *school-site management;* advocates of market solutions, or relatively unfettered parental choice; and advocates of systemic reform, or greater centralization on certain dimensions (notably curricula, teacher training, student assessment, and finance) and less centralization on others (notably governance and specific instructional decisions). These reforms reflect deep division over who the relevant constituents are for public education. The advocates of market solutions argue that the content of public education should become, in effect, the sum of the individual decisions of parents and students. Advocates of administrative decentralization argue that the content of public education should be the sum of decisions made by local school governance structures, which include parents, teachers, and administrators. Advocates of systemic reform argue that the content of public education should be determined by some combination of "tight" central control on dimensions related to systemwide quality and "loose" central control, or decentralized decision making, on dimensions related to the tailoring of curricula and teaching to specific settings and students. Advocates of systemic reform argue, in effect, that the content of public education should be the sum of state and national decisions that set quality standards and local and school decisions that determine how to meet these quality standards in the context of specific communities and groups of students (Malen, Ogawa, and Krantz, 1990; Chubb and Moe, 1990; Smith and O'Day, 1991).

Historically, then, political debates over centralization and decentralization in American education are only superficially about the efficiency, effectiveness, or accountability of specific structural arrangements. More fundamentally, they are debates about how to construct a public for public education. For advocates of decentralizing reforms, "the people" are parents and community members who have a direct interest in specific schools and who often were deliberately or unintentionally excluded from participation under earlier forms of organization. For the advocates of centralizing reforms, "the people" means the broader, more diffuse community of citizens, including not only those with immediate connections to specific schools but also those with a general interest in the collective results of the entire system. Advocates of decentralizing reforms accuse centralizers of deliberately concealing the interests of specific constituencies—education professionals and business interests, for example—in their appeals to a broader public. Advocates of centralizing reforms accuse decentralizers of making public education the private preserve of narrow, parochial, often corrupt constituencies that are less concerned about the general improvement of education than about serving their own interest in money and influence.

Morone (1990, p. 29) argues that this ambivalence over who constitutes "the people" runs through the entire fabric of American political institutions, and the ambivalence is symptomatic of the fact that "Americans have failed to institutionalize a communal spirit," a problem he characterizes as "a dilemma of political practice and institutional design."

In education, arguably the most political of American governmental functions, this dilemma of political practice and institutional design takes a special form. Debates in education over institutional structure are not just debates about who constitutes the public; they are also debates about the legitimacy of professional educators to speak with authority on matters of educational practice. In a society obsessed by the competing claims of various political interests, educators are increasingly treated by political decision makers—and, indeed, increasingly see themselves—as one among many political interests with a stake in public decisions about the enterprise. Many reforms, of both the centralizing and decentralizing sort, are explicitly and calculatedly designed to undermine claims by educators to any special knowledge about teaching and learning and to any special right to use that knowledge in ways that would increase their influence in educational policy (see, for example, Sykes, 1990.) Reformers may disagree about who constitutes "the people" for the purpose of any particular reform; but, at least since the 1960s, reformers usually agree that educators are not to be trusted, any more than any other parochial special-interest group, with major decisions about the direction or content of public education. If war is too important to be left to the generals, the argument goes, then education is certainly too important to be left to the educators (see, for example, Finn, 1991).

This general tendency to treat educators as one among many political constituencies has had many effects (including marginal professional status for teachers), but none has been more pervasive than the disconnection between policy and practice in educational reform. The politics of structural reform in education has increasingly become a politics about the authority and legitimacy of various institutional arrangements, disconnected from any serious treatment of whether these arrangements can be expected to have any impact on what students learn in school. The stakes of structural reform are largely reckoned in terms of who gains and who loses influence within the governance structure, not in terms of whether structural change leads to changes in the conditions of teaching and learning. To treat conditions of teaching and learning as central to reform would mean treating knowledge about teaching and learning as authoritative in political decision making, and this would be to adopt a view that is at odds with the political role of educators as representatives of specific political interests.

Lest my argument be interpreted as special pleading for educators, let me add that educators themselves have been among the most enthusiastic partisans of disconnecting structural reform from teaching and learning. Site-based management, the major form of administrative decentralization at the moment, is almost entirely the product of education professionals, yet there is little or no evidence that it has any direct or predictable relationship to changes in instruction and students' learning. In fact, the evidence suggests that the implementation of site-based management reforms has a more or less random relationship to changes in curriculum, teaching, and students' learning (Malen, Ogawa, and Krantz, 1990). Educators have learned to play the game of structural reform in ways that are consistent with the prevailing form of interest-group politics: rationalize structural changes not in terms of how they will affect teaching and learning but in terms of who will gain access and influence to political decisions about schooling.

Debates about centralization and decentralization in American education, then, are mainly debates about *who* should have access to and influence over decisions, not about *what* the content and practice of teaching and learning should be or *how* to change those things.

## The Contradictions of Structural Reform

The interplay of political interests around centralization and decentralization leads not only to the uncoupling of structural change from educational practice but also to a number of contradictions in the basic design and operation of administrative structures. These contradictions center on basic questions: Who are the intended beneficiaries of decentralization? To whom are schools accountable? In what terms are the alleged benefits of decentralization to be reckoned?

### *Decentralization to Whom?*

To say that authority and responsibility for key decisions should be "decentralized" in an educational system is to say very little, in the absence of some set of beliefs about who are the objects or beneficiaries of decentralization, whose interests are to be served by decentralization, and how decentralization is supposed to serve those interests. To see how these questions are resolved in real settings, consider the case of New York City.

New York City's 1969 decentralization grew, in part, out of a bitter and divisive teachers' strike, in which the United Federation of Teachers (UFT) protested the authority of a community organization in the Ocean Hill-Brownsville section of Brooklyn to hire, fire, and reassign teachers and principals. Between May and November 1968, the UFT struck the citywide system three times. The "community control" project in Ocean Hill-Brownsville, one of three model projects in the city, had been the brainchild of officers at the Ford Foundation and was subsequently joined by education reformers in the city and by community activists in the neighborhood.

The reformers saw an opportunity to break what they regarded as the pernicious control of the citywide board of education and to force recognition of the poor quality of schooling for black and Puerto Rican children. The UFT, for its part, saw the More Effective Schools program—a pilot, school-based program that brought substantial resources to schools with heavy concentrations of disadvantaged students—as a progressive solution to the citywide problems of quality, and the UFT saw the attempt of the community organization to assert control of hiring, firing, and reassignment as a direct challenge to its hard-won efforts to ensure fair treatment and decent working conditions for its members across the whole city (Mayer, 1968).

Preceding and running parallel to the battle over community control in Ocean Hill-Brownsville was a broader policy debate, at the city and state levels, over decentralization. In 1897, New York City had moved from a system in which each borough had its own board to one in which there was a centralized board for the whole city. In 1902, forty-six local boards of education were established, their members appointed by the borough presidents, and each of the boards sent a representative to the central board. In 1917, the local boards were reduced to an advisory capacity, and the central board was reduced to seven members, appointed by the mayor and the borough presidents. This system of weak local boards continued into the 1960s. In 1961, in the aftermath of a scandal over corruption in school construction, the state legislature established thirty new local boards, whose members were to be appointed by the central board but whose responsibilities remained advisory (Zimet, 1973).

By the late 1960s, the city's racial and ethnic composition had changed dramatically. Between 1950 and 1960, for example, there was a net emigration of over 1,000,000 whites from the city, and there was an immigration of nearly 400,000 African-Americans and Hispanics into the city. White school enrollment declined by over 20 percent, from over 650,000 to under 500,000, while African-American and Hispanic enrollment more than doubled, from about 300,000 to over 600,000 (State Charter Commission for New York City, 1974). Between 1960 and 1965, the city schools underwent at least three separate attempts to desegregate, each less successful than the last, which left a legacy of frustration and demoralization among the city's civil rights leaders. By the late 1960s, the increased political mobilization of minority citizens, brought about by the civil rights and desegregation struggles and coupled with increased alienation and dissatisfaction with city political institutions, given the repeated failure of desegregation efforts, resulted in increased political support for community control among minority community leaders (Zimet, 1973; Fantini, Gittel, and Magat, 1971).

Before the first of the three 1968 teachers' strikes, Mayor John V. Lindsay appointed an advisory panel, chaired by McGeorge Bundy of the Ford Foundation. The panel proposed that responsibility for school governance be decentralized to community school district boards, jointly constituted by mayoral appointments and by community elections. This plan was rejected by both the New York City School Board and the State Board of Regents. In May 1968, the state legislature passed a law allowing the mayor to appoint four additional members to the city board. The mayor promptly appointed members sympathetic to decentralization. This newly constituted board began its work at the peak of the teachers' strike and submitted its own proposal for decentralization to the state legislature. That proposal was passed in the spring of 1969, and this bill forms the basis of the present system of decentralization in New York City (Zimet, 1973).

Under this system, the citywide board of education is constituted by the mayor's appointment of two members and by the election of the remaining five members from the city's five boroughs. Each of the city's thirty-two community districts is governed by a board elected from within that district. The citywide board of examiners and the chancellor retain responsibility for determining the fitness of candidates for teaching and administrative posts, but community boards are responsible for specific personnel decisions within their districts. The community boards are also responsible for specific curriculum decisions and subject to citywide and state policies, but the chancellor can suspend or remove a community board, or any member of it, if a district fails to meet city or state minimum curricular standards. The citywide board of education retains responsibility for all the city's high schools (Zimet, 1973).

Notice that there are several answers to the question "Decentralization to whom?" in the politics of decentralization in New York City. Various generations of policy makers at the state and local levels have answered the question largely by balancing the interests of various constituencies, responding opportunistically to the changing ethnic and racial composition of the city, and correcting what they saw as abuses of whatever structure was in place. Policy makers, in other words, could not answer the question "Decentralization to whom?" without first determining whose interests needed attention. The advocates of community control subscribed to the idea that community members should have responsibility for making virtually all decisions affecting schools (*community* was defined not in terms of the participants in a given school but in terms of a geographically defined neighborhood). The citywide Board of Education subscribed to the idea that the whole structure had to be governed by a political body accountable to the electorate of the city as a whole, whatever provisions were made for decentralized administration of the schools. Educators held to the notion that the school as an organizational unit should be the object of decentralization for certain specific instructional decisions, while other matters—notably policies affecting conditions of work—should be decided at the citywide level. Policy makers resolved these various conflicting views not by choosing a single constituency to exercise authority over the schools but rather by building a structure that balanced various constituencies against each other. The community boards were given circumscribed authority over elementary and secondary schools; the citywide Board of Education retained authority over most budget matters, the personnel system, and the high schools. Educators retained a considerable degree of school-level influence, largely because of fragmented authority at the higher levels.

Even in the more recent and arguably more radical form of decentralization in Chicago, one can see much the same ambiguity over who is to be the object of decentralization. As in New York, decentralization in Chicago grew out of a bitter and divisive teachers' strike. The resulting plan—the outcome, as in New York, of outside reformers' acting through state government—put decision-making authority for hiring principals and formulating and implementing school-improvement plans (among other things) in the hands of 542 local school councils. The plan reconstituted the citywide board as a delegate assembly of local board members, and it set targets for reducing staffing in the central administration of the citywide board. Nevertheless, the plan is quite prescriptive where the responsibilities of local school councils are concerned; for example, it lays out in some detail how councils should go about constructing and overseeing the implementation of school-improvement plans (see Hess, 1991). The state law also prescribes overall objectives for the Chicago schools and a monitoring mechanism for seeing whether the system achieves those objectives. The reform has left Chicago's structure for collective bargaining with teachers virtually intact. While the focus of reform is on decentralization to the school community, that feature is nested in a broader structure, which implies that schools are ultimately responsible to a wider constituency at the citywide and state levels.

A similar pattern of ambiguity concerning who is the object of decentralization can be seen in the myriad school-site management schemes implemented by local districts over the last decade or so. Reviews of the literature on school-site management find that the authority of schools and of school-site councils—which typically represent some combination of parents, administrators, and staff—is either very vaguely specified or highly circumscribed; seldom if ever does school-site management actually mean real control over the core elements of the organization (budgeting, staffing, curriculum, organizational structure, and governance). In most instances, school-site management means some incremental shift of responsibility from central administration to the school site on some limited set of dimensions. Nor does school site management ever fundamentally alter the web of policies, many of which originate not from the local district but from the state and federal levels, within which schools operate. The idea that school-site management involves decentralization of authority and responsibility to "the school," then, is a convenient fiction that masks considerable ambiguity and disagreement over who is the object of decentralization and what decisions are supposed to be made at the school-site level (Malen, Ogawa, and Krantz, 1990; Clune and White, 1988).

### *Accountability to Whom?*

To say that decentralization increases "accountability" in educational systems is to say very little in the absence of some set of beliefs about who is to be accountable to whom for what. On the surface, most decentralizing efforts express a common theme on the subject of accountability: schools are to be held accountable to the public for the results that they produce with students. Below the surface of this simple (some would say simplistic) formula lie roiling ambiguity and outright contradiction.

One source of ambiguity centers on the issue of who constitutes the public. As noted at the beginning of this chapter, there is in republican government a deep-seated ambiguity concerning whether "the people" means the public at large, as represented through democratic institutions, or the public writ small, as represented in particular geographical constituencies, special-interest groups, or factions. In New York, decentralizing to the community level created a new set of official institutions—community boards—which were, in theory, expected to be more responsive to the immediate needs of parents and students because the interests of the community could be represented more specifically and immediately through these institutions. In practice, however, the community boards' politics is at least as factionalized as citywide politics; and when factions assume control of community districts, they are at least as exclusionary in their policies and practices toward minority factions within their geographical constituencies as larger-scale institutions are. To be an African-American in East Harlem, where community politics is effectively dominated by Puerto Rican Hispanics, is to be in an even smaller minority than an African-American would be in the city at large. To say, then, that creating smaller institutions that are closer to "the people" increases accountability to "the people" is as often as not to substitute democratic sentiment for analysis. In fact, an equally compelling case can be made—and has been made, by James Madison in the tenth and fifty-first *Federalist* papers—that the best protection against factionalism and repression of minorities is to be found in the "Chinese box" design of the federal system, which allows citizens who feel that they have been poorly treated at one level of government to have redress at other levels (Hamilton, Madison, and Jay, [1787–1788] 1941). In this model, the matter of who constitutes "the people" for any specific question of public policy depends entirely on the level of the system at which the issue is addressed. There is no absolute presumption that "the people" at one level are any wiser, more informed, or better equipped to make decisions than "the people" at any other level; the only presumption is that factional interests will exert different influences at different levels of aggregation.

Another source of ambiguity in the relationship between accountability and decentralization is the hierarchical relationships concealed in decentralization schemes. These relationships may become evident only over time. Decentralization in both New York City and Chicago is a creature of state policy. In both instances, reformers at the city level took their case to the state legislature and were able to gain significant changes in the institutional structure of the local education system. After theses policies are set in motion, local actors tend to treat the institutional framework as given, rather than as an artifact of politics at a higher level of government, which can be changed whenever the politics at the level change. To say, then, that community district decentralization in New York or school-site decentralization in Chicago makes schools more accountable to their immediate communities is to say something important about the short-term incentives operating on schools, but it is also to ignore something important about the longer-term dynamics of accountability in the system at large. When charges of corruption are leveled at community districts in New York City (as they have been with increasing frequency), the authority of the citywide Board of Education and the state attorney general is invoked to resolve such charges. In other words, the community boards are also "accountable" to a citywide and statewide constituency for their fiscal and personnel practices. One wonders what will happen as the Chicago experiment in school-site decentralization progresses to the point where it becomes clear that certain schools are performing at consistently low levels or that certain communities have somewhat different ideas about how to manage personnel decisions. It seems unlikely that these problems will be resolved entirely in terms of "accountability" to local constituencies, since those local constituencies will be implicated in the problems that the schools have produced. It seems more likely that various higher-level jurisdictions will become involved, according to the seriousness of the problem and its visibility, and that these jurisdictions will represent the interests of very different constituencies.

A final source of ambiguity is vagueness about what the schools will be held accountable for in decentralized schemes. Policy analysts and good-government reformers take for granted that decentralization is about producing better results for children, through whatever outcome measures may be fashionable at the moment. In operation, decentralization schemes involve much more complex and ambiguous means-ends relationships. The Ford Foundation officers and professional reformers who put together the New York City decentralization plan clearly believed that the city's schools had to become more closely connected to the emerging minority political activists in the city and that this connection would ultimately fuel an improvement in the quality of education for children. This relationship has turned out to be much more complex and problematic than the reformers assumed. The reformers could have taken an initial cue from the fact that the key disputes in the Ocean Hill–Brownsville conflict did not have much to do with the quality of classroom instruction in the neighborhood's schools, but rather with who had the authority to fire and replace existing school staff. After watching Rody McCoy, the chief administrator in Ocean Hill–Brownsville, Martin Mayer observed:

> When I arrived at Ocean Hill that month [March 1968] . . . , I found McCoy working desperately hard with his principals and staff—some white, some Negro—to put a head of steam under a number of new programs in reading, math, Negro and Puerto Rican culture, bilingualism, etc. He had begun small-scale training programs for "paraprofessionals." . . . He was planning for teacher teams, nongraded classrooms, programmed instruction—everything in the way of educational innovation that might help in a neighborhood where most children were as far behind as they were in Ocean Hill. I visited four of the district's schools on as many days, and returned to tell McCoy that I had seen a good deal of routine and some substandard teaching, and that the schools seemed dominated by a fear of disorder which impeded teaching. He said he knew, that he was working to establish a climate in which teachers could teach, and that once he had the climate he was going to judge who was good and could give help, who needed help, and who ought to be eliminated from the district. It was all intelligent, level-headed and very sad [Mayer, 1968, pp. 35-36).

With one hand, McCoy was attempting to improve instruction in the schools; with the other, he was attempting to respond to community pressure for another kind of accountability—involving employment in the schools—by firing and reassigning career teachers and principals. He was being "accountable" on both hands, but being accountable did not necessarily result in better education for children. In fact, two potentially conflicting conceptions of accountability were at work in McCoy's actions—accountability for students' learning and accountability to adults' demands for access. In the end, educational improvement and accountability for students' learning fell by the wayside: the politics of accountability to adults' demands for access was more pressing.

Systems of decentralization that attempt to draw schools into closer relationships with their communities inevitably entail such conflicting notions of accountability. To say that such schemes increase "accountability" is not, after all, to say much about their likely effect on students.

### *What Sort of Efficiency?*

Centralized bureaucracy is always an attractive target, and reformers usually see decentralization as opening up opportunities for more efficient government through the reduction of the overhead costs associated with centralized administration and through the use of those resources for direct delivery of services at the lowest level of the system. To say that decentralization increases efficiency, however, is to say very little in the absence of knowledge about the level of aggregation at which efficiency is important and in the absence of knowledge about how resources are used in so-called decentralized systems.

One could argue, for example, that in New York City (with the city as a whole as the relevant level of aggregation) the introduction of community school districts has been an extremely inefficient measure. Community districts have simply replicated the organizational model of the larger system, creating locally run administrative bureaucracies that oversee schools and provide staff support to community boards. With the community district as the relevant level of aggregation, one can argue that important efficiencies have occurred in certain specific cases. In Community District 4, in East Harlem, for example, the central administration has shifted resources significantly away from central administration and toward the schools and has experimented at the school level with staffing arrangements that eliminate administrative and support staff and reallocate those resources to teaching (Elmore, 1990). In the system as a whole, however, these efficiencies are idiosyncratic.

In Chicago, the citywide administration is under state mandate to meet certain targets for reduction in central staff and reallocation of resources to individual schools. At the moment, individual schools are grappling with what it means to have each school governed by its own elected board and with the implications of that system of governance for the use of resources in the system. One thing seems clear, however, by analogy to New York City: one cannot assume that just because resources are being used at the school level, they are being efficiently allocated for maximum impact on students' learning. It may be that school-site decision making is at least as inefficient in its use of resources as centralized decision making is, if cost per unit of output is used as the criterion of inefficiency. One could imagine, for example, the consequences of some five hundred schools all inventing their own curricula, staff development plans, and building maintenance programs. In fact, the reformers have already anticipated this problem and are busily developing more "efficient" (and, incidentally, more centralized) mechanisms for accomplishing these tasks. For the reformers, these mechanisms are "good" centralization in that they are controlled by people sympathetic to the reforms, rather than representing the "bad" old form of centralization at the district level. Whether there is much difference, in terms of effects on students, between the "good" new centralization and the "bad" old centralization is, as they say, an empirical question.

For our purposes, however, it is sufficient to observe that the relationship between decentralization and efficiency in education is tenuous at best. There is no simple formula for establishing a relationship between decentralized authority and efficient use of resources; there is only a series of complex, interrelated puzzles.

## Rediscovering Madison, or What's Loose and What's Tight

The debate about centralization and decentralization in American education is, like the debate between Swift's Big-Endians and Little-Endians, one of great intensity, in which the gains and losses are reckoned in political terms, but this debate has few apparent consequences for what students learn. It is a debate in which complex and puzzling issues are defined in simplistic terms and in which policy and administrative structure are uncoupled from the central task of the enterprise—teaching and learning. It is a debate in which issues of instructional improvement are heavily politicized through the association of improvements in the quality of teaching and learning with the self-serving political interests of educators. For these reasons, policy debates about centralization and decentralization are unlikely to produce any improvements in schooling.

If the historical debate tells us anything, it is that the central policy question should not be whether to centralize or decentralize authority, but rather what should be loosely controlled from any given level of government and what should be tightly controlled. In the practical world of political and administrative decisions, no absolute values attach to centralization or decentralization; there are only relative values, gained from balancing the interests of constituencies at various levels of aggregation around the central task—teaching and learning. In the world of political rhetoric, however, centralization and decentralization are often treated as issues of absolute value. The orthodoxy of the moment dictates one extreme or the other, with little or no thought for the practical consequences.

Political decision makers and policy analysts can exert some influence over the debate by framing questions of authority less in terms of a dichotomy between centralization and decentralization and more in terms of the question "What should be loosely governed, and what should be tightly governed, from any given level of the system?" Implicit in this question is the assumption that multiple levels of government, as well as their constituencies, all have an interest in the governance of the schools, but that if they all attempt to assert equal influence over all matters of schooling, the system will collapse of its own organizational complexity. Thus the issue is not *whether* one level of government or another should influence education but rather *how much* influence of *what kind* any given level of government should exert over *what factors*.

It would seem reasonable, for example, for the federal government and for states to have a substantial interest in knowing how well students are gaining the knowledge and skills that will equip them to function economically and politically, but it seems less reasonable to expect that specific decisions about how to create settings in which students learn could be prescribed from the federal or the state level. Likewise, it would seem reasonable to expect schools to have a substantial interest in how well particular students perform and in whether their parents are engaged in students' learning and satisfied with the results. Between these two widely separated levels, it would seem reasonable to expect localities to have an interest in whether students are equipped for the specific social, political, and economic conditions they will face when they leave school.

Meshing these various interests is a problem of institutional design that is simply a more specific version of the broader puzzle that Madison described in the tenth and fifty-first *Federalist* papers. In Madison's formulation, certain groups with well-defined political interests will, if left to their own devices, tend to capture local political institutions and use them for their own purposes. According to Madison, the institutional structure of government should be constructed to introduce countervailing interests at higher levels of aggregation, to ensure that specific and general interests are constantly vying for the loyalties of citizens. This institutional structure succeeds when it causes citizens to evaluate public decisions not simply in terms of their own parochial interests but also in terms of the broader interests of the larger polity in which they reside.

At the level of policy design, solving Madison's problem involves deciding which institutions at different levels of government should have which responsibilities, focusing policy on those responsibilities, and radically reducing or eliminating everything else. If, for example, states have a primary interest in ensuring that students are prepared to participate effectively in the economic and political life of the community, then states may well choose to focus most or all of their attention on ensuring that students know what they need to know. In other words, state policies would focus mainly on students' performance. If localities have a primary interest in the relationship between schools and specific local constituencies, then they may focus mainly on designing institutions that create a sense of influence and ownership on the part of parents and citizens. If schools have a primary interest in serving the needs of particular students and their families, then they may focus mainly on designing institutions that tailor the broad aims of the state and of localities to differences among students. Such systems of interdependent relationships become complex and unmanageable only when disagreement and distrust among levels of government become so intense that the higher levels attempt to dictate what the lower levels should be doing. This is what Morone (1990) means when he says that Americans have a tendency to substitute adversarial solutions for communitarian solutions to democratic problems. Greater agreement among levels of government on the specific responsibilities of each level means, in effect, greater recognition of the limits of one level's ability to solve the problems of other levels, as well as greater recognition of the special problems of translating general policies into specific solutions.

In this context, the cyclical political wrangles over centralization and decentralization in American education can be seen as a protracted evasion of the central question: What should be loosely controlled, and what should be tightly controlled, from what level of the system? This "loose-tight" issue will not be resolved by simple formulas that stress the superior competence of one level of government for all purposes. Rather, it will be resolved through the designing of institutions and policies that emphasize the particular interests and competencies of each level.

## References

Chubb, J. E., and Moe, T. M. *Politics, Markets, and America's Schools.* Washington, D.C.: Brookings Institution, 1990.

Clune, W. H., and White, P. *School-Based Management: Institutional Variation, Implementation, and Issues for Further Research.* New Brunswick, N.J.: Center for Policy Research in Education, 1988.

Cohen, D. "Governance and Instruction: The Promise of Decentralization and Choice." In W. H. Clune and J. F. Witte (eds.), *Choice and Control in American Education.* Vol. 1: *The Theory of Choice and Control in American Education.* New York: Falmer Press, 1990.

Elmore, R. *Community District 4: A Case of Choice.* New Brunswick, N.J.: Center for Policy Research in Education, 1990.

Fantini, M., Gittell, M. and Magat, R. *Community Control and the Urban School.* New York: Praeger, 1971.

Finn, C. *We Must Take Charge: Our School and Our Future.* New York: Free Press, 1991.

Hamilton, A., Madison, J., and Jay, J. *The Federalist.* New York: Modern Library, 1941. (Originally published 1787–1788.)

Hess, G. A. *School Restructuring, Chicago Style.* Newbury Park, Calif.: Corwin, 1991.

Malen, B., Ogawa, R., and Krantz, J. "What Do We Know About School-Based Management? A Case Study of the Literature—A Call to Research." In W. H. Clune and J. F. Witte (eds.), *Choice and Control in American Education.* Vol. 2: *The Practice of Choice, Decentralization, and School Restructuring.* New York: Falmer Press, 1990.

Mayer, M. *The Teachers' Strike, New York, 1968.* New York: HarperCollins, 1968.

Morone, J. A. *The Democratic Wish: Popular Participation and the Limits of American Government.* New York: Basic Books, 1990.

Smith, M. S., and O'Day, J. "Systemic School Reform." In S. Fuhrman and B. Malen (eds.), *The Politics of Curriculum and Testing.* New York: Falmer Press, 1991.

State Charter Commission for New York City. *Impact of School Decentralization in New York City on Municipal Decentralization.* New York: State Charter Commission for New York City, 1974.

Swift, J. *Gulliver's Travels.* London: Oxford University Press, 1947.

Sykes, G. "Fostering Teacher Professionalism in Schools." In R. F. Elmore (ed.), *Restructuring Schools: The Next Generation of Educational Reform.* San Francisco: Jossey-Bass, 1990.

Tyack, D., and Hansot, E. *Managers of Virtue: Public School Leadership in America, 1820–1980.* New York: Basic Books, 1982.

Zimet, M. *Decentralization and School Effectiveness: A Case Study of the 1969 Decentralization Law in New York City.* New York: Teachers College Press, 1973.

# 3

# Control Versus Legitimation: The Politics of Ambivalence

**Hans N. Weiler**

This chapter seeks to shed light on the political dynamics of the debate over decentralization in educational governance by placing it within the theoretical context of the state's exercise of power. The key conceptual categories in this context are *control, conflict,* and *legitimacy.* My principal thesis is that the state, in exercising its power, has a dual interest: ensuring effectiveness and maintaining control, on the one hand, and enhancing and sustaining the normative basis of its authority (its legitimacy), on the other. Conditions of conflict, endemic in modern and pluralistic societies, highlight the fundamental contradiction between these two interests: many otherwise effective strategies for maintaining control tend to be detrimental to the state's legitimacy, and measures to enhance the state's legitimacy tend to be used at the expense of maintaining control. Nowhere does the "politics of ambivalence" become clearer than in the debate over the "optimal scale of governance" (Scharpf, n.d., p. 2)—that is, over greater centralization or decentralization in the conduct of policy. While the state's interest

*Note:* The ideas developed in this chapter go back to lectures given at the University of Luleå, Sweden, in 1988 and at the Norwegian Research Council for Applied Social Science in Oslo in 1989. The support of these institutions, of the Center for Advanced Study in the Behavioral Sciences, and of the Spencer Foundation is gratefully acknowledged. The author received valuable suggestions for improving the initial draft of this chapter from Jane Hannaway and David Tyack. This chapter is a substantial revision of earlier writings on the topic of decentralization that have appeared in *Educational Policy* (Weiler, 1989a), *Evaluation as Policymaking* (Weiler, 1990c), and *Educational Evaluation and Policy Analysis* (Weiler, 1990a).

in maintaining effective control over policy is normally best satisfied through centralized forms of governance, decentralization holds out the competing dual attraction of serving as an instrument of conflict management and "compensatory legitimation" alike.

Drawing on observations from among advanced industrialized and developing countries, this chapter pursues this line of reasoning by critically examining some of the arguments that are commonly and most prominently advanced in favor of greater decentralization in educational governance and by showing that these arguments reveal the basic contradictions that result from the principal interests of the state. This examination will be followed by a discussion of two points: that decentralization, whatever else its advantages may be, suggests itself from the point of view of the state as an attractive instrument of both conflict management and compensatory legitimation; and, this attractiveness notwithstanding, that the state's interest in maintaining control keeps getting in the way of serious decentralization. The persistent tension between considerations of control and of legitimation is further highlighted when the issue of decentralization is seen in the context of evaluating the performance of educational systems. It is here that my general thesis—"that policies of decentralizing the governance of educational systems carry the seeds of their own contradictions" (Weiler 1990a, p. 433)—finds another and more specific illustration.

In the analysis of educational policy, both in the United States and in a more comparative perspective, the issue of centralization versus decentralization has loomed particularly large in recent years. The meaning and referents of this debate, however, have varied considerably. At one end of the spectrum, the critical issues, especially in the United States, have to do with "restructuring" and "school-based management" (see Elmore and Associates, 1990; Timar, 1990; Tyack, 1990; and, for a comparative perspective, see Hanson, 1990), including the decentralization of the governance structure of large urban school systems, such as in New York City. At the other end of the spectrum, a great deal of attention has been directed at the role and limitations of national-level educational authority in such federally constituted polities as the United States, Australia, or the (old and new) Federal Republic of Germany. The emergence of supranational jurisdictions, notably in the case of the

European Community, has begun to extend the scope of the centralization-decentralization debate even further.

Outside the United States, and on slightly different terms, inquiries into the conditions and effects of greater or lesser degrees of decentralization in education have been similarly voluminous and often embedded in broader considerations of decentralized power arrangements in the modern state (Sharpe, 1979; Lauglo and McLean, 1985). As cases in point for the prominence of the decentralization issue in educational policy, France (Périé, 1987), Australia (Birch and Smart, 1990), Germany (Baumert and Goldschmidt, 1980), and Norway (Granheim, Kogan, and Lindgren, 1990) have been particularly well documented. A somewhat different collection of literature has addressed the particular challenges of decentralization in educational management under conditions of underdevelopment (Cheema and Rondinelli, 1983; McGinn and Street, 1986).

## Decentralization in Educational Policy: Prevailing Arguments

Advocacy of decentralization in educational governance normally takes the form of one of three arguments: the *redistribution* argument, which has to do with the sharing of power; the *efficiency* argument, which is geared to enhancing the cost-effectiveness of the educational system through a more efficient deployment and management of resources; and the *cultures of learning* argument, which emphasizes the decentralization of educational content. These arguments are predicated on three different rationalizations for decentralizing the governance of educational systems. They are meant to respond to different political and social dynamics and to have different effects on both the educational system and its environment.

In reviewing these three arguments, I will show that each of them, although for different reasons, reveals a basic ambivalence about the relative merits of centralization and decentralization in educational governance. This conclusion will lead to the search for alternative perspectives (decentralization as a means of both conflict management and compensatory legitimation), which may provide a better account of the political dynamics surrounding decentralization policies in education.

### *Decentralization and the Redistribution of Authority*

In education, as in other policy areas, authority over policy is effectively exercised in two ways: through the regulation of behavior (institutional and individual) and through the allocation of resources (human, material, or financial). Typically, this authority is exercised by the state and its agencies. With some significant exceptions and variations, it is predominantly exercised in rather centralized ways. It is usually the state that sets standards of qualification for students at different levels (often both at the point of entry into and the point of exit from the educational institution) and for teachers and other educational personnel. These standards are set in the form of curricular prescriptions, examination requirements, or certification and accreditation rules. In addition, although sometimes in less tangible ways, standards for educational qualification are enforced by skill- and competence-based criteria for entry into different parts of the labor market (including public service) and by the terms under which public funding is made available to educational institutions.

Similarly, the state effectively exercises its authority over the allocation of resources, at least to that part of the educational system that is "public," but often (at least indirectly) over allocations to "private" institutions as well. Through its budgetary authority, the state deals with the educational system's need for financial resources, but it tends also to control and regulate the supply of duly qualified human resources and of material resources (such as land, space, equipment, teaching materials, and so on). Part of the authority of the state over the allocation of resources consists of setting the terms for the contributions made to education by other entities (such as students, families, local and regional authorities, philanthropic organizations, and so on). There is less direct control by the state over the resources of private educational institutions (as in the large private sector of secondary and higher education in the United States), although there is a great deal of indirect but rather effective influence by the state over the resource conditions of private education through such measures as rules on taxation, inheritance, trusts, indirect cost recovery, student loan eligibility, and so on.

In most countries around the world, the state's regulatory

and allocative functions alike tend to be exercised in rather centralized ways. This is more clearly the case where there is one single center of policy authority at the national level, as in France, Mexico, or Malaysia. Federal systems, such as those of the Federal Republic of Germany, the United States, Switzerland, and Nigeria, represent a certain degree of decentralization, even though their component parts (*Länder,* states, *Kantone*) could be seen as "multiple centers," with some of the same kinds of centripetal dynamics. This is particularly true for recent developments in the United States toward "state-level centralization" (see Chapter One, this volume). It may be too early to say in what direction the governance structures of the former socialist systems of Eastern Europe will develop; the initial indications from developments in the former Soviet Union point in the direction of a major trend toward decentralization. East Germany, as part of its incorporation into the Federal Republic of (West) Germany in 1990, has also moved from its highly centralized past to a federal structure.

Rationales for centralized forms of decision making in education seem to be remarkably similar across different systems. As far as the state's regulatory function is concerned, the principal rationale advanced is the need for standardization: curricula, qualifications, and examinations need to be reasonably similar across the national or subnational unit, so as to facilitate mobility, the exchange of personnel, the mutual recognition of diplomas across different regions, and so on. In the "cooperative federalism" of Germany, educational policy is in the hands of the second level of political organization (the sixteen *Länder* of the "new" Federal Republic), but even there a major effort is made—through the Permanent Conference of State Ministers of Education (the Kultusministerkonferenz, or KMK)—to standardize the main parameters of educational regulation across the *Länder,* so as to achieve homogeneity for the country as a whole (Baumert and Goldschmidt, 1980).

Where the state's allocative authority is concerned, the argument for centralization appears in two forms: centralization in the allocation of resources is supposed to enhance equity by reducing or eliminating whatever disparities exist between different parts of the country in terms of resources and to increase effectiveness by utilizing economies of scale and allowing greater movement of resources to where they are most needed. When the responsibility for educational financing in California and a number of other states shifted, quite dramatically, from the local to the state level in the 1970s (Elmore and McLaughlin, 1982), one of the key arguments for this shift was that it would reduce the effect of disparities in the local property-tax bases from which local school districts had traditionally derived their main income.

Against the background of this strong tradition of, and ostensibly cogent rationale for, centralized forms of educational decision making, attempts to redistribute the exercise of regulatory and allocative authority through more decentralized arrangements have been conspicuous for their frequency, but not necessarily for their success. The situation in the United States has been more complex than elsewhere in that at least four different trends have manifested themselves more or less simultaneously:

- A significant concentration of authority at the state level (mostly at the expense of the local level), as a consequence of shifts in the financing of education
- A further weakening, throughout the Reagan and Bush administrations, of the already rather feeble role of the federal government in educational policy, especially in terms of resource allocation
- A trend toward further decentralization in the movement for school-site management (see Chapter Two, this volume)
- A highly visible campaign for a national curriculum and a standardized national achievement test

Even where there has been serious and tangible decentralizing of at least some of the central authority's functions, however, it is common to find mixed appraisals of the experience. The second Organisation for Economic Co-operation and Development (OECD) review of Norwegian educational policy, while impressed with the boldness and determination of the 1987 reforms, sees "potential difficulties" in decentralization with regard to both equity and standards (1988, pp. 40–41); McGinn and Street, after reviewing three instances of decentralization efforts in Latin America (Peru, Chile, Mexico), reaffirm the central role of the state's political "project" as the main determinant of whether decentralization does or does not move beyond the level of rhetoric (1986, pp. 489–490). The ambitious plans of the West German *Bildungsrat,* in the early 1970s, for a major decentralization of educational governance (very much in the direction of "school-site management") encountered insurmountable political difficulties (Deutscher Bildungsrat, 1973; Weiler, 1990b) and have not had any lasting impact on the structural arrangements for the governance of the West German educational system. There was at the same time, in West Germany as elsewhere, a great deal of local initiative in launching major reform projects in the 1960s and early 1970s; some of the early experiments with the "Gesamtschule" model of comprehensive secondary schooling are a case in point (Weiler, 1983a, 1983b). There again, however, most of this initiative was subsequently absorbed into the existing centralized and semicentralized structures of educational governance.

Why this should be so is really not too difficult to explain, in the context of our theoretical understanding of the nature of the modern state (Offe, 1984; Scase, 1980; Carnoy, 1984; Weiler, 1983a). The proposition of a genuine sharing of the state's allocative and regulatory power seriously affects two key conditions for the maintenance of state authority, especially in advanced capitalist societies: the need to maintain control under conditions of increasing and multiplying "centrifugal" and control-avoidance tendencies and the need to ensure, as effectively as possible, the reproduction of existing social relations, with the help of the educational system. Both of these preoccupations contrast sharply with the sharing-of-power notion of decentralization: almost by definition, a wider and more diffuse distribution of the authority to regulate and allocate multiplies both the levels and the sources of control over the educational system (McGinn and Street, 1986). Similarly, a decentralized system of governance tends to introduce into the processes of regulation and allocation certain interests (such as those of parents and local communities) that may disturb the relatively smooth and privileged interaction between the state and the agencies of capital accumulation (Naschold, 1974; Preuss, 1975).

Given this basic incompatibility between the power-sharing logic of decentralization and the interest of the modern state in maintaining control, it is not surprising that forms of decentralization that involve the genuine redistribution of authority remain rather rare. Wherever they are attempted, they tend to raise concerns over the loss of control or lead to questions about whether, in the words of the OECD examiners of Norwegian educational policy, "the central authorities are satisfied that, given the ambitious drive towards decentralization, . . . they have retained sufficient involvement in the shaping of policy" (Organisation for Economic Cooperation and Development, 1988, p. 51).

### *Decentralization and Efficiency*

A second rationale for introducing more decentralized structures of governance is based on the claim that decentralization may yield considerable efficiency in the management of educational systems (World Bank, 1988). This claim involves two sets of expectations: that greater decentralization will mobilize and generate resources that are not available under more centralized conditions and that decentralized systems can utilize available resources more efficiently.

The first of these expectations has to do with the possibility of bringing hitherto untapped local and private resources into the overall resource pool available to education. While there are traces of this strategy in the industrialized world (as in the symbiotic industry-university arrangements of "technology parks"), it has also become a particularly prominent feature of the educational policy debate in developing countries, largely under the influence of the World Bank (World Bank, 1980; Jimenez, Paqueo, and Lourdes de Vera, 1988). The reasoning goes like this: to the extent that decentralized systems of educational governance do more actively involve a broader range of societal institutions and groups, the same institutions and groups can be expected to contribute resources that previously, under more centralized forms of governance, were not available or were used for other purposes. This expectation is directed particularly at the local community, which in return for a greater role in making educational decisions under more decentralized governance arrangements, is expected to express a stronger sense of commitment to the overall educational enterprise by generating added resources for school construction and maintenance, teachers' salaries, and so on. Similar but somewhat more diffuse expectations are associated with greater involvement of the private sector in educational decision making and governance, which is expected to lead to the commitment of more private resources for covering the overall cost of education.

The second of the expectations that link decentralization with greater efficiency has less to do with how resources are raised than with how they are used. The argument recognizes that decentralization, in the short term, may involve a certain loss of efficiency as a result of diminished economies of scale. Over the medium term and the long term, however, the expectation is that decentralized systems of governance will use available resources more wisely and efficiently. This expectation is based on the assumption that decentralization will increase familiarity with local conditions and needs, which in turn will lead to a better match between demand and supply and thus to a more economical utilization of limited resources (Cheema and Rondinelli, 1983).

The validity of this argument rests on whether there is going to be a favorable trade-off between loss of economies of scale, on the one hand, and enhanced efficiency in the use of resources, on the other. There is some initial evidence that the balance does indeed come out in favor of a more decentralized generation and utilization of resources (Rondinelli, McCullough, and Johnson, 1989), but the overall picture is still not very encouraging (Bray and Lillis, 1988). In the poorer countries of the Third World, dramatic erosion of the resource bases of national governments may outweigh whatever economies are being effected through decentralization at the local or regional levels (Cheema and Rondinelli, 1983; Bray, 1984). In more affluent countries, the argument about more efficient use of resources under decentralization may well carry more weight. To determine whether it actually does, however, requires a return to the earlier argument about decentralization and efficiency.

This argument, which focused on the possibility of raising added resources through decentralization, contains a very important—and, as I have shown in a previous section, somewhat precarious—premise, which is that additional resources would be provided by local and private institutions in return for their greater involvement in the process of making and implementing educational policy. The expectation of mobilizing new resources is, in other words, contingent on a real sharing of power in the decision process. Local communities or private firms are unlikely, however, to make added resources available to an educational system over which they will have just as little influence as they had before. This contingency brings the matter of resource mobilization back to the issue of redistribution of authority, about which there are grounds for a good deal of skepticism. The link between decentralization and resource mobilization is rather complex, but it is reasonable to conclude that, without any real transfer of influence away from the central authority of the state, significant new resources are unlikely to be forthcoming from either the local level or the private sector. As Bray and Lillis (1988, p. 12) conclude their comparative study of community financing of education in the developing world, "Decentralization and community participation are frequently just a model to which it is fashionable to pay lip service. Governments are pleased to accept the resources and the grass roots initiatives which coincide with their own concepts; but they are rarely willing to relinquish control and place themselves in a position where their policies can be undermined."

### *Decentralization and the Cultures of Learning*

A third and somewhat different argument for the decentralization of educational systems is being advanced with regard to the nature and the context of the learning process. This line of reasoning focuses on the decentralization of educational content, arguing that decentralization "can provide greater sensitivity to local variations" (Bray, 1984, p. 9) or, in the words of the Norwegian report to OECD, "[adapt] the educational efforts to local conditions, both in terms of local economic activities, and in terms of knowledge and understanding of the special characteristics of the local region" (Royal Ministry, 1987, p. 124). This argument seeks to overcome a situation in which centralization is seen as producing a mismatch between a student's and a school's specific learning environment (which tends to reflect local and regional cultures and traditions), on the one hand, and a centrally defined learning agenda or curriculum, on the other. A variant of the same argument has to do with the language of instruction in multilingual societies, where initial instruction in the students' mother tongue, which is likely to be a local or subnational language, is seen as providing a more functional bridge between learning at home and learning in school (Bamgbose, 1976). Another facet of this issue is the increasingly intense debate over the "deskilling" of teachers, who have less and less control over curriculum content and instructional decisions under increasingly centralized systems (Apple, 1982; Fullan, 1982).

As a diagnostic matter, the point seems well taken. Except in very small or culturally very homogeneous societies, most countries vary considerably across regions, communities, and language groups in terms of cultural and social frameworks of learning. The frames of reference for the study of history, botany, social studies, and other fields vary obviously and significantly between southern and northern Italy, Alabama and California, or Bavaria and Berlin. Differences such as these, in countries such as the Federal Republic of Germany and the United States, historically have sustained the argument for a federal or local structure of educational governance and for varying degrees of cross-regional differentiation, as far as the content of education is concerned.

Here again, however, competing priorities seem to get in each other's way. On the one hand, the importance of culturally specific learning environments and learning media (such as language) is being increasingly recognized; on the other hand, the demands of modern labor markets and communication systems seem to require more generalized and uniform competencies, skills, and certifications at the national and, indeed, the international levels (Royal Ministry, 1987). The link between culture and learning tends to get replaced by the link between learning and technology: the link between culture and learning tends to benefit from a more decentralized, disaggregated notion of learning and educational content; by contrast, the link between learning and technology tends to require more homogeneity and uniformity, as far as the content and outcome of education are concerned (Nandy, 1978/79).

### *Decentralization in Education: An Interim Assessment*

In reviewing the three arguments that are most commonly advanced in favor of greater decentralization in educational governance, we have found a rather equivocal picture so far. While all three arguments do seem to make a certain amount of sense in the abstract, it turns out on closer inspection that all of them encounter, to varying degrees, substantial difficulties, either on theoretical grounds or in terms of implementation, or both:

1. The notion of decentralization as redistribution of power seems largely incompatible with the modern state's manifest interest in maintaining effective control and discharging some of its key functions with regard to economic production and capital accumulation.
2. Decentralization as a means of enhancing the efficiency of educational governance, both by generating additional resources and by using available resources more effectively, seems to have some potential, especially where the utilization of resources is concerned, but it also appears to rest on the premise of a real division of authority, which seems, on closer examination, difficult to uphold.
3. The notion of decentralizing the contents of learning as a means of recognizing and accommodating the diversity and importance of different cultural environments in one society is generally considered meaningful and valid. At the same time, however, it encounters the conflicting claims of different conceptions of knowledge, which contrast a kind of learning that is more geared to the specifics of cultural contexts with the national and international universalities of dealing with modern systems of technology and communication.

The question thus remains: Why, if decentralization is such a precarious and problematic proposition, does it continue to loom so large on the agenda of educational policies and reforms in so many countries? The next section will suggest an answer, which has to do with the fact that an overt commitment to decentralization in educational governance has its important political utilities, largely independent of the kinds of considerations I have discussed so far. These political utilities tend to keep the notion of decentralization on the agenda of educational policy, notwithstanding the difficulties involved in implementing it.

## The Political Utilities of Decentralization

As I have shown in the preceding section, some of the more widely used rationales for decentralization in education seem to be of limited value, not only as adequate descriptions of policy options but also as theoretical constructs for understanding the nature of the policy process. This section argues that two other conceptions of decentralization more adequately describe the political dynamics of the debate over how much centralization or decentralization there should be in educational governance. These alternative conceptions involve two of the more serious challenges with which the modern state has to cope: the increase in conflict and the loss of legitimacy.

### *Decentralization as Conflict Management*

There is nothing dramatically new about the observation that conflict is endemic to modern societies (Dahrendorf, 1967; Offe, 1984). Theorists of politics argue over the sources of conflict and the possibility and modes of conflict resolution, but hardly over the ubiquity of conflict in contemporary society.

To go beyond this general observation, however, educational policy has shown a particular propensity for conflict. Few policy issues—besides, say, nuclear energy and, at least until recently, questions of national and international security—have generated as much controversy in as wide a variety of settings as education has, especially in situations where major changes in educational policy have been proposed. The bitter debate over the introduction of comprehensive schools in Britain and West Germany; the succession of confrontations over university reform in France, from 1968 to the winter of 1986-87; the earlier conflicts over desegregation, and the more recent conflicts over religion in the schools in the United States; the competition between universalizing primary education and expanding secondary and higher education in many developing countries—these and many other examples provide ample evidence for the potential of educational policy to generate conflict.

Nor is it surprising that this should be so. After all, education is closely interwoven with the two major threads of any society's social fabric: it plays a key role in allocating social roles and status, and thus in determining and sustaining social hierarchies; and it is the principal instrument through which societies transmit their values and norms and inculcate them in successive generations of citizens. The salience of these functions makes education particularly susceptible to controversy and conflict, especially where (as is the case in most modern societies) there is substantial and profound disagreement over both the desired nature of social relations and the normative bases of human and social behavior.

Conflict is thus a fairly constant element in the pursuit of educational policy in most countries and tends to become particularly intense when it comes to plans for reforming the educational system in some major way (Weiler, 1985). Since the resolution or elimination of conflict over educational policy by central fiat usually proves unrealistic, the management of conflict becomes a critically important challenge for the state.

In this context, decentralization becomes a potentially promising strategy for coping with highly conflictive situations. The overt advantage of decentralization, from the point of view of conflict management, is that it allows the state to diffuse the sources of conflict and provide additional layers of insulation between them and the rest of the system. A classic (and disarmingly obvious) example of the use of this strategy was the reorganization of the University of Paris after the disruptive events of the May 1968 student protests. When the once unified mega-University of Paris was broken up into a dozen or more separate entities, in such a way that the major elements of insurgency and dissent were concentrated and isolated in two of those entities—Vincennes (later Vincennes-Saint Denis) and Nanterre—the thrust of the protest movement was effectively deflected and channelled into parallel structures that could be more easily contained and monitored (Prost, 1981).

The modest degree of decentralization inherent in the federal system of educational governance in the Federal Republic of Germany has served a similar role in the conflict over the introduction of comprehensive schools *(Gesamtschulen)* in the late 1960s and 1970s. Even with this element of diffusion, a good deal of conflict has remained, but one can easily imagine how much more intense the conflict over this particularly sensitive issue would have been had it been played out in a unitary, centralized system of educational policy. As it was, states *(Länder)* of different political persuasions were largely free to go their own ways as far as introducing or not introducing comprehensive schools was concerned, and this arrangement served to defuse the issue enough to keep it from being the political dynamite that it had the potential of becoming. In retrospect, however, one also has to note that this fragmentation of the reform effort contributed in no small measure to the ultimate defeat of the comprehensive school reform. To judge by the West German case, at least, decentralization does not always and necessarily work to the advantage of implementing controversial reforms (Eliason and Weiler, 1989).

The ability either to create new forms of decentralized governance (as in the University of Paris case) or to use existing ones (as in West Germany) adds measurably to the state's ability to manage and contain the kind of conflict that tends to arise around critical educational policy issues. At the same time, these two examples also highlight the substantial cost involved in the use of decentralization in highly conflictive situations. Decentralization can and does contain and isolate the sources of conflict, but it also tends to fragment reform movements and deprives the system as a whole of the full innovative thrust of proposals for reform and change. In other words, decentralization as an instrument of conflict management also tends to function as a device to reduce innovation and change to localized phenomena of limited impact.

### *Decentralization as Compensatory Legitimation*

The previous section dealt with the state's interest in developing its ability to manage conflict and with the potential of decentralization to serve that interest. This section starts from a different but related premise: namely, that the modern state faces a particularly severe challenge in the erosion of its own legitimacy. The theoretical basis of this argument has a rich and complex history, which goes back to the work of Max Weber and the more recent contributions of Habermas (1975), Offe (1984), Wolfe (1977), Crozier, Huntington, and Watanuki (1975), Weiler (1983a, 1985, 1988), and others. The meaning of *legitimacy* in this tradition varies, but there is common ground in that the term refers to the normative basis for the state's authority, or the state's "worthiness of recognition" (Habermas, 1979, p. 178). For the purposes of our argument here, it will suffice to restate the basic premise that derives from this theoretical ancestry: the modern state, for reasons having to do with both the volume and the nature of the demands placed on it, as well as with its structurally limited capacity for responding to them, faces an increasingly serious "delegitimation of authority" (Crozier, Huntington, and Watanuki, 1975, pp. 162–163). The normative basis of the state's authority, in other words, has become increasingly precarious, to the point where authors of different theoretical persuasions speak of a "crisis of legitimation" (Habermas, 1975) or of a "crisis of governability" (Crozier, Huntington, and Watanuki, 1975).

In speaking of "compensatory legitimation," we assume that those who act on behalf of the state—politicians, legislators, policy makers, senior administrators—are very much aware of this erosion of the state's legitimacy and have an interest in preserving or recapturing as much as possible of this rather precious commodity (upon which rests, after all, the credibility of their own actions). This assumption led me to suggest in some of my earlier work that an important consideration for those who design policies is not only what outcomes these policies will achieve (greater equity, more efficient schools, more employment of graduates, and so on) but also how these policies will, as a matter of "compensatory" or remedial strategy, more broadly affect the state's search for added legitimacy (Weiler, 1983a, 1983b).

A wide array of policy strategies could be shown to serve as putative sources of compensatory legitimation; the utilization of expertise and research, the invocation of rational planning procedures, and the involvement of legal institutions and norms are cases in point. Among them, decentralization may well play a particularly important role, for two reasons.

First, the problem with the legitimacy of the modern state seems to lie, at least in part, in its (real or perceived) overcentralized nature, its distance from the "basis" of the political system, its monolithic quality, its structural inability to attend to important variations within the society, and the often "impersonal, coercive, and dehumanizing" quality of its administrative bureaucracy (Freedman, 1978, p. 262). If this assessment is correct, then anything that can make the state appear less centralized and monolithic, as well as more attentive to internal variations of needs and conditions, may be seen, from the point of view of the state, as a potential source of added legitimacy.

Second, for reasons already mentioned in the first part of this chapter, there is a particular preoccupation in many modern societies with the adverse effects of overcentralized educational systems. The resurgence of cultural regionalism, of local languages, dialects, and cultural and folkloric traditions, and of subnational alternatives to national conceptions of cultural identity have led to more emphasis on the limits of centralization in education. These developments have further reinforced (and been reinforced by) the perception that centralized state structures (other things being equal) tend to be greater obstacles to democratic expression than decentralized structures tend to be.

Thus, there is a dual utility in the notion of decentralization, which makes it particularly attractive in the calculus of compensatory legitimation and which may well explain the strong currency of the idea of decentralization in many countries. A dilemma arises, of course, when it comes to assessing the trade-off between the benefits of enhanced legitimacy and the cost of losing control. As I have argued, all real decentralization (in the sense of genuinely shared regulatory and allocative power among levels of governance) does imply a loss of control for the center. If it is true that decentralization also holds out the attractive prospect of compensatory legitimation at a time when legitimacy is in short supply, a major challenge for the modern state lies in reconciling two conflicting objectives: retaining as much (centralized) control over the system as possible without severe loss of legitimacy and simultaneously appearing, at least, to be committed to decentralization, thus reaping the benefits in legitimation to be derived from such appearance. The frequent wavering between centralized and decentralized modes of policy behavior—or, to be more exact, between decentralization rhetoric and centralization behavior—may have to do with the difficult task of walking the fine line between the conflicting imperatives of control and legitimacy.

## Decentralization and Evaluation: A Case in Point

Against the background of this assessment of the politics of decentralization, I would now like to examine more specifically the relationship between decentralization and evaluation. The importance of this relationship lies not only in the fact that it looms large in the policy debate of many countries but also in the fact that it highlights some of the critical political dynamics of the decentralization debate. I am arguing that this relationship is problematic for three different but interrelated reasons, each of which goes back to some of my earlier observations. First, modern pluralist societies increasingly lack consensus on the objectives of education and hence on the criteria for evaluating the performance of educational systems. Second, there is (protestations to the contrary notwithstanding) a very close and inevitable link between evaluation and control, which is often difficult to reconcile with the basic premises of decentralization. Third, evaluation tends to be seen and used as a means of "compensatory legitimation" in its own right—that is, more for its legitimating than for its informative capacity.

### *Evaluation and Lack of Consensus*

In principle, there should not be much of a problem. Should it not be possible to evaluate a decentralized system of education just as well as a centralized one? Could one not ascertain just as well under centralized as under decentralized conditions whether teachers teach what they are supposed to teach, whether students learn what they are supposed to learn, and whether the schools are clean and the accounts properly kept?

On closer inspection, the answer is not quite that easy. There certainly are elements of education where one set of performance criteria is equally valid and acceptable in all the different parts and segments of a society and can thus usefully serve as the basis of a systemwide evaluation of how education is doing. There is probably little disagreement over what to look for in assessing the physical quality of the school plant or in determining the level of health of schoolchildren or the punctuality of the staff, even though there may well be variations in the relative importance attached to any of these measures. Beyond these elements, however, things tend to get more problematic. Expectations about what educational systems should accomplish vary considerably, not only from one society to another but also across the different regions and groups of all but the most homogeneous societies. Multilingual societies face the dilemma of which language or languages to accord priority in the educational system: groups that are heavily involved in external commerce will consider proficiency in international languages (and in modern accounting and management methods) more important than the preservation of the country's cultural traditions and local languages. Those whose children grow up in more privileged and stimulus-rich circumstances will judge an educational system more by how well it cultivates outstanding talent and ability, while the parents of less privileged children will attach greater importance to the system's ability to foster more equitable learning opportunities for a larger number of people. Even standards for something supposedly as universally valid and desirable as those for competence in dealing with technology turn out to be subject to profound disagreements once one moves beyond some rather obvious premises about the importance of mathematical ability (Nandy, 1978/79). As the Norwegian government's report for the second OECD review states, not only is there tension between the criteria of "relevance and practical usefulness," on the one hand, and "quality," on the other, but the very notion of "quality" is "open to widely different interpretations" (Royal Ministry, 1987, p. 145). This is an admission that is as rare, especially in official pronouncements on education, as it is insightful. More often, the deceptive facility of standardized testing seems to have lured many in the world of educational policy into simplistic assumptions about how "quality" in education should be conceived and measured (National Commission on Testing and Public Policy, 1990). The preoccupation, in national as well as international circles, with cognitive achievement as the sole legitimate measure of educational outcomes has some of the same qualities of oversimplification (Weiler, 1991).

The massive evaluation exercise that accompanied the experimental comprehensive school program in the Federal Republic of Germany in the 1970s provides an instructive example for how lack of consensus on educational objectives affects evaluation. The point of departure was the claim that a scientific basis was needed for arriving at a decision on whether to maintain the conventional three-tier system of postelementary education or to introduce a comprehensive secondary school. On this basis, the evaluation program was set up to compare the performance of the two types of schools in an experimental design, using the conventional system as the "control" group and the pilot comprehensive schools as the "treatment" group (Weiler, 1983a, 1989b). The program could not have been more thorough, rigorous, competently staffed, and generously funded; and yet, when all was said and done, and when the findings on the comparative performance of the two types of schools became available, each side in the policy dispute claimed, with some justification, that the data proved its own point. Those who all along had advocated maintaining the existing system, on the grounds that it did better in producing educational excellence, found their views largely confirmed by the data on the achievement of gifted children in the selective *Gymnasium.* At the same time, the advocates of the *Gesamtschule,* more interested in greater equality of educational opportunity and in raising the level of education for larger groups of less privileged children, found that the comprehensive school did rather well what they had expected it to do (Eliason and Weiler, 1989; Weiler, 1989b). In fact, the two frames of reference proved so utterly irreconcilable that the federal-state commission set up to monitor the experimental program, after submitting its findings in 767 pages of painstaking detail, declared itself unable to formulate an assessment of the experiment that all its members could accept (Bund-Länder-Kommission, 1982, pp. 19–20). The lesson is clear enough: where there are many irreconcilable objectives, evaluation is likely to be inconclusive at best and a source of further conflict at worst.

Decentralization is related to this dilemma in a slightly paradoxical way. In one sense, a decentralized system of governance is likely to make the multitude of priorities for educational objectives more clearly transparent, forcing evaluation into a more complex and less standardized mode than it might otherwise adopt. In another sense, however, the very complexity of a decentralized system may lead to the kinds of concerns that in turn prompt new demands for evaluation, precisely for the sake of reestablishing a certain degree of homogeneity—of "asserting the national norms" (Organisation for Economic Co-operation and Development, 1988, p. 41)—and hence for the sake of greater centralization.

### *Evaluation, Information, and Control*

The relationship between decentralization and evaluation is problematic in another sense as well. Evaluation is rarely a disinterested activity, least of all in a domain like education, where values and status play such critically important roles. While evaluation is about the gathering of knowledge, the gathering of knowledge is by no means all that evaluation is about. It is not at all surprising that fundamental ambiguity on this issue permeates discussion and writings about decentralization in many settings. Another look at the recent decentralization debate in Norway is instructive. The Norwegian government's report to the OECD on the state of educational policy in Norway is rather low-key on the issue of evaluation. It notes that what little inspection there used to be was in the process of turning into "pedagogical support services" (Royal Ministry, 1987, p. 101) and records, without much apparent enthusiasm, "political claims for more central control of a core curriculum and performance indicators" (p. 144). By contrast, claims of that sort loom conspicuously large in the ensuing report of the official OECD examiners of Norway's educational policy (Organisation for Economic Co-operation and Development, 1988). The report reflects a veritable preoccupation with the issue of evaluation. Notwithstanding the claim that they "are concerned not with the reintroduction of national controls but with considering ways in which good norms of educational practice can be established and disseminated better in Norway" (p. 45), the OECD examiners are quite obviously troubled by the "lack of a clear ideological role for the ministry" (p. 43), and especially by the fact that "there is no effective system for monitoring standards" (p. 40). This concern leads them to argue for reappraisal of the role of the "centre" (that is, the national government), which should "establish its influence by asserting the national norms which should be expected of all local authorities and their schools, by creating means of monitoring and evaluating and by publishing their evaluations" (pp. 40–41).

This position illustrates one of the critical dilemmas in the relationship between decentralization and evaluation. If evaluation were merely a matter of gathering information about students, schools, and teachers, there would hardly be a problem, but because that information is then not only made public but also interpreted authoritatively, it becomes an obvious and major instrument of control and intervention. The many ways in which scores on standardized achievement tests (such as the Scholastic Aptitude Test) in the United States have become a matter of eagerly awaited publicity (as when local newspapers report the mean scores of the local high schools) and high-level interpretation (as in governmental invocations of comparative achievement data's bearing on the country's future) are a case in point. Here, "evaluation" is not merely the gathering and dissemination of information; it also has something to do with the authoritative interpretation of standards of knowledge and is endowed with a considerable amount of force, both real and symbolic.

That may well be the way this or another country wants it to be; what I am arguing here is that such a conception and role of evaluation tend inherently to be at odds with the notion and the practice of decentralization as a genuine delegation of power. Where, and to the extent that, the ultimate goal of evaluation is to "assert the national norms" for the performance of schools, students, and teachers, evaluation enters into a competitive relationship with the basic premises of decentralization.

### *Evaluation as Compensatory Legitimation*

My third observation on the problematic nature of evaluation goes back to the earlier argument about decentralization as a strategy of "compensatory legitimation." What I propose here is that evaluation, because of the eminence of scientific rationality in our contemporary world view, enjoys a particularly high measure of prestige as an element in the policy process. This prestige makes evaluation a perfect and virtually irresistible target for those in search of added sources of legitimation for the policy process and its outcomes. There can be little doubt that the phenomenal rise of evaluation, as part of both the discourse and the practice of policy, is in no small part due to its (real or perceived) capacity for conferring on the policy process the added virtue of scientific respectability; for the policy process, in whatever field, to include explicit provisions for systematic and rigorous evaluation has become a mark of wholesomeness and is seen as an effective way of providing added legitimation to a process that is often badly in need of remedial credibility. I would not follow Lundgren in ascribing "mythological capabilities" to evaluation, but he is certainly right in describing one of the important functions of evaluation as the preservation of "the belief in a rational paradigm for policy making" (Lundgren, 1989, p. 33). The relationship between evaluation and legitimation has become particularly pronounced in the field of curriculum policy, which has encountered special legitimation problems, especially in the context of major curriculum reforms, and has seen the device of systematic evaluation emerge as one way of dealing with those problems (Weiler, 1990b; Hameyer, 1976; Raschert, 1977; Wulf, 1975).

This line of argument moves the function of evaluation into an entirely different context. To the extent that evaluation is being seen as a strategy of compensatory legitimation, its importance lies perhaps much less in the evidence it gathers, the insights it generates, and the improvements that thereby become possible than in its connotations of scientific solidity and respectability, almost regardless of its findings. This is not to suggest that the legitimating role of evaluation is uppermost in the mind of everybody who talks about, recommends, or is involved in evaluation. What it does suggest, however, is the need for much greater awareness of the multiple contexts in which the argument for evaluation can be and is being conducted. Evaluation, whether we like it or not, is a profoundly political process, and its potential for legitimating the authority of the evaluator (such as the state) is a key element of this process. According to Noblit and Eaker (1989, p. 127), "All evaluation designs have the potential of realigning political power and redefining what is credible knowledge" (see also Palumbo, 1987).

To behave as if evaluation were a strictly technical, descriptive, and hence "neutral" activity will make it either irrelevant or misleading.

## Conclusion

Understanding the political dynamics of centralization and decentralization in educational policy requires going beyond the kinds of arguments that are typically advanced for greater decentralization. Decentralizing the making and the implementation of educational policy affects, in important ways, the nature and the interests of the state, particularly its ability to cope with the dual problems of policy conflict and the erosion of its own legitimacy. With regard to these two issues, the idea of decentralization proves fundamentally paradoxical and precarious, presenting the state with one of its more profound and intractable dilemmas.

This dilemma becomes particularly acute in the attempt to reconcile the competing rationales of decentralization and evaluation. For reasons that concern the loss of consensus on the objectives of education, the real or symbolic force with which the dissemination and interpretation of evaluation results may affect an educational system, and the profoundly political nature of evaluation, this reconciliation attempt seems a noble but extraordinarily difficult task. Both decentralization and evaluation ultimately have to do with the exercise of power, and there is always the possibility that the power that decentralization gives away with one hand evaluation may take back with the other. Reconciling the two may well turn out to be an exercise in contradiction.

## References

Apple, M. W. "Curricular Form and the Logic of Technical Control: Building the Possessive Individual." In M. W. Apple (ed.), *Cultural and Economic Reproduction in Education: Essays on Class, Ideology and the State.* New York: Routledge & Kegan Paul, 1982.

Bamgbose, A. *Mother Tongue Education: The West African Experience.* London: Hodder and Stoughton, 1976.

Baumert, J., and Goldschmidt, D. "Centralization and Decentralization as Determinants of Educational Policy in the Federal Republic of Germany (FRG)." *Social Science Information,* 1980, *19*(6), 1029–1098.

Birch, I., and Smart, D. "Economic Rationalism and the Politics of Education in Australia." In D. E. Mitchell and M. E. Goertz (eds.), *Education Politics for the New Century: The Twentieth Anniversary Yearbook of the Politics of Education Association.* New York: Falmer Press, 1990.

Bray, M. *Educational Planning in a Decentralised System: The Papua New Guinean Experience.* Sidney, Australia: Sidney University Press, 1984.

Bray, M., and Lillis, K. *Community Financing of Education: Issues and Policy Implications in Less Developed Countries.* Elmsford, N.Y.: Pergamon Press, 1988.

Bund-Länder-Kommission für Bildungsplanung und Forschungsförderung. *Modellversuche mit Gesamtschulen: Auswertungsbericht der Projektgruppe Gesamtschulen* [Experimenting with comprehensive schools: Evaluation report of the project team]. Bühl/Baden, Germany: Konkordia, 1982.

Carnoy, M. *The State and Political Theory.* Princeton, N.J.: Princeton University Press, 1984.

Cheema, G. S., and Rondinelli, D. A. (eds.). *Decentralization and Development: Policy Implementation in Developing Countries.* Newbury Park, Calif.: Sage, 1983.

Crozier, M. J., Huntington, S. P., and Watanuki, J. *The Crisis of Democracy: Report on the Governability of Democracy to the Trilateral Commission.* New York: New York University Press, 1975.

Dahrendorf, R. *Society and Democracy in Germany.* New York: Doubleday, 1967.

Deutscher Bildungsrat. *Zur Reform von Organisation und Verwaltung im Bildungswesen. Teil I: Verstärkte Selbständigkeit der Schule und Partizipation der Lehrer, Schüler und Eltern* [Organizational and administrative reform in education. Part I: Increased autonomy of the school and participation of teachers, students, and parents]. Bonn, Germany: Deutscher Bildungsrat, 1973.

Eliason, L. C., and Weiler, H. N. "The Politics of Educational

Reform in Western Europe: Do Policy Systems Learn from Past Experience?" Paper presented at the annual meeting of the Western Political Science Association, Salt Lake City, Utah, Mar. 30–Apr. 1, 1989.

Elmore, R. F., and Associates. *Restructuring Schools: The Next Generation of Educational Reform.* San Francisco: Jossey-Bass, 1990.

Elmore, R. F., and McLaughlin, M. W. *Reform and Retrenchment: The Politics of California School Finance Reform.* New York: Ballinger, 1982.

Freedman, J. O. *Crisis and Legitimacy: The Administrative Process and American Government.* Cambridge, England: Cambridge University Press, 1978.

Fullan, M. *The Meaning of Educational Change.* Toronto: Ontario Institute for the Study of Education Press, 1982.

Granheim, M., Kogan, M., and Lindgren, U. P. (eds.), *Evaluation as Policymaking: Introducing Evaluation into a National Decentralised Educational System.* London: Kingsley, 1990.

Habermas, J. *Legitimation Crisis.* Boston: Beacon Press, 1975.

Habermas, J. *Communication and the Evolution of Society.* Boston: Beacon Press, 1979.

Hameyer, U., and others (eds.). *Bedingungen und Modelle der Curriculuminnovation* [Conditions and models of curricular innovation]. Weinheim, Germany: Beltz, 1976.

Hanson, E. M. "School-Based Management and Educational Reform in the United States and Spain." *Comparative Education Review,* 1990, *34*(4), 523–537.

Jimenez, E., Paqueo, V., and Lourdes de Vera, M. *Does Local Financing Make Primary Schools More Efficient?* Washington, D.C.: World Bank, 1988.

Lauglo, J., and McLean, M. *The Control of Education: International Perspectives on the Centralization-Decentralization Debate.* Portsmouth, N.H.: Heinemann Educational Books, 1985.

Lundgren, U. *Educational Policy Making, Decentralisation and Evaluation: An Invititation to Papers.* Oslo, Norway: EMIL, 1989 (mimeographed).

McGinn, N., and Street, S. "Educational Decentralization: Weak

State or Strong State?" *Comparative Education Review,* 1986, *30*(4), 471–490.

Nandy, A. "The Traditions of Technology." *Alternatives,* 1978/79, *4*(3), 371–385.

Naschold, F. *Schulreform als Gesellschaftskonflikt* [Educational reform as social conflict]. Frankfurt, Germany: Athenäum, 1974.

National Commission on Testing and Public Policy. *From Gatekeeper to Gateway: Transforming Testing in America.* Chestnut Hill, Mass.: Boston College, 1990.

Noblit, G. W., and Eaker, D. J. "Evaluation Designs as Political Strategies." In J. Hannaway and R. Crowson (eds.), *The Politics of Reforming School Administration: The 1988 Yearbook of the Politics of Education Association.* New York: Falmer Press, 1989.

Offe, C. *Contradictions of the Welfare State.* Cambridge, Mass.: MIT Press, 1984.

Organisation for Economic Co-operation and Development, Education Committee. *Review of Educational Policy in Norway: Examiner's Report and Questions.* Paris: Organisation for Economic Co-operation and Development, 1988.

Palumbo, D. J. (ed.). *The Politics of Program Evaluation.* Vol. 15: *Sage Yearbooks in Politics and Public Policy.* Newbury Park: Calif.: Sage, 1987.

Périé, R. *L'Education nationale à l'heure de la décentralisation: Changements et continuité* [National education at the time of decentralization: Changes and continuity]. Paris: La Documentation Française, 1987.

Preuss, U. K. *Bildung und Herrschaft: Beiträge zu einer politischen Theorie des Bildungswesens* [Education and Power: Contributions to a Political Theory of Education]. Frankfurt, Germany: Fischer, 1975.

Prost, A. *Histoire générale de l'enseignement et de l'education en France. Tome IV: L'Ecole et la famille dans une société en mutation* [General history of instruction and education in France. Vol. 4: School and family in a transforming society]. Paris: Nouvelle Librairie de France, 1981.

Raschert, J. "Problem der Legitimation von Lehrplänen und Richtlinien" [The Problem of Legitimating Curricula]. In H.-D. Haller and D. Lenzen (eds.), *Wissenschaft im Reformprozess:*

*Aufklärung oder Alibi?* [Scholarship and reform: Enlightenment or alibi?] Stuttgart: Klett-Cotta, 1977.

Rondinelli, D. A., McCullough, J. S., and Johnson, R. W. "Analysing Decentralization Policies in Developing Countries: A Political-Economy Framework." *Development and Change,* 1989, *20,* 57–87.

Royal Ministry of Cultural and Scientific Affairs and Royal Ministry of Church and Education. *Reviews of National Policies for Education: Norway.* Oslo: Government of Norway, 1987.

Scase, R. (ed.). *The State in Western Europe.* New York: St. Martin's Press, 1980.

Scharpf, F. W. "The Joint-Decision Trap: Lessons from German Federalism and European Integration." Unpublished paper, n.d.

Sharpe, L. J. (ed.). *Decentralist Trends in Western Democracies.* Newbury Park, Calif.: Sage, 1979.

Timar, T. B. "The Politics of School Restructuring." In D. E. Mitchell and M. E. Goertz (eds.), *Education Politics for the New Century: The Twentieth Anniversary Yearbook of the Politics of Education Association.* New York: Falmer Press, 1990.

Tyack, D. "'Restructuring' in Historical Perspective: Tinkering Toward Utopia." *Teachers College Record,* 1990, *92*(2), 172–191.

Weiler, H. N. "Legalization, Expertise, and Participation: Strategies of Compensatory Legitimation in Educational Policy." *Comparative Education Review,* 1983a, *27*(2), 259–277.

Weiler, H. N. "West Germany: Educational Policy as Compensatory Legitimation." In M. Thomas (ed.), *Politics and Education: Cases from Eleven Nations.* Elmsford, N.Y.: Pergamon Press, 1983b.

Weiler, H. N. "Politics of Educational Reform." In R. L. Merritt and A. J. Merritt (eds.), *Innovation in the Public Sector.* Newbury Park, Calif.: Sage, 1985.

Weiler, H. N. "The Politics of Reform and Non-Reform in French Education." *Comparative Education Review,* 1988, *32*(3), 251–265.

Weiler, H. N. "Education and Power: The Politics of Educational Decentralization in Comparative Perspective." *Educational Policy,* 1989a, *3*(1), 31–43.

Weiler, H. N. "Why Reforms Fail: The Politics of Education in

France and the Federal Republic of Germany." *Journal of Curriculum Studies,* 1989b, *21*(4), 291–305.

Weiler, H. N. "Comparative Perspectives on Educational Decentralization: An Exercise in Contradiction?" *Educational Evaluation and Policy Analysis,* 1990a, *12*(4), 433–448.

Weiler, H. N. "Curriculum Reform and the Legitimation of Educational Objectives: The Case of the Federal Republic of Germany." *Oxford Review of Education,* 1990b, *16*(1), 15–27.

Weiler, H. N. "Decentralisation in Educational Governance." In M. Granheim, M. Kogan, and U. P. Lindgren (eds.), *Evaluation as Policymaking: Introducing Evaluation into a National Decentralised Educational System.* London: Kingsley, 1990c.

Weiler, H. N. "The International Politics of Knowledge Production and the Future of Higher Education." Paper prepared for an international conference on the future of higher education, Caracas, Venezuela, May 1991.

Wolfe, A. *The Limits of Legitimacy: Political Contradictions of Contemporary Capitalism.* New York: Free Press, 1977.

World Bank. *Education Sector Policy Paper.* (3rd ed.) Washington, D.C.: World Bank, 1980.

World Bank. *Education in Sub-Saharan Africa: Policies for Adjustment, Revitalization, and Expansion.* Washington, D.C.: World Bank, 1988.

Wulf, C. "Funktionen und Paradigmen der Evaluation" [Functions and Paradigms of Evaluation]. In K. Frey and others (eds.), *Curriculum-Handbuch.* Munich, Germany: Piper, 1975.

# 4

# Deinstitutionalization and School Decentralization: Making the Same Mistake Twice

**Dan A. Lewis**

We are in the midst of a revolution in the organization of human services. From public schools, where the revolution is just beginning, to state mental hospitals and correctional facilities, where we are three decades into the change, there has been a metamorphosis in service organization and ideology that rivals the birth of these institutions over 150 years ago. The reliance, in the nineteenth century, on institutions is being replaced by a new service ideology, which emphasizes community programs and client choice. The monopoly of the state on service provision has been broken. The revolution is fueled by a critique of bureaucratic institutions that legitimizes the privatization of care, control, and now education.

Our understanding of this revolution is both informed and distorted by the very ideology that supported the change and is now the conventional framework for analyzing its impact. The *problem,* so the argument goes—in mental health, corrections, and now education—is the very institutions we have built to handle the situation. The *solution* to our policy problems is to do away with the state hospital, the prison, and now the public school. It is the *institution* that causes the problem and must be transformed, if not destroyed, if society is to improve its human services. This emphasis on institutional analysis focuses our attention on how organizations socialize clients and not on what precedes and follows those institutional experiences. The results in mental health and correctional policy have not been encouraging. The "total" institution was originally meant by its inventors to provide a mobile and fast-changing society with a method of controlling deviance through a benign form of environmental manipulation (Rothman, 1971). It rapidly degenerated into an organization that deformed those who were recruited to the status of inmate and excluded them from the rest of society. But current mental health policy has led to the twin consequences of little control of the dangerous mentally ill and poor service provision for those in need who pose no threat (Lewis and others, 1991). Correctional institutions still segregate, and rates of incarceration have climbed steadily while community services for the less dangerous have also grown (Krisberg and others, 1987). Reliance on deinstitutionalization and community programs has failed either to remove "total" institutions or to improve society's capacity to deal with deviance.

Prisons, mental hospitals, and juvenile corrections facilities were transformed in the middle of the twentieth century as reformers and scholars attacked these institutions and argued for community alternatives. Now public schools are being attacked in a similar fashion. The result is an emphasis on decentralization and choice as ways to improve schooling. In this chapter, I will relate the deinstitutionalization movement in human services to current reforms in public schooling and suggest how the experience of the other human services, especially the mental health system, can shape our thinking about the changes taking place in public education.

The modern reforms in education and human services are driven by an ideology that rationalizes the privatization of service in the name of freedom and equality. This new educational system will draw the poor and the black into civil society through a set of arrangements that blur the lines between private and public and reaffirm the hierarchical relations between races and classes (Eckstein, 1984). Special-interest groups are incorporated into state mechanisms to regulate and legitimate the new arrangements. Local school councils and school-based management schemes draw constituencies into governance. These new forms of participation and special-interest representation protect and legitimate the new private service sector (Cawson, 1986). Recent decentralization efforts in Chicago and Miami are examples of this new form.

In education, deinstitutionalizing reforms are called *choice* and *decentralization*. They legitimize the privatization of schooling.

They differ in their reliance on political or economic metaphors to describe how the new system will work, but they both attack the institution of public education. While the current educational debate over school reform pits choice against decentralization, I believe that these two ideologies will be blended in the near future to legitimize the new system. In both mental health and corrections, the early battles over competing reform alternatives—that is, over which kind of community programming made the most sense—dissolved into a practice that differed little from the original institutional practice that was the cause of so much concern (Cohen, 1985). The emerging new order legitimizes "policy talk" about parents for the choice advocates, and "policy talk" about community for the proponents of decentralization as the critique of bureaucracy squeezes out other explanations of the failure of public education. The same process took place in mental health and correctional reform and has resulted in a new system of care, which leaves the poor devastated and the private sector much enhanced.

The same basic ideology informs both the mental health movement and the educational reform movement, separated only by a generation of experience. Public schooling is headed down the road to a deinstitutionalized school system, which will undermine public authority and responsibility for education while enhancing the control of private agencies and interests. The pervasive belief is that the institution is the problem, and the community is the solution. Until we break this perspective's hold on our thinking, we will be doomed to repeat the same errors made by well-intentioned reformers who hoped to improve other human services.

## Ideology and Institutionalism

American institutional analysis is rooted in a political philosophy that emphasizes rationalism, a benign human nature, and the notion that evil behavior flows from poorly designed institutions (Burnham, 1986). Rational solutions to difficult problems can be found in the rearrangement of the organizations that claim expertise over the problem. Women, children, and men can be changed by these organizations, and the problems will be solved. These basic assumptions were concretized in the late 1950s and early 1960s in the work of foundations and federal government programs that aimed to improve how human services operated by forcing them to turn outward to meet the challenges of poverty and race relations (Marris and Rein, 1982).

As more modest projects to improve the bureaucracies failed to achieve their objectives, and as desegregation efforts met massive resistance in large American cities, commitment to the notion that bureaucracies could improve themselves lost legitimacy. Professionals and the bureaucracies that housed them were seen as incapable of improving the situation. The very nature of the hospital, prison, or school made it impossible for it to help those in need. The belief in the 1960s was that public bureaucracies, especially school systems, were not responsive to the needs of the poor and that urban problems were caused by this unresponsiveness:

> Poverty and delinquency were perpetuated by an inherited failure to respond through ignorance, apathy and discouragement to the demands of urban civilization. The institutions of education and welfare had grown too insensitive and rigid to retrieve these failures, from a characteristic, morbid preoccupation with the maintenance of their organizational structure. The processes of assimilation were breaking down, and could only be repaired by an enlargement of opportunities. But this emancipation would only come about as the enabling institutions of assimilation—the school, the welfare agencies, the vocational services—recognized their failure, and became more imaginative, coherent, and responsive [Marris and Rein, 1982, p. 53].

The assumption was that rational reform could succeed: that human nature was at worst malleable and would respond to institutional shifts in activity, and that better-designed institutions would work. The mad could be cured, the criminal restored to conventional behavior, and the poor child educated if the institutions were transformed. Destroy the bureaucracy, and you change the opportunities of the poor. Enter deinstitutionalization.

Theories of deinstitutionalization have their foundation in the Chicago school of sociology. Goffman (1961) and Becker (1963) adapted earlier theories of occupational careers to the worlds of deviance and institutions. Their theories were built on a social psychology of identity formation that treated interaction as the source of the self. Identity was based on how others related to you; you were who others said you were. If institutions were "total," then who you were followed from the roles you played institutionally. In this way, the institution created the self. Goffman and Becker applied this approach to the bottom rather than the top of the social scale. Where others had looked at medical careers, scholars now looked at patients and prisoners. Deviance lay not in the personality of the criminal or the mental patient but in the definitions that the institution applied to those it recruited to these subordinate roles.

If institutions by definition created the very people they were supposed to change, then reform meant destroying the factories of deviant identity. The theory was supported by empirical work on the institutions of social control, which were overflowing in the 1950s. Large, crowded, and understaffed, these places came to be seen as the causes of problems. Schools, of course, are not "total institutions" (Tyack, 1974). They do not have complete control over the lives of students. Students go home at the end of the day, play hookey, transfer, and have sources of identity provided by peers, parents, and others. But the public school did have many features in common with other institutions, and by the mid 1950s schools had become as insulated, bureaucratized, and professionalized as the deviance-control agencies (Tyack, 1974).

The movement to reform urban schools in the late 1960s was driven by the deinstitutionalization paradigm. Fantini (1970), Gittell (1972), and others used this perspective to shape a reform strategy for public schooling. The bureaucracy was the problem, and external control by "the community" was the solution. For Fantini (1970), the term *institution* referred to the set of arrangements by which public education was delivered—bureaucratic, professional, and insulated arrangements. Public schooling had been "taken out of politics" by these institutional forces, and the city reformers (Rogers, 1968) of the late 1960s wanted to put politics back in: if the institution could be controlled politically by external forces, schooling would improve.

In other words, it was thought that the urban environment (meaning the social and economic arrangements) around the institution was essentially neutral and that it would not affect either the schooling enterprise or the students' chances for success later on. This reduction of educational achievement to changes in governance decontextualized the complicated matter of who does well in school. Public education was seen by the reformers as separate and aloof from the poor, cut off and unresponsive. To reformers, what mattered was who ran the institution, not how how the economy or the family worked. Given that analysis, if the right people were in charge of schools, the schools could perform better, as if they were operating in isolation from the rest of society. The reform dilemma was articulated as a choice between two school systems; one, operated by the community, that was open and innovative and another, operated by professionals, that was closed and insulated:

> The accumulated evidence indicates a basic sickness in the school structure: The total environment of the system prevents progress and changes that would meet new situations and serve new populations. Studies analyzing all aspects of city school systems have identified as the fundamental malady an insensitive system unwilling to respond to the demands of the community. With this new understanding, the insulated centralized bureaucratic structure has come increasingly under attack, and school-reform movements have replaced the efforts for integration [Gittell and Hevesi, 1969, p. 8].

Accordingly, if you open the institution, you solve the problem. Table 4.1 gives a graphic example of how this kind of thinking worked. Institutions could generate either learning or failure, according to who controlled them. If the community ran a school, it would not only improve but also be transformed. The paradigm emphasizes political power and the political advancement of poor parents at the expense of professional discretion and bureaucratic

**Table 4.1. Characteristics of Traditional and Reformed School Systems.**

| *Distinguishing Feature* | *Traditional System* | *Reformed System* |
|---|---|---|
| Center of Control | Professional monopoly | The public (the community) |
| Role of parents' organizations | To interpret the school to the community for public relations | To participate as active agents in matters substantive to the educational process |
| Bureaucracy | Centralized authority, limiting flexibility and initiative to the professionals at the individual school level | Decentralized decision making, allowing for maximum local lay and professional initiative and flexibility, with central authority concentrating on technical assistance, long-range planning, and systemwide coordination |
| Educational objectives | Emphasis on grade-level performance, basic skills, cognitive achievement | Emphasis on both cognitive and affective development; humanistically oriented objectives (for example, identity, connectedness, powerlessness) |
| Test of professional efficiency and promotion | Emphasis on credentials and systematized advancement through the system | Emphasis on performance with students and with parent-community participants |
| Institutional philosophy | Negative self-fulfilling prophecy; student failure blamed on learner and background | Positive self-fulfilling prophecy; no study failures, only program failures; accountable to learner and community |
| Basic learning unit | Classroom, credentialized teacher, school building | The community, various agents as teachers, including other students and paraprofessionals |

*Source:* Fantini, 1970, p. 46. Reprinted with permission of The Brookings Institution.

autonomy: "The advocates of decentralization are obviously correct to assume that the pedagogical problems which afflict the schools are ultimately political problems; that the children will not learn to read, will not accept the confinements of civilization and the responsibilities of citizenship, until a substantial shift of power has taken place within the city" (Epstein, 1968, p. 299).

A commitment to improved education demanded more democracy and less bureaucracy. The problem had been that the institution was insulated from democracy and thus pathological. If the poor had control of the schooling enterprise, then they could make it work by directing the school toward the interests of those being served. Professionals would either respond to the authority of the new governance structure or be removed. If the community (meaning the people who lived near the school) and the parents of school-age children had more voice in the schooling enterprise, then there would be more parental satisfaction with the schools and more commitment to the educational process. The result would be improved educational attainment. The democratization of the governance process and the representation of parental and community interests would lead to improved schooling.

These deinstitutionalized theories of reform suggested that if bureaucracies could be made more responsive, then the poor, especially the minority poor, could lift themselves out of poverty. The paradigm focused on who has authority in the school—who gets to tell whom what to do. It had little to say about other aspects of the situation that may affect low achievement. It also assumed that parents want this decision-making responsibility and that authority can be granted through legislative action. Finally, the reformers assumed that parents' political power would lead to more parental commitment to the institution and more involvement with schooling (volunteering, helping with homework, even parents' building up their own skills and educational interests), especially as the school became more responsive. Schools were thought to create students; new schools could create new students.

In the deinstitutionalization model, parents are treated as agents of change, with common interests and a common motivation to change how the schools are operating. The victim of bureaucracy becomes its master. These parents can articulate their shared interests, in opposition to the interests of other groups or classes that have controlled the educational process in the past. Reformers and activists help parents in that articulation process by amplifying and clarifying those interests. If the governance structure changes to accommodate parental interests and treat parents with respect, then parents will soon be able to articulate their own interests and develop their own leadership. Community organizations and protest organizations that purport to represent parents' interests are very important in the reform process, for they teach parents not to accept the powerlessness that professionals impute to them, and they draw parents together to act politically. In this way, more democracy transforms the institution and creates a better educational system.

The same emphasis on institutional analysis is also the basis of more conservative contemporary reforms. Chubb and Moe (1990a) suggest that the same simple choice between institutional systems will improve schooling. Where the liberal approach suggested more democracy, the current conservative one suggests less. The left opts for more politics; the right, for more markets. Both assume that institutional paralysis is the problem and that the introduction of private interests, defined as parents, is the solution. Many conservative thinkers believe that America suffers from too much democracy and that the way to improve matters is to break the hold of government on individual decisions informed by the market. Twenty years after decentralization, it is now the public authority that creates the bureaucracy that must be changed:

> The fundamental causes of poor academic performance are not to be found in the schools, but rather in the institutions by which the schools have traditionally been governed. Reformers fail by automatically relying on these institutions to solve the problem—when the institutions are the problem.
>
> The key to better schools, therefore, is institutional reform. What we propose is a new system of public education that eliminates most political and bureaucratic control over the schools and relies instead on indirect control through markets and parental choice. These new institutions naturally function

> to promote and nurture the kinds of effective schools that reformers have wanted all along [Chubb and Moe, 1990b, p. 5].

Deinstitutionalizing the schools would free them to be more responsive. State-run institutions cannot do a good job. Something else, not the public institution, would be better. In this view, services will be delivered by noninstitutional actors. Here, the market is the antidote to the institution. "Community" mental health and "community" corrections turned out to mean privately controlled services delivered by people who did not work for the state but depended on the government for support. The outlook for the same kind of system in education is favorable. Prisons and mental hospitals survived and, in some cases, flourished, serving as selective feeders to the private sector by releasing those who could be served by the private sector and holding on to those who were too difficult for the private agencies to handle.

The problem for the conservatives was not in the mental patient or in the student, nor was it in the society or in the economy where that person was embedded. It lay in how the institution was governed. This analysis was informed by the near-monopolies on human service enjoyed by the governing authorities and service bureaucracies. But the economic metaphor mystifies the public nature of the choice approach. The deinstitutionalization paradigm generally hid the possibility that other factors were responsible for the problem and that, without the current organization, unanticipated factors would come into play when it was changed. Indeed, actors in institutions could modify their behavior to maintain their power, learning how to manipulate the new system to maintain their advantage.

## Deinstitutionalized Practice

Current strategies to reform urban public schools have as their foundation a theory of deinstitutionalization that undermines the legitimacy of the state and privatizes its functions. That theory of deinstitutionalization has shaped reform efforts in other human service areas and has led to changes in service organization and delivery that have been devastating for the poor and have enhanced the resources of the middle class. This theory focuses on the conflict between bureaucracy and the individual, and it expresses that conflict as a problem of socialization (Meyer, 1978). The left-wing variant of the theory emphasizes the political dimension (Bastian and others, 1986); the right-wing variant focuses on economics; both undermine the state's legitimacy.

For most of the twentieth century, institution building and reform were synonymous. The building of institutions, the training of professionals, and the insulation of the service enterprise from politics were seen as ways to make progress in helping those in need. In education, this process of institution building was completed within a decade of the end of World War II. The "one best system" was composed of a strong superintendent, a school board above politics, and a professional cadre of teachers who were judged by educational standards. Public education involved what went on inside the school building and was the domain of school professionals and elected representatives. Revisionist and conservative scholars have emphasized what was lost in the battle to build that system (Ravitch, 1983), but with the development of a service economy came the need for new markets, as well as the need to break the state's monopoly on the delivery of human services so that private enterprises could expand. Enter deinstitutionalization, a reform that legitimizes that shift.

The deinstitutionalized mental health system does not look the way its advocates thought it would (Rochefort, 1989). Much of our understanding of this "community revolution" (Bell and Held, 1969) comes from those scholars and activists who write about the evils of the old bureaucratic or institutional system and describe the new arrangements as progress. This discourse promotes the new social-control system by comparing its potential with the evils of the old system; it avoids the question of how the new system supports the status quo. These researchers see the innovations as ways to remedy problems that the government has failed to address; they see a breakdown of effective democratic government. The result is that issues of effectiveness and redistribution are masked by a rhetoric that hides the consequences of the reforms behind a veil of false dichotomies.

Deinstitutionalization theory offers a very poor map to those who want to understand how the new system works. To improve that map, we need a conceptual framework that moves beyond describing the new operations and legitimizing innovations. I propose the concept of *inclusion* to capture this new reality. Inclusion is a complex concept that, better than the term *deinstitutionalization,* expresses the confusing currents and cross-currents in the modern-day transformation of human services. I shall first describe inclusion as it applies to mental health care.

The concept of inclusion refers to three different but related trends. The first trend is the general shift in the care of the mentally ill away from the traditional, large-scale state hospital to those social institutions that make up the fabric of community life. For example, despite the popular image of the homeless discharged mental patient, the majority of state mental patients are discharged to their families (Kiesler and Sibulkin, 1987). Thus, for the majority of patients, the burden of care and control rests with their families. Similarly, when patients need income, they rely on the institutions of work or government-sponsored income support, just as those who are not mentally ill do. When they need shelter, they have to rely on the low-income housing market—or, when the market fails them, on family or government support—just as other low-income groups do. In short, the term *inclusion* expresses the reality that, for patients and their immediate environment, clinical issues have become fused with problems of living.

Second, the notion of inclusion refers to the growing popularity of nonsegregative services for the treatment of the seriously mentally ill. For example, the number of psychiatric episodes in state hospitals has decreased since the mid 1950s, while the number in general hospitals has increased. In 1982, general hospitals accounted for 62.0 percent of all inpatient psychiatric episodes, while state hospitals accounted for only 17.6 percent (Kiesler and Sibulkin, 1987). In strictly quantitative terms, the general hospital is now the preferred site for treatment of acute mental disorders. Nevertheless, the emergence of the general hospital as the major provider of acute inpatient psychiatric care is not a case of the care of the seriously mentally ill being transferred from a custodial to a community setting. General hospitals have become part of a new, greatly expanded market for the treatment of mental disorders. This development is largely the result of the growth in mental health coverage in private (Blue Cross/Blue Shield) and federal (Medicaid and Medicare) insurance programs since the 1950s (Mechanic, 1987), and the population treated by general hospitals differs in important respects from the population treated by state hospitals. Both the acute treatment of the mentally ill and their long-term care have been dispersed over community-based facilities (Shadish, Lurigio, and Lewis, 1989). With operating costs underwritten by social security funds, a vast network of community residential institutions (such as board-and-care facilities, nursing and group homes, halfway houses, and single-room-occupancy hotels) has emerged since the 1960s. These facilities have been promoted as less restrictive alternatives to the long-term wards of the state hospital. In actual practice, however, their mode of controlling the resident often has a great deal in common with the custodial, punitive style of the large-scale mental institution (Lerman, 1982). Thus, this second aspect of inclusion could be described as the penetration of the institution into civil society.

The third aspect of inclusion represents the reverse: the penetration of civil society into the institution (Jacobs, 1977). The traditional state hospital has never ceased to play its central role in the care and control of the mentally ill, particularly the indigent mentally ill. The way it performs this role, however, has changed dramatically during the last three decades. The traditional authoritarian, coercive style of the state mental institution became more and more untenable in light of the structural changes in social organization and the moral values of postwar society. The institution's response to the mental patient converged with society's changing attitude toward minorities and marginal groups. The hospital became more egalitarian and came largely to rely on the patient's voluntary participation in treatment (Wagenaar and Lewis, 1989). These changes transformed the patient-provider relationship and gave the deinstitutionalized system its characteristic inclusionary tenor. Along with the transformation of the patient-provider relationship came profound social and economic changes that threw more and more patients into poverty (Lurigio and Lewis, 1989).

## Likely Consequences of Deinstitutionalized Schooling

If public education can anticipate a similar experience, then the central characteristics of the deinstitutionalized mental health system will appear in public education. I shall now highlight four such characteristics, as well as the potential difficulties that deinstitutionalizing innovations are likely to present.

### *Mandatory Reassignment of Clients*

The segregation of mental health clients inside institutions, which were walled off from the outside world both politically and clinically, was forcibly ended. In urban education, this was and is being done through desegregation plans, magnet schools, and choice plans. Students find themselves assigned to new places, on the basis of the notion that their assignment to segregated institutions was violating American laws and values. The notion that someone must be schooled in a segregated setting is no longer acceptable, either to the general public or to policy makers (Taylor, 1986). Similar movements have taken place in the mental health and correctional fields, as community corrections (Lewis and Darling, 1990) and community mental health (Lewis and others, 1991) have become guiding metaphors in legitimizing contemporary approaches to treatment.

### *Private Sector Penetration*

The monopoly of state control over the delivery of mental health services was broken as private agencies were given a share of state resources to deliver services to part of the client group (Fisher, Dorwart, Schlesinger, and Davidson, 1991). This arrangement has been given many different names, "community" appearing in most of them; in urban education, it is legitimized in the name of "choice" and is in the early stages of development. Both mental health and corrections have seen private sector penetration become a reality, as larger and larger proportions of state budgets for treatment go to private agencies that deliver services to clients.

### *Voluntary Compliance*

While exclusion was found to be illegal and unacceptable, the integration of client populations was made voluntary in the mental health system. Clients were not coerced to accept service in nonsegregative settings. After a few false starts, governmental authorities allowed market forces and personal preferences to determine who went to which services. The discretion of both the client and his or her family, as well as the receptivity of the available institutions, allocated clients across settings. For public schools, the same process has meant that state coercion was kept to a minimum after considerable original resistance to integration, and families now decide where to send their children to school. Segregation is against the law, but integration has been made voluntary outside the South.

### *Intransigence of the Original Conditions*

Many critiques of the exclusionary service system were based on theories of socialization that treated the "total" institution as the cause of the problem (crime, mental illness, ignorance). Theories that are used in an inclusionary perspective are "person-blame" rather than "system-blame" theories (Murray, 1984). They tend to place blame for problems inside people ("They are just that way") rather than inside institutions. In education, this has led to an emphasis on the importance of parents, the community, and students' attitudes as causes of poor achievement. The ascendancy of these newer theories makes it clear that private sector agencies and new inclusionary services should not be held responsible for how the client does. Rather, in this new world the clients themselves, or hard-to-control factors, are seen as causes of the problems, and the services are viewed as dealing with the consequences of problems that are beyond the reach of public policy. This new world and the arrangements we have just outlined are legitimized in the eyes of reformers merely on the basis of their contrasts with the old world of exclusion. The new system is justified by a critique of the old. The reformers tend to focus on the new system as an alternative to the older system of segregation and exclusion, rather than charting how the new system regulates and stratifies.

## Conclusion

The conventional debate over innovations such as decentralization usually appears as a fight between those who maintain the institutions to be changed (in this case, the public school bureaucrats—the insiders) and those who push for the new, "community" alternative (school reformers—the outsiders; see Moore and Davenport, 1990). In the reform process, research is often used to support challenges to the exclusionary approach. Researchers typically accept the reform position as credible and often assume it as embodying the proper theoretical stance from which to define research issues (for example, lack of innovation in a school district or resistance to change). By allowing reformers' views to determine the issues, however, researchers also adopt reformers' assumptions. In doing so, researchers often miss the important processes that are put into play when a system "transforms" itself from an exclusionary to an inclusionary one. The reform position certainly highlights the problems of the exclusionary system, but it is of little help in describing how the new inclusionary system operates. Reformers, as well as their supporters in the government and in foundations, push resistant bureaucracies and entrenched politicians to open up the governing process, but they do not explore how the new arrangements work. We must deinstitutionalize the way we think about school reform.

## References

Bastian, A., and others. *Choosing Equality: The Case for Democratic Schooling.* Philadelphia: Temple University Press, 1986.

Becker, H. *Outsiders: Studies in the Sociology of Deviance.* New York: Free Press, 1963.

Bell, D., and Held, V. "The Community Revolution." *Public Interest,* 1969, *3,* 142–171.

Burnham, J. *Suicide of the West: An Essay on the Meaning and Destiny of Liberalism.* Washington, D.C.: Gateway Editions, 1986.

Cawson, A. *Corporatism and Political Theory.* Cambridge, England: Basil Blackwell, 1986.

Chubb, J. E., and Moe, T. M. "America's Public Schools: Choice Is a Panacea." *Brookings Review,* 1990a, 4-12.

Chubb, J. E., and Moe, T. M. *Politics, Markets, and America's Schools.* Washington, D.C.: Brookings Institution, 1990b.

Cohen, S. *Visions of Social Control.* Cambridge, England: Polity Press, 1985.

Eckstein, H. "Civic Inclusion and Its Discontents." *Daedalus,* 1984, *113,* 107-145.

Epstein, J. "The Politics of School Decentralization." *New York Review of Books,* 1968, *10,* 26-32.

Fantini, M. "Quality Education in Urban Schools." In H. M. Levin (ed.), *Community Control of Schools.* Washington, D.C.: Brookings Institution, 1970.

Fisher, W. H., Dorwart, R. A., Schlesinger, M., and Davidson, H. "Contracting Between Public Agencies and Private Psychiatric Inpatient Facilities." *Medical Care,* 1991, *29,* 766-774.

Gittell, M. "Decentralization and Citizen Participation in Education." *Public Administration Review,* 1972, *32,* 670-686.

Gittell, M., and Hevesi, A. G. (eds.). *The Politics of Urban Education.* New York: Praeger, 1969.

Goffman, E. *Asylums: Essays on the Social Situations of Mental Patients and Other Inmates.* New York: Doubleday, 1961.

Jacobs, J. B. *Stateville: The Penitentiary in Mass Society.* Chicago: University of Chicago Press, 1977.

Kiesler, C. A., and Sibulkin, A. E. *Mental Hospitalization: Myths and Facts About a National Crisis.* Newbury Park, Calif.: Sage, 1987.

Krisberg, B., and others. "The Incarceration of Minority Youth." *Crime and Delinquency,* 1987, *33,* 173-205.

Lerman, P. *Deinstitutionalization and the Welfare State.* New Brunswick, N. J.: Rutgers University Press, 1982.

Lewis, D. A., and Darling, C. "The Idea of Community in Correctional Reform: How Rhetoric and Reality Join." In J. Murphy and J. Dison (eds.), *Twenty Years of Correctional Reform.* Newbury Park, Calif.: Sage, 1990.

Lewis, D. A., and others. *Worlds of the Mentally Ill: How Deinstitutionalization Works in the City.* Carbondale: Southern Illinois University, 1991.

Lurigio, A. J., and Lewis, D. A. "Worlds That Fail: A Longitudinal Study of Urban Mental Patients." *Journal of Social Issues,* 1989, *45,* 79–90.

Marris, P., and Rein, M. *Dilemmas of Social Reform: Poverty and Community Action in the United States.* (2nd ed.) Chicago: University of Chicago Press, 1982.

Mechanic, D. *Mental Health and Federal Policy.* Englewood Cliffs, N.J.: Prentice-Hall, 1980.

Meyer, J. W. "The Effects of Education as an Institution." *American Journal of Sociology,* 1978, *83,* 55–77.

Moore, D. R., and Davenport, S. "School Choice: The New Improved Sorting Machine." In W. L. Boyd and H. J. Walberg (eds.), *Choice in Education: Potential and Problems.* Berkeley, Calif.: McCutchan, 1990.

Murray, E. *Losing Ground.* New York: Basic Books, 1984.

Ravitch, D. *The Troubled Crusade: American Education, 1945–1980.* New York: Basic Books, 1983.

Rochefort, D. A. (ed.). *Handbook on Mental Health Policy in the United States.* New York: Greenwood Press, 1989.

Rogers, D. *110 Livingston Street: Politics and Bureaucracy in the New York City School System.* New York: Random House, 1968.

Rothman, D. *Discovery of the Asylum.* Boston: Little, Brown, 1971.

Shadish, W. R., Lurigio, A. J., and Lewis, D. A. "After Deinstitutionalization: The Present and Future of Mental Health Policy." *Journal of Social Issues,* 1989, *45*(3), 79–90.

Taylor, D. G. *Public Opinion and Collective Action.* Chicago: University of Chicago Press, 1986.

Tyack, D. B. *The One Best System: A History of American Urban Education.* Cambridge, Mass.: Harvard University Press, 1974.

Wagenaar, H., and Lewis, D. A. "Ironies of Inclusion: Social Class and Deinstitutionalization." *Journal of Health Politics, Policy and Law,* 1989, *14,* 503–522.

# 5

# Fiscal Decentralization and Accountability in Education: Experiences in Four Countries

**Donald R. Winkler**

Educational decentralization is in vogue throughout the world, although the policies and practices employed to implement decentralization vary widely across countries, as well as across states within the United States. Two typologies are useful in describing worldwide decentralization efforts. One typology distinguishes between *deconcentration,* which is the delegation of some decision-making authority to local agencies of central administrative units, and *decentralization,* which is the assignment of such extensive decision-making responsibility to the elected officials of local agencies (Rondinelli and others, 1983). The other typology makes a distinction in the level of decision-making authority, ranging from the national level to the individual (Uphoff, 1986).

The popular meaning of educational decentralization is very much country-specific. In some Latin American countries with a history of complete centralization of decision-making power in the central government's education ministry, decentralization is the delegation of powers to the regional offices of the ministry. In other countries, it refers to the constitutional transfer of such power from the central government to regional or local governments. In the United States, which by either of these standards is already highly decentralized, it typically refers both to deconcentration of the school district's central administrative decision-making authority to

*Note:* The findings, interpretations, and conclusions expressed in this chapter are entirely those of the author and should not be attributed in any manner to the World Bank. Alec Gershberg provided indispensable research assistance.

local school personnel (for example, teacher empowerment) and to transfer of authority to elected local school councils.

This chapter is concerned with the distribution of decision-making power among national, regional, and local governments and does not specifically address its distribution within local governments. Furthermore, the chapter focuses on fiscal decentralization, or the shift of governmental responsibility for the management of financial resources, since this is arguably the single most important administrative function. The chapter examines the theory and practice of primary-secondary education finance in intergovernmental systems and distills lessons for decentralization policies and their management, with special attention to the implications of decentralization for accountability.

This chapter begins with a typology of educational centralization-decentralization models, analyzes the advantages and disadvantages of those models, compares these ideal models with practice among both higher-income and lower-income countries, and draws lessons learned from experience. While the principal purpose of this analysis is to inform decentralization policy debates in developing countries, the lessons are equally important for higher-income countries. This analysis pays special attention to four countries having distinctly different organizational arrangements for financing and providing education—Australia, the United States, Brazil, and Chile. In Australia, educational finance and provision are the responsibility of the states. In the United States, states are also responsible for education, but most states further devolve most decision making to special education districts. Brazil is similar to the United States in devolving much decision making for primary education to local governments. Chile, where regional governments are simply administrative units of the central government, is often viewed as having made one of the most radical transitions from highly centralized to decentralized provision of education among developing countries.

The popularity of decentralization is attributable to a wide variety of factors. These can be grouped into four broad categories: educational finance, efficiency, accountability and effectiveness, and redistribution of political power. While these factors are examined here with respect to developing countries, they apply equally well in explaining the increasing popularity of community control of schools in the United States.

The financial arguments for decentralization are a recent phenomenon. The proportion of school-age children enrolled in primary and secondary schools has grown rapidly over the past two decades, and educational expenditures have grown rapidly as well. Central governments now find themselves facing severe fiscal constraints to continued expansion of educational opportunities. Hence, shifting part of the burden for support of primary and secondary education to subnational units of government, to community and voluntary organizations, and to parents has become an increasingly attractive alternative. The form of shifting advocated in decentralization plans varies with a variety of country characteristics, including the form of government, colonial administrative heritage, and traditions of community involvement.

The efficiency rationale for decentralization argues that centralized planning and administration, both at the national level and in large urban school districts, have resulted in expensive education, which is decreasing in quality. One explanation for high costs is inadequate governmental capacity to administer a centralized educational system. Another explanation is the cost of decision making in a system where even the most minor local education matters must be decided by a geographically and culturally distant bureaucracy. Yet another explanation is the frequent application by the education authorities of nationwide standards for curriculum, construction, teacher quality, and so on, which thereby prevents cost savings through adjustments of educational inputs to local or regional price differences.

The effectiveness rationale argues that centralized systems reduce the accountability of schools to their customers. After independence, many developing countries nationalized and centralized their educational systems, sometimes at the expense of community and mission schools. Similarly, school consolidation policies in the United States and other countries served to centralize decision making and increase the distance between schools and parents. Administration and accountability can be improved in education, it is argued, if schools are made more responsive to parents and to the local community and if the need for the central government (or the central administration in large urban school districts) to make decisions on local education matters is eliminated. These arguments are buttressed by examples of greater cost-effectiveness in the private sector.[1] An example of these arguments for decentralization is given in the sixth five-year plan of Pakistan: "The nearly comprehensive nationalization of educational institutions and the accompanying policy of free education ten years ago had at least two casualties. An already impoverished government was landed with a large financial burden, which restricted it from expanding education. And many of the schools of high quality, some of them run by education-conscious communities, lost their excellence under the public control. This, in both quantity and quality, was counter-productive" (Government of Pakistan, 1982, pp. 318–319).

Redistribution of political power is rarely stated as an objective of decentralization, but democratization or inclusion of marginal groups in society is a frequently stated goal. An example is the 1972 Peruvian educational reform, which quite explicitly attempted to include Indians and other disadvantaged groups in educational decision making. Some would argue that redistribution of political power is the primary objective of decentralization (McGinn and Street, 1982). With that as the objective, decentralization may be undertaken to empower groups in society that support the central government's policies or to weaken groups that pose obstructions to those policies. Thus, decentralization in Mexico has served to reduce the power of the teachers' union by transferring salary negotiations from the central to the state government level. From this perspective, decentralization is less concerned with the transfer of power from one level of government to another than with the transfer of power from one group to another. Ironically, one consequence of decentralization may be to increase the effective control of the central government, or at least that of key decision makers within the central government.

## Organizational Arrangements for Education

While the focus of this chapter is fiscal decentralization, it is useful to consider the organization of financing and spending within the broader context of governmental functions and responsibility for education. Governments are involved in many aspects of primary and secondary education: school organization, curriculum and teaching methods, supervision, setting of examinations, recruitment and compensation of teachers, financing of recurrent and capital expenditures, school construction, evaluation, and audit. The degree of centralization of decision making may differ widely by component, even within a given intergovernmental system (country or state). For example, curriculum decisions may be highly centralized; at the same time, school construction may be very decentralized.

The typology of education functions presented here can be combined with the typology of alternative modes of shifting decision making downward (deconcentration versus decentralization) and the typology of levels of decision making. The resulting mixes of decision-making power with respect to education functions, decision-making modes, and levels of government are what lead to the description of an entire educational system as "centralized" or "decentralized." Table 5.1 shows the mixes most commonly found in educational systems described as centralized, decentralized, and mixed. Quite clearly, each of these typologies could be extended in great detail. For example, a more extreme decentralized model might include school-based decision making or family decision making through the use of vouchers.

For any given intergovernmental system, the degree of centralization with respect to each component can be determined through the examination of the constitution, legislation, and regulations that set out the responsibilities of each level of government and constituent ministries or departments. But there is often a discrepancy between what is written or reported and what is practiced. In particular, the central government often sets guidelines for curriculum, teacher qualifications, school construction standards, and so on, that are unrealistically high, given the income and human resources of the country. As a result, what appear to be strict central government regulations and mandates may not be enforced and may in fact be largely ignored by the providers of educational services.

Table 5.1 provides a centralized-decentralized typology for the principal governmental activities found in public education. The discussion that follows describes that typology with some country-based examples.

**Table 5.1. Centralization-Decentralization Typology.**

| | *Centralized Model* | *Mixed Model* | *Decentralized Model* |
|---|---|---|---|
| Curriculum and teaching methods | Curriculum, teaching materials, preservice and in-service instruction provided by the central ministry of education | Curriculum, teaching materials, and in-service instruction established and provided by the central government or through its regional delegations | Basic contents of curriculum set centrally; textbooks may be selected and purchased locally; in-service instruction may be provided locally |
| Examinations and supervision | Examinations set and evaluated by central ministry of education; responsibility for direct supervision often lies with regional administrative offices | Examinations set centrally but usually administered and evaluated regionally; supervision of local instruction often carried out through regional or district offices | Examinations set and evaluated locally or through voluntary associations; central or regional governments usually provide limited supervision of teachers and schools |
| Teacher recruitment and compensation | Central government sets accreditation standards, provides teacher education, sets teacher pay scales, and directly pays the teachers | Teachers may be selected by the local school authority, but central or regional government typically prescribes pay scales; accreditation standards also set centrally | Teachers selected and pay scales set by local government; accreditation standards typically set by central government but may not be enforced |

**Table 5.1. Centralization-Decentralization Typology, Cont'd.**

| | *Centralized Model* | *Mixed Model* | *Decentralized Model* |
|---|---|---|---|
| Financing of recurrent expenditures | All current expenditures fully funded by central government except minor user fees; non-teacher resources distributed to schools | Central or regional government provides most funding of local schools, with some portion of educational expenditures funded by local revenue sources; local community has some influence on total expenditure levels | Local government funds elementary and secondary education from local revenue sources; user fees or "voluntary" contributions to parent-teacher associations may be required; categorical or project grants may be provided by central government |
| School construction | Central government sets construction standards, which may be uniform for the entire country, and covers all construction costs, although the local community may be required to provide labor and/or some construction materials | Construction standards set by central government; matching funds often provided for school construction, sometimes in the form of a promise by the central government to cover some portion of recurrent expenditures | Land and materials for school construction provided by local community; labor may be voluntary; local construction standards used |
| Financial and management audits | Review of central government ministry of education carried out by internal and external auditors | Internal audit of central government ministry complemented by external audit of use of the central government funds by local agencies | Local government responsible for internal control and managing external audit of school agencies; central government may audit use of its funds by local agency |

### School Organization

The term *school organization* refers to the establishment of minimum schooling requirements, the structure of elementary and secondary schooling, and the rights of children to education. With the exception of a very few federalist systems (for example, the United States), decisions about school organization are highly centralized. Despite a high degree of centralization, however, large differences in compliance with organizational standards, especially in providing educational opportunities (for example, number of grades of education offered) to all children, are found in almost all school systems (Carron and Chau, 1980). The major difference between decentralized and centralized school systems lies in the level of government that makes resource-allocation decisions that result in unequal opportunities. In the centralized model, unequal educational opportunities are the result of resource-allocation decisions made in the ministry of education itself. In the decentralized model, unequal educational opportunities are usually the result of differences in wealth or tax bases among local or regional governments responsible for financing elementary and secondary education.

### Curriculum and Teaching Methods

Like school organization, curriculum standards are usually regulated by the central government, which also usually provides teacher education. In most countries, public school curriculum standards are also extended to private schools. Curriculum is typically viewed as the domain of experts, who mainly reside in teacher colleges or in the ministry of education. Teacher education is also typically viewed as the responsibility of the central government (or of the regional government in large decentralized systems).

Centralization of curriculum-related decision making need not imply a uniform curriculum. Several centralized countries have attempted to differentiate the curriculum to meet the instructional needs of different social groups. A tightly controlled pedagogy can be one policy response to the problem of poorly qualified teachers.

### *Examinations and Supervision*

Perhaps the most crucial questions about educational supervision concern who selects the chief administrative officer of a school or group of schools and what power that individual has over the various educational functions. The chief administrator is typically appointed by the ministry (or by the regional education secretariat) in a highly centralized system and may have relatively few powers other than the power to send personnel evaluations to the ministry and monitor the education and examination system to ensure compliance with ministry guidelines. In a decentralized system, by contrast, the chief administrator may be directly elected by the local community or may be appointed by an elected mayor or council. Between these two extremes is the administrator who is appointed by the ministry and given considerable decision making authority over resource allocation in the schools. In many developing countries, transportation is sufficiently difficult and human resources sufficiently scarce that there is very little effective supervision of the schools, regardless of how the administrator is selected. In many countries, administrators are also responsible for supervising private schools, and that fact only exacerbates this resource problem.

Examinations provide a standard for measuring and evaluating learning. Variation is perhaps more extreme in examination control and procedures than in any other educational function. In many former British colonies (for example, countries in the West Indies), exams are set and graded in England. At the other extreme are most countries in Latin America, which have no national examinations; as a result, the criteria set for passing from one grade or one level to the next are set at the school level and vary greatly. In between these two extremes are countries that set and grade exams regionally. Although a system of national examinations is typically found in the centralized model, Latin America demonstrates that local control of examinations and promotion standards can coexist in relatively centralized systems.

### *Teacher Recruitment and Compensation*

Accreditation standards for teachers are almost always set centrally (a notable exception is the United States, where state governments license teachers), but the criteria set for accreditation are often ideal standards, which cannot be met in practice. The local or regional labor market for teachers determines de facto local or regional accreditation standards, even in highly centralized school systems.

Teacher recruitment and promotion practices vary greatly among countries. In a highly centralized country, the central government (through either the education ministry or the civil service ministry) recruits, appoints, promotes, and moves teachers; nationally recruited teachers are also likely to enjoy civil service protection. In a decentralized country, the community itself may recruit teachers, and employment and promotion may be politically determined in part (say, through patronage of the elected mayor). Teacher compensation practices are highly correlated with recruitment procedures. When recruitment and promotion are centralized, there is typically a national pay scale, which does not vary with working conditions. When recruitment is decentralized, teachers are usually paid in accordance with conditions in the local labor market.

### *Financing of Recurrent Expenditures*

In a highly centralized educational system, the government both finances and directly provides all inputs, with no local contributions (except minor matriculation fees). In a decentralized system, the local community finances and directly provides inputs, either through local tax revenues (the United States, Brazil) or through "voluntary" fees (Kenya). A mixed system would include the central government's financing and provision of some educational inputs (books, supervision), categorical grants to regional or local governments, and some local community control over use of those funds.

### *School Construction and Finance*

In the centralized model, the central government sets uniform construction standards and directly carries out all school construction. In the decentralized model, the local community finances and constructs schools (in low-income countries, this arrangement may take the form of local voluntary contributions and construction with local materials and standards). In the mixed model, the central government may construct schools, using different regional standards; or the community that constructs its own school may be required to follow governmental standards in order for the school to be accredited and staffed. In practice, school construction and finance tend to be more decentralized than the other components of elementary and secondary education, especially in Africa and Asia. In many developing countries (Zimbabwe, India), the central government offers an implicit matching grant, promising to staff the school constructed by the local community.

### *Evaluation and Audit*

The locus of financial control, auditing, and performance evaluation typically lies with the government that provides the revenues for education. The central government almost always exercises internal control over its own use of funds (for example, in the centralized model) and either undertakes audit or requires external audit of the use of its funds by other levels of government (for example, in the decentralized model). Local governments, by contrast, typically control only those funds derived from local revenue sources. Performance evaluations typically include the administration of standardized examinations.

### *An Assessment*

Two important questions can be posed about the alternative models presented in Table 5.1. First, what determines which model is selected by a particular country (or state, in the United States)? Answering this question is an exercise in political economy. The choice may be related to perceptions of the relative efficiency or effectiveness of alternative models; more likely, however, the choice is determined by historical, cultural, and political factors. I have seen no rigorous examination of this question, and to attempt an answer would be too ambitious a task for this chapter.

Second, which model is best? The answer to this question depends partly on the values of the respondent and partly on empirical evidence. Those who assign a high value to equality may argue for a centralized model or a mixed model with strict regulations to limit inequality. Those who assign a high value to freedom of choice would most likely argue for a highly decentralized model. Finally, those most interested in efficiency would select centralized provision of activities where economies of scale are large and decentralized decision making for activities where input prices (such as teachers' salaries) vary widely. The average citizen, of course, may desire some mix of these values, according to the trade-offs involved. Although interested in efficiency, the average citizen may be willing to incur higher costs to ensure greater equality of educational opportunity across jurisdictions. Unfortunately, empirical evidence on these trade-offs is wanting, and the absence of such evidence prevents any firm answer to the question. Still, experience in various countries can at least suggest an answer to the question of which models appear to satisfy which criteria best. This chapter limits the review of countries' experiences to fiscal activities, for practical reasons of space and time.

## Fiscal Decentralization: A Scenario

Fiscal decentralization is the reassignment of revenue-raising and expenditure responsibilities from the central to subnational governments; in terms of Table 5.1, it is the movement from the "centralized" to either the "mixed" or the "decentralized" model. Fiscal decentralization is the core of any educational decentralization policy. Changes in revenue and expenditure assignments alter organizational incentives and behavior, with important implications for efficiency and equity.

In the original, centralized state of the world, the central government collects all revenues and makes all expenditure decisions. A competitive and iterative budgeting process, usually between the education and finance ministries and the legislature, leads to a budget for primary and secondary education. Within political and other constraints, the education ministry determines the allocation of the budget across budget categories and across schools, communities, or regions within the country. Communities or regions desiring new schools, more teachers, more grade-level or course offerings, or more of other educational resources must solicit such resources from the education ministry. Additional resources are "free" to the solicitor, who is thus not concerned about either their efficient use or the cost implications to the central government. The education ministry, however, is concerned with these efficiency and cost issues and takes them into consideration in responding to solicitations. Nevertheless, the technicians of the ministry are sometimes frustrated to find that political relations between the ministry and elected officials at the subnational level often dominate technical evaluations. Finally, since the education ministry directly provides physical resources, it need not be concerned about the proper use of funds, although it is concerned about the proper use of resources and for that purpose carries out periodic supervision of schools.

Critics of this centralized world focus on three principal problems. First, centralization implies a considerable degree of uniformity in policies, salaries, and procedures, regardless of local and regional differences in educational needs and input prices. Second, the geographical distance between decision makers and parents and the lack of any mechanism to accurately reflect parents' and taxpayers' preferences lead to a large amount of dissatisfaction.[2] Third, the education ministry's effective monopoly (with the exception, perhaps, of a small private education sector) restricts both parental choice in schooling and educational innovation. These problems could be ameliorated in the context of centralized educational finance and provision through policies to permit regional variations in curriculum, salaries, and course offerings; introduction of mechanisms to provide parental feedback and participation; and development of policies to encourage innovation. Let us assume, however, that because of resource limitations and institutional or political constraints, such changes are not possible. As a result, the country decides to decentralize authority for revenues and expenditures to local and/or regional governments.

To continue this scenario, the government decides that if there are problems with centralization, then radical decentralization must be the solution. Therefore, it adopts the constitutional changes required to give each local government both its own sources of revenue (mainly the property tax) and the authority to decide rates of taxation on those revenue sources, as well as the authority to decide how much to spend on a variety of local services, including education. Furthermore, local governments are responsible for teachers' recruitment (subject to the central government's minimum qualification standards) and remuneration, as well as for the provision of school supplies and texts, school construction, and building maintenance. Given their constitutional autonomy, local governments are neither required to submit financial reports to the central government nor subject to mandatory external audits.

Initially, local citizens are euphoric over their new powers, but criticisms soon arise. The first and major criticism is that local governments with low fiscal capacity (that is, a low property-tax base) cannot raise and allocate sufficient revenues to provide the quantity and quality of education that was provided earlier. These jurisdictions complain that their children have less educational opportunity than children fortunate enough to live in jurisdictions with high fiscal capacity. Relatively well-off jurisdictions join in, complaining that they lack the large revenues required to undertake new school construction.[3] Another criticism erupts from the national teachers' association, which complains that teachers of similar qualifications are receiving very different salaries within the country, and some receive only poverty-level wages. Parents also join the chorus, complaining that their input is sometimes ignored by elected officials who have different spending priorities; furthermore, they argue, the schools fail to provide them with even basic information on spending and performance. The central government soon realizes that it cannot rid itself so easily of the responsibility for educational finance, and it begins to consider policies for correcting the major problems. A search for policy options would naturally begin with an assessment of those policies already in practice in countries with federal or decentralized systems of government. This assessment would also begin with a more precise definition of the criteria that could be employed to assess those systems—the topic to which we now turn.

## Criteria and Options

The litany of complaints about both centralized and decentralized arrangements for education financing and spending suggest at least some criteria that could be employed in a technical evaluation of policy options. As shown in Table 5.2, these criteria would at least include the capacity of the system to satisfy taxpayers' or consumers' preferences, guaranteed minimum levels of educational quantity and quality, mechanisms for holding decision makers accountable to the payers and users of education, and a satisfactory level of equality of educational opportunity.[4] Variables measuring these criteria are not necessarily easy to define or quantify, but it is at least possible in all cases to specify some of the conditions that positively or negatively affect their size.

Satisfaction of consumers' and taxpayers' preferences is related to both voice and choice. The louder the voice that taxpayers and parents have in determining taxing and spending for education, the greater their satisfaction with the outcomes should be.[5] In most circumstances, the smaller the jurisdiction making decisions on taxing and spending, the louder this voice. Alternatively, if

**Table 5.2. Criteria for the Evaluation of Policy Options.**

| *Criteria* | *Comments* |
|---|---|
| Satisfaction of consumers and taxpayers' preferences regarding taxes and educational services | The larger the jurisdiction, the more homogeneous the service; the more heterogeneous the preferences of the population concerning education, the poorer the match between citizens' preferences and the services they receive |
| Guaranteed minimum levels of educational quantity and quality | The high mobility associated with human capital results in interjurisdictional spillovers of education benefits |
| Accountability for educational performance and use of funds | Accountability requires clear assignment of responsibilities, public information on performance and finance, and rigorous finance and management audit |
| Equality of educational opportunity | High correlations between educational quantity and quality and family income or local tax base are commonly interpreted as low equality of educational opportunity |

citizens have choice in selecting jurisdictions or schools, they can choose the schools that best match their preferences, with income and other constraints giving some citizens greater choice than others. Both voice and choice become more important with greater heterogeneity in the citizens' preferences for taxing and spending. These arguments suggest the proposition that decentralization increases consumers' and taxpayers' satisfaction.

The human capital requirements of democratic and industrial societies and the high mobility of human capital imply that failure on the part of some jurisdictions to provide some minimum quantity and quality of educational services may result in lower productivity and higher public service costs elsewhere. Thus, there is an externality argument for ensuring that all citizens attain some minimum level of knowledge.[6] In practice, this is defined as jurisdictions' provision of minimum educational services, in terms of both minimum years of education and minimum per-pupil expenditure levels. The analysis given here focuses solely on minimum expenditures. If the central (or state) government does not ensure minimum expenditures, and if the fiscal capacity of the schools varies widely, then decentralization is hypothesized to increase the proportion of students receiving less than the required minimum expenditures.

Accountability means holding public officials responsible for their actions and is thus a necessary condition for satisfying any other criteria by which one can judge alternative arrangements for education financing and spending. Accountability requires clear assignment of responsibility for financing and provision of education, congruence between public policy and implementation, financial reporting and auditing to ensure proper uses of funds, program evaluations to assess school performance, and free and easy access by education consumers to financial and performance information. Decentralization is likely to have ambiguous effects on accountability. While it may encourage parents and voters to monitor the school more closely, it may also reduce the information available to those doing the monitoring (presuming that central ministry officials have, on the average, better information than parents and voters do).

While most societies wish to ensure some degree of equality

of educational opportunity, specification and definition of the term vary widely. Typically, equality is considered to be low when there exist large differences in expenditures and educational attainment among a country's regions, ethnic groups or races, or socioeconomic groups. The existence of high positive correlations between educational expenditures and family income or between educational expenditures and fiscal capacity of the jurisdiction is also a reflection of low equality of educational opportunity. To the extent that large variations exist in family income or fiscal capacity across schools, decentralization is hypothesized to reduce equality of education.

## Experiences in Four Countries

Two higher-income and two lower-income countries constitute the sample of countries reviewed here for the purpose of distilling lessons for governments that are considering further decentralization of education finance. Even though the sample is small, these four countries reflect significantly different models of fiscal decentralization in education, as summarized in Table 5.3. Two of the countries—Australia and Chile—have large central government revenue-sharing programs, which significantly reduce subnational government fiscal disparities. The other two countries—the United States and Brazil—have large subnational government fiscal disparities, even after federal categorical and revenue-sharing transfers.

Australia is a federation of states with weak municipal governments. The central government, or commonwealth, provides a large share (59 percent) of total state revenues through redistributive revenue sharing (Groenewegen, 1984). As a result, fiscal capacity is relatively equal across states, and differences in revenues largely reflect regional preferences. By contrast, the United States provides no revenue sharing to either state or municipal governments, with resulting large disparities in fiscal capacity.[7] The Brazilian federal government provides both automatic revenue sharing and discretionary transfers to state and municipal governments.[8] Nevertheless, interstate and intermunicipal fiscal disparities remain very large.[9] In addition, federal and state government transfers play a small role in reducing fiscal disparities among municipalities. Finally, Chile

**Table 5.3. Organization of School Finance and Expenditure.**

| *Country* | *Financing of Recurrent Expenditures* | *Financing of Capital Expenditures* | *Teacher Recruitment and Remuneration* | *Evaluation and Audit* |
|---|---|---|---|---|
| Australia | States responsible for financing of state and nongovernment schools, with some federal transfers (11% of total for state schools); state plus federal transfers to private primary schools represent 38% of total expenditures | Government school construction financed out of general state revenues, general-purpose capital grants, and categorical commonwealth grants | State governments have overall responsibility, with recent local involvement in recruitment | Commonwealth audit of its categorical grants through ad hoc agreements with state agencies |
| United States | States and localities share responsibility for finance of local schools, with small federal contribution (6% of total); wide variation in education finance between states | Local governments have principal responsibility for finance, largely through bond proceeds, with some state aid | Responsibility of local governments, with state role usually limited to accreditation standards and regulation of pension plans | Local government usually responsible for arranging external audits, with state overview and federal audits of federal transfers; states responsible for evaluation and testing |
| Brazil | States finance state schools, municipalities finance municipal schools, with small federal contribution (10% of total) | Each government level responsible for financing its own school constructions | Each government level responsible for recruitment and remuneration of its teachers, with state role limited to accreditation standards | State government responsible for audit of both state and municipal accounts, with emphasis on preaudit; no evaluation or testing |
| Chile | Central government finances municipal schools, with small municipal contribution (10% of total) | Central government finances and constructs municipal schools | Municipal government responsible for recruitment and remuneration, subject to central government standards, including minimum teacher salary scale | Central government audits municipal accounts, with emphasis on preaudit, and administers national standardized tests; no program evaluation |

has both revenue sharing and categorical programs that redistribute revenues among the thirteen regions and 334 municipalities; the remaining fiscal disparities are small, by comparison to both the United States and Brazil.[10]

### *Financing of Recurrent Expenditures*

All four countries assign responsibility for providing education to subnational governments, but their methods of doing so vary greatly. The substantial fiscal equalization among states in Australia means that commonwealth education transfers can focus on special needs, rather than being concerned with state fiscal capacity. Still, commonwealth categorical grants represent 11 percent of total revenues of state schools. With the exception of private schools, which represent 30 percent of total primary and secondary enrollments, education is directly provided by the state governments. Therefore, there is no need for state grants to municipalities, although state budgeting allocations to individual schools reflect local differences in services and costs (Mathews, 1983).

By contrast to Australia, U.S. federal government transfers do little to compensate for interstate disparities in fiscal capacity or interstate education spending differences. Indeed, the U.S. Constitution does not assign the federal government any specific role in education. State governments, which do have a specific role, typically delegate the responsibility for providing primary and secondary education to local special districts, which are often coterminous with general local government boundaries. Federal categorical grants represent 6 percent of total education financing, while state governments, on the average, provide about half the financing for education through redistributive block and categorical grants, and local own-source revenues represent a little less than half the total.[11] Nevertheless, there are large differences among states; for example, local governments in Alabama provide 18 percent of total revenues, and local governments in Nevada generate 56 percent of total revenues. Federal and state categorical transfers alike are numerous and complex and emphasize the compensation of local authorities for special education costs or special needs. In addition, the state governments have adopted various alternatives to reduce inequities in per-student educational expenditures. California equalizes spending by prohibiting districts with high fiscal capacity from increasing their expenditures. Minnesota establishes a high level of state-guaranteed minimum expenditures per student. Missouri has legislated (but not yet funded) a power-equalizing formula, which ensures that all districts receive identical increases in spending for the same tax-rate increase.

Brazil's primary and secondary education finance is complex, given Brazil's unique dual school system, especially at the primary level. State governments operate state primary schools, while municipalities, often in the same jurisdiction, operate municipal primary schools.[12] Federal government education transfers to states and municipalities are equalizing but represent only 10 percent of total state and municipal government primary and secondary education expenditures; these transfers primarily take the form of project grants negotiated with state education secretariats (World Bank, 1986). In addition, the federal government provides some textbooks and school meals to students in all public schools. Despite large intrastate variations in fiscal capacity among municipalities, state governments in general have not adopted either block or categorical education grants, although the existence of state schools reduces education's demands on municipal budgets. Municipal and state governments are both constitutionally required to allocate 25 percent of specified revenues to education.

Education finance in Chile is relatively simple. Municipalities have the responsibility of providing public education, either directly or through semiautonomous corporations, but the central government has the principal responsibility for educational finance. Central government finance represents 90 percent of municipal primary and secondary education expenditures and takes the form of transfers per pupil, weighted by special need and cost factors. Nonprofit schools, which represent 32 percent of total primary and secondary enrollments, are also eligible to receive the same per-pupil transfers; since parents can select their children's schools, these transfers operate like education vouchers. Municipalities finance the remaining 10 percent of their education expenditures out of own-source revenues.[13]

### *Financing of Capital Expenditures*

Capital investment (primarily school construction and rehabilitation), like financing of recurrent expenditures, differs greatly among the four countries. In Australia, state governments finance capital investment out of their general state revenues and their share of general-purpose commonwealth capital grants, financed through the issuance of government bonds; the central government's role in direct finance of capital investment is minimal. In the United States, by contrast, local authorities are responsible for financing capital investment, largely through general-obligation bonds, with some state regulation and aid. Municipalities and states in Brazil are responsible for financing capital investment in education from their general revenues and from negotiated federal transfers. Finally, the central government in Chile is principally responsible for financing and constructing municipal schools, mainly through municipal applications to the National Development Fund.[14] While these applications are given a technical evaluation, political links between the central government and the municipal government are important in allocating these discretionary grants.[15]

### *Teacher Recruitment and Compensation*

Salaries of personnel typically account for 90 percent of total recurrent outlays; therefore, responsibility for recruitment and remuneration of teachers largely determines expenditure authority. In Australia, this authority lies with the state government, although there have been recent experiments with local involvement in recruitment. In the United States, this responsibility lies with local authorities, although the state sets accreditation standards and often manages a statewide teacher pension plan. In Brazil, municipalities and state governments are responsible for recruitment and remuneration of teachers in their respective schools. In Chile, this authority is given to municipalities, although the central government recently passed a minimum pay scale for teachers, applicable to all schools receiving public subventions.

### *Evaluation and Audit*

No country in this sample of four can be said to do an adequate job of financial audit and program evaluation. In Australia, the commonwealth is responsible for the audit of its categorical programs, which typically are not included in state government budgets. There is no single consistent procedure for audit and evaluation; instead, agreements for review are reached with implementing state agencies (Else-Mitchell, 1986). In the United States, the federal government does follow a consistent audit procedure, with a designated federal agency given the authority to carry out a single audit of all federal programs for a given state. While this arrangement avoids many audits by many federal agencies, the large number of federal grant programs (392 categorical programs in 1984) and of detailed grant conditions reduces effective enforcement. In the United States, municipal governments typically audit the use of state categorical transfers, with overall review by state authorities. In addition, most states have annual testing programs, which provide feedback to parents and communities on some indicators of school performance.

In both Brazil and Chile, audit practices emphasize preaudit compliance with legal authorities for expenditures; grant conditions, other than for the use of funds, are not usually included in such audits; the central government's ministries usually lack the capacity to provide substantive program evaluations; and central government grants are not appropriated by states or municipalities. In other respects, however, the countries differ significantly. In Brazil, state tribunals audit both state and municipal accounts. Nevertheless, financial reports by municipalities to states and to the federal government do not follow common accounting practice, which requires careful reworking to generate comparable data, a process that involves years before publication is possible. In addition, Brazil has no school examination or evaluation program to provide feedback on performance. The controller general of Chile, by contrast, carries out throrough periodic audits of all municipal accounts, including central government transfers, and applies harsh penalties in the event of mistakes. In addition, the ministry of education administers a nationwide educational testing program but does not widely disseminate or analyze the results (Schiefelbein, 1991).

## Assessment of Fiscal Decentralization

The following brief description of fiscal decentralization and the evaluation criteria given earlier provide the basis for a qualitative assessment, which is summarized in Table 5.4. Two of the criteria posited earlier—minimum education expenditures and equality of opportunity—can be defined and measured, and empirical evidence on these exists for each of the four countries. The other two criteria—consumers' and taxpayers' satisfaction and accountability—are not easily defined and measured, and the only information available for assessing these variables in the four countries comes from the existence of conditions that, in principle, are conducive to their attainment.

### *Consumers' and Taxpayers' Satisfaction*

No unambiguous evidence exists on the relationship between consumers' and taxpayers' satisfaction and decentralization. Several likely determinants of satisfaction were noted earlier—size of jurisdiction, authority to tax and spend, choice of schools or jurisdictions, and community input in resource allocation or management (including selection of school management)—but there is little or no confirming (or disconfirming) evidence. Still, it is at least useful to identify how the four countries compare on these variables. In Australia, for example, the jurisdictions for providing education are very large geographically, and citizens can only elect state general government leaders, who can be selected regardless of their views on education. Brazilian state schools are similar in this respect to those of Australia, although Brazilian states also face significant constraints in increasing their own-source revenues for whatever purpose. Brazilian municipalities, however, offer a mixed picture, with large municipalities such as São Paulo being considerably larger than some states and rural municipalities in the northeast providing choice in terms of selection of leaders but little choice in raising own-source revenues or moving to nearby jurisdictions. Chilean

**Table 5.4. Assessment of Fiscal Decentralization in Four Countries.**

| *Country* | *Consumers' and Taxpayers' Satisfaction* | *Minimum Education Expenditures* | *Accountability* | *Equality of Opportunity* |
|---|---|---|---|---|
| Australia | States can determine revenues and education expenditures, but very limited local control; large government subsidies to private schools | No national minimum standards; states guarantee minimum expenditure levels in state schools | Consumer or taxpayer has small voice in finance decisions but can select private school alternative; finance system transparent, but state budgets exclude commonwealth categorical transfers | High equality of spending among states and among state schools; average spending in Catholic schools 72% of that in state schools |
| United States | Local districts choose education tax rates and expenditure levels, subject to state government controls; school boards elected | No national minimum standards; states guarantee minimum expenditure levels and regulate minimum quality | Consumer or taxpayer has relatively large voice in finance decisions; complexity of finance reduces transparency; rigorous audits and open information on state examinations | Highly unequal spending among states; inequalities within some states significantly reduced through redistributive state aid |
| Brazil | Municipalities choose education expenditure levels but have limited power to increase revenues; mayors and councils elected | Federal constitution requires state and local governments to allocate 25% of revenues to education; no state minimum standards | Consumer or taxpayer has some voice concerning municipal school expenditures; lack of information on school performance and use of funds | Highly unequal spending among and within states, despite redistributive federal aid; stats fail to equalize spending differences across municipal schools |
| Chile | Municipalities choose education expenditure levels but very limited power to increase revenues; mayors and councils currently appointed | National minimum expenditure level set by level of per-pupil voucher | Consumer or taxpayer potentially has large voice concerning municipal school expenditures and can select private school; financial and performance information not disseminated | Highly equal spending across municipal and subsidized private schools |

municipalities also suffer from own-source revenue constraints but can choose to alter education expenditures within those constraints. The appointment of mayors and councils clearly limits the influence of citizens, but this is a situation inherited from the previous military government, and it will soon change. Larger cities, however, comprise several municipalities, an arrangement that provides some possibility for citizens' choice, and the opportunity to use vouchers to send children to nonprofit schools increases that choice, at least in urban areas. With significant exceptions, consumers' and taxpayers' choice and voice are relatively significant in the United States. Schools are usually governed and administered by special districts, led by elected directors; those districts often have great discretion to determine both taxes and spending. Some urban areas, however, have single school districts, with as many pupils as the entire municipal school system has in Chile. Moreover, state constraints on taxing and spending have essentially eliminated such discretion for many school districts; for example, in California, the state with the largest number of public school students, education taxing and spending decisions are made largely at the state level.

If the relationships postulated earlier held true, a practical model for ensuring consumers' satisfaction might combine features from Chile and the United States and would attempt to satisfy the following conditions:

1. School districts would be no larger than necessary to realize economies of scale.
2. Parents would be permitted to exercise some choice in selecting schools.
3. The board of directors for the school district would be directly elected.
4. The community would have some collective choice regarding education tax and expenditure levels.

In other words, in the ideal model, educational finance and resource-allocation decisions would be assigned to local rather than regional or national governments. Education would be provided through special districts, rather than by general-purpose governments. Neither expenditures nor local tax rates would be constrained by higher levels of government. There is no assurance, of course, that other factors (such as corruption, fatalism, lack of an informed citizenry, lack of local administrative capacity) might not render this ideal model unworkable.

### *Minimum Expenditures*

Unlike satisfaction, the quantity and quality of education can be directly (if imperfectly) measured, usually proxied by education expenditures. Furthermore, the differences among the four countries are striking. Brazil fails to establish effective levels of minimum expenditures either between or within states. Although the federal constitution does require that state and municipal governments allocate a minimum of 25 percent of specified revenues to education, that condition is not effectively audited and enforced. Even if it were enforced, wide disparities in fiscal capacity would ensure large state and municipal differences in the minimum quantity and quality of education.

Like Brazil, the United States has no national levels of minimum quality and quantity. Each state, however, does establish its own minimum years of schooling and minimum expenditures per pupil. Attainment of minimum expenditures is ensured through variable matching-grant programs, which typically mandate a minimum tax rate on a tax base (usually the property tax), compute each district's revenues from that tax rate, and provide transfers to bring all schools up to the specified state minimum. The specified minimum varies greatly by state.

By contrast with Brazil and the United States, both Australia and Chile provide the conditions to ensure minimum expenditures per pupil. Australia sets no national standard, but its system of interstate fiscal equalization ensures that each state has the fiscal capacity to expend adequate amounts in public schools; minimum intrastate spending is dictated by state resource-allocation rules. Chile, through its per-pupil subvention or voucher rate, effectively sets the minimum expenditure per pupil in both municipal and nonprofit schools.[16]

Since human capital is mobile across both local and regional boundaries, a preferred model would have the central government ensuring minimum expenditures nationally, with regional governments free to set higher minimum expenditures within their boundaries. More important than the minimum itself may be the mechanisms for ensuring minimum expenditures. These include mandates, pupil grants, and variable matching grants. Mandates are the least preferred alternative. The Brazilian mandate to allocate a specified percentage of the budget to education does not account for variations in subnational government revenues or for differences in percentages of respective populations in public schools. A program mandating subnational governments to spend a specified amount per pupil would work poorly in situations of high variation in fiscal capacity, but it would work well where fiscal capacity has been largely equalized (for example, in Australia) through redistributive revenue sharing.[17] Per-pupil grants (as in Chile) neither distort expenditures nor impose fiscal stress, but they are costly, in terms of the magnitude of required transfers from the central to subnational governments, and they provide identical subventions without regard to fiscal capacity. Finally, matching grants are lower in cost to the central government, and matching rates may vary with fiscal capacity.

### *Accountability*

As noted earlier, accountability requires clear assignment of responsibilities, public information on finance and performance, and mechanisms by which to hold decision makers responsible. In Brazil, responsibility for financing and providing primary education is unclear in practice, federal government transfers lack transparency, and information on finance and performance is neither collected nor disseminated systematically. Australia provides clear assignment of responsibilities and transparency in finance but has weak electoral mechanisms by which to ensure accountability by educational decision makers to consumers and taxpayers. The United States provides public information on finance and performance and, for smaller jurisdictions, a mechanism by which consumers and taxpayers can hold educational decision makers responsible, but the complexity of school finance is reflected in lack of clarity, both in finance and in expenditure assignment. Chile's system of school finance is transparent, and it generates reliable information on finance and performance, but that information is not disseminated to inform taxpayers and consumers of public education; in addition, there is now only a very indirect mechanism—election of national leaders—by which voters can hold educational decision makers accountable.

An ideal intergovernmental model of educational accountability would include features borrowed from each of these four countries. It would include the following elements:

- Precise legal assignment of revenue and expenditure responsibility by level of government
- Transparent finance of education, including transparency and simplicity in intergovernmental transfers
- Rigorous reporting and audit of educational finance, expenditures, and performance
- Dissemination to the public of accessible information on finance and performance
- Establishment (as feasible and consistent with other objectives) of a link between costs and benefits, through requirements for local voters to incur the costs of education services (cost sharing in intergovernmental transfers, financing of expenditures beyond minimum levels by local own-source revenues, and loans rather than grants for capital outlays)

### *Equality of Educational Opportunity*

The four countries differ greatly in terms of equality. Per-pupil expenditures vary widely among and within states in Brazil. For example, average municipal school expenditures in the northeast are one-third of those elsewhere in the country, and expenditures in northeast state schools are triple those of municipal schools (World Bank, 1986). High inequality in per-pupil expenditures is also found in the United States. The average per-pupil expenditure in New York, for example, is more than double that of Alabama, and almost twice as much is spent on high-expenditure (95th percentile of expenditures) as on low-expenditure (5th percentile) schools within New York (Schwartz and Moskowitz, 1988). By contrast, there is a high degree of equality in Australia and Chile, despite very different systems of school finance.

These four countries employ four different policies for reducing inequalities in spending:

- Redistributive revenue sharing to general-purpose local governments (Australia and, to a lesser extent, Brazil and Chile)
- Per-pupil grants, possibly adjusted for cost differences, to local governments (Chile and the United States)
- Categorical grants targeted to student populations that are especially needy or especially costly to education (Australia and the United States)
- Spending limitations on governments with high fiscal capacity (United States)

In the first three cases, effective reduction of inequality in educational expenditures has much more to do with the size of transfers (revenue sharing, or per-pupil grants) than with the specific policy. Redistributive revenue sharing accounts for a larger portion of state government revenues in Australia than in Brazil. Per-pupil grants constitute a much higher percentage of average expenditures in Chile than in the United States. The fourth policy—spending limitations—reduces the size of the outlays that the granting government must make to equalize spending.

### *Propositions Restated*

In theory, as noted earlier, fiscal decentralization should lead to greater satisfaction of consumers and taxpayers, increased failure to meet minimum required spending levels, reduced equality of educational opportunity, and ambiguous effects on accountability. These propositions are not easily tested, especially with the limited data provided in this review of four countries. Still, this review suggests a few restatements of earlier propositions:

1. The potential of decentralization to satisfy consumers' and taxpayers' preferences on education expenditures is limited when jurisdictions are large (for example, the states in Australia or

large cities in the United States) or when own-source revenues are fixed (for example, in the municipalities of Chile).

2. Mandated minimum (Brazil) or maximum (California) education expenditures can reduce the magnitude of the intergovernmental transfers required to ensure minimum spending and relative equality in spending.
3. To ensure equality of educational opportunity is expensive, and it often requires central and regional government transfers to constitute a high percentage of average educational costs (for example, in Australia and Chile).
4. The absence of a strong role for central government in equalizing fiscal capacity or educational spending contributes to large spending differences among subnational jurisdictions (for example, in Brazil and the United States).
5. The complexity of educational finance (for example, in California and Minnesota) reduces the transparency and understanding of legal assignments, thereby reducing the potential for accountability to elected officials and voters.
6. Easily available information on school finance, performance, and the use of funds (as found in the United States but not in Brazil) is critical to ensuring accountability in a democratic setting.
7. Cost-sharing grants or matching grants (such as those found in the United States) increase political accountability at the local level; the absence of cost sharing in discretionary and project grants (as in Chile) requires strict reporting by the grantee on performance and the use of funds.[18]
8. In all decentralized educational systems, the role of the central or regional government is critical to ensuring minimum spending and equity, protecting minority interests, providing comparative information on school finance and performance, and stimulating and disseminating innovations to reduce costs or improve performance.

## Notes

1. While this argument is frequently made, it is controversial and only partly substantiated.

2. In terms of public choice, the central education ministry can be seen as offering services that reflect the preferences of some median customer or voter, thereby leaving most customers dissatisfied.
3. Local jurisdictions find themselves unable to borrow for capital investment, a frequent phenomenon in developing nations.
4. As noted earlier, these technical criteria may differ significantly from those used by political actors involved in decision making, but the results of the technical analysis may at least inform (if not constrain) the political debate.
5. This statement presumes mechanisms by which voices can be expressed fairly and presumes no systematic discrimination against minority interests.
6. In principle, such minimum achievement standards would imply considerably higher expenditures on students with learning difficulties, a disproportionate number of whom are from disadvantaged socioeconomic backgrounds.
7. The U.S. revenue-sharing program operated only from 1972 to 1980; its complex formula did not result in significant redistribution. Federal grants-in-aid, which are only mildly redistributive among states, currently represent about 18 percent of total state and lcoal outlays (Advisory Commission on Intergovernmental Relations, 1990).
8. Total federal transfers to the state and municipal governments account for 22 percent of current direct administration revenues (excluding public enterprises); federal total and revenue-sharing transfers to the states alone represent 23 and 7 percent, respectively, of direct administration revenues.
9. While per-capita federal transfers to the northeastern states are triple the amount given to the southeastern states, the northeastern states' expenditures per capita are less than half as large.
10. Central government transfers account for 56 percent of current total municipal government revenues.
11. There are large differences among states. For example, local authorities provide 17.9 percent of financing in Alabama, versus 55.8 percent in Nevada; see Schwartz and Moskowitz (1988).

12. The 1988 constitution gave municipalities the responsibility for primary education and states responsibility for secondary schools. In practice, however, dual systems continue to function, especially at the primary level.
13. There are three types of schools in Chile—municipal public (59 percent of enrollments), subvened nonprofit (32 percent of enrollments) and tuition-financed private (9 percent of enrollments); the latter receive no central government subventions.
14. The ministry of education plays only an advisory role to the National Development Fund in project selection. Nonprofit schools are not eligible for government finance of capital investment, which means that their recurrent costs must be kept below the value of the vouchers received.
15. In particular, each region's director, who is appointed by the president, has final say on National Development Fund grants. Project applications from mayors who are of the same political persuasion as the director reportedly receive favored treatment.
16. This subvention rate has declined in real terms, however, since the establishment, in 1982, of this education finance system.
17. Jurisdictions with low fiscal capacity could find their spending patterns seriously distorted and their fiscal status strained by spending mandates.
18. An interesting study of Philippine education shows that cost-effectiveness in education increases with local share of finance (Jimenez, Paqueo, and Lourdes de Vera, 1988).

## References

Advisory Commission on Intergovernmental Relations. *Significant Features of Fiscal Federalism.* Vol. 2. Washington, D.C.: Advisory Commission on Intergovernmental Relations, 1990.

Carron, G., and Chau, T. N. *Regional Disparities in Educational Development: Policy Implementation in Developing Countries.* Paris: International Institute for Educational Planning, 1980.

Else-Mitchell, J. R. *Accountability in Intergovernmental Fiscal Transfers,* Occasional Paper no. 38. Canberra: Federalism Research Centre, Australian National University, 1986.

Government of Pakistan. *The Sixth Five-Year Plan, 1983–1988.* Islamabad: Planning Commission, Government of Pakistan, 1982.

Groenewegen, Peter D. *Public Finance in Australia: Theory and Practice.* Englewood Cliffs, N.J.: Prentice-Hall, 1984.

Jimenez, E., Paqueo, V., and Lourdes de Vera, M. *Does Local Financing Make Primary Schools More Efficient?* Washington, D.C.: World Bank, 1988.

McGinn, N., and Street, S. "The Political Rationality of Resource Allocation in Mexican Public Education." *Comparative Education Review,* 1982, *20,* 178–198.

Mathews, R. *Fiscal Equalization in Education.* Canberra: Australian National University Press, 1983.

Rondinelli, D. A., and others. *Decentralization in Developing Countries: A Review of Recent Experience.* World Bank Staff Working Papers, no. 581. Washington, D.C.: World Bank, 1983.

Schiefelbein, E. "The Use of National Assessments to Improve Primary Education in Chile." Unpublished paper, 1991.

Schwartz, M., and Moskowitz, J. *Fiscal Equity in the United States.* Washington, D.C.: Decision Resources, 1988.

Uphoff, N. *Local Institutional Development.* West Hartford, Conn.: Kumarian Press, 1986.

World Bank. *Brazil: Finance of Primary Education.* Washington, D.C.: World Bank, 1986.

# 6

# Decentralization in Two School Districts: Challenging the Standard Paradigm

**Jane Hannaway**

Structural reforms are high on the current national reform agenda in education. The emerging conventional wisdom is that drastic changes in the way education goes about its business are necessary to improve school productivity. In this chapter, I consider one of these reforms—decentralization. My purpose is to explore its implications for the amount of serious attention and effort teachers give to teaching and learning activities. I begin by laying out the standard theoretical argument for decentralization in organizations and consider its applicability to educational organizations. Finding the argument wanting, I go on to develop a line of reasoning that, I suspect, is better suited to education. My discussion is informed by the results of two case studies of school districts, recognized by many as exemplary cases of decentralization. I conclude that decentralization can have marked effects, both beneficial and deleterious, on how work in education is carried out. These effects are heavily dependent on the particular characteristics of the decentralization

*Note:* This is a substantially revised version of a paper prepared for the Consortium for Policy Research in Education Forum on Decentralization, Washington, D.C., November 1991. The research reported here was supported by the Consortium for Policy Research in Education with a grant from the U.S. Department of Education, Office of Educational Research and Improvement, grant OERI-G008690011. It is part of a larger research program conducted in collaboration with Martin Carnoy. The research assistance of Michelle Ennis, Barbara Hibino, Shari Seider, and Hua Yang is gratefully acknowledged. Comments on this chapter by Robert Calfee and Rodney Ogawa and by the other contributors to this volume, as well as discussions with George Papagianis, and especially with Henry M. Levin, were helpful.

plan and the context of the school. Drawing on the case study results, I attempt to identify some of these conditions in this chapter.

## Standard Arguments and Education

Arguments for organizational decentralization are typically information-based arguments.[1] Different structural arrangements provide openings for expression and influence by different actors who hold different amounts and types of information. The basic principle presumed to guide decentralization in organizations is simple: those actors with the best information about a particular subject should have the discretion to make decisions about that subject. Consistent with this argument, empirical research has shown that two conditions—large organizational size and complex or dynamic technology—are likely to lead to decentralized organizational structures (see Jennergren, 1981, for a review of this research). In the case of size, it is presumed that decision demands, at some point, outstrip the decision-making capacity of top management. Management is simply not able to process the large volume of information and make all the decisions necessary to manage the organization effectively. Thus, out of sheer necessity, management delegates decision-making responsibilities to lower levels in the hierarchy (Blau and Schoenherr, 1971; Child, 1973; Hinings and Lee, 1971; Khandwalla, 1974; Pugh and others, 1969). In the case of a complex or dynamic technology, the reasoning is similar: top management, not able to keep abreast of technologically required adaptations, delegates responsibility for such decisions to lower-level agents who are closer to the relevant information (Galbraith, 1977). In delegating responsibility, organizations presumably weigh the increased coordination and monitoring costs produced by decentralization against the increased efficiency that results from the decisions of more knowledgeable agents. The central decentralization problem for firms is the design of incentives and contracts that ensure that agents (with discretion) behave in accordance with the preferences of the principals. This is commonly known as the *principal-agent* problem.

In education, decentralization proponents argue that the technology of teaching is complex and dynamic and that decision making about what goes on in the classroom should therefore be located with the classroom teacher, or at least somewhere within the school. Proponents assume, quite reasonably, that teachers understand, better than central authorities, the requirements of the classroom teaching and learning process. Proponents also presume that the autonomy and discretion of lower-level units, meaning schools and the actors within them, are constrained by higher authorities. If these constraints were lifted, it is argued, and schools (particularly teachers) were empowered to use with more discretion the information that they possess, then they would do things differently and better. The expectation is that school-level actors, freed from state and district prescriptions, would focus their efforts in ways that would lead to greater student achievement.

While this thinking has some theoretical justification (and considerable political appeal), it is difficult to reconcile it with theories of "loose coupling" (Bidwell, 1965; March and Olsen, 1976; Meyer and Rowan, 1977; Weick, 1976) and with significant empirical evidence that educational organizations are not tightly connected and managed (see, for example, Meyer and Scott, 1983; Hannaway and Sproull, 1979). Teachers work fairly autonomously in classrooms,[2] schools operate fairly independently of school districts, and school districts function with considerable freedom from state and federal governments, at least with regard to central teaching and learning tasks (Bidwell, 1965; March and Olsen, 1976; Meyer and Rowan, 1977; Weick, 1977; Meyer and Scott, 1983). In other words, this literature claims that schools and teachers already have, to a very large extent, the latitude to behave on the basis of the information they possess. If decentralization to school-level actors has beneficial effects on what happens in terms of classroom teaching and learning—and many observers of school practice would claim that it has—then arguments better grounded in an educational context are needed for understanding why. Something else must be going on in education.

To uncover what decentralization means in practice in education, I investigated the operation of two highly reputed decentralized school districts. What I observed is that the problems faced in the process of decentralization, as well as the benefits that accrue from it, differed markedly in four ways from what one would expect from the standard decentralization (principal-agent) literature.

A key assumption, for instance, in the principal-agent literature is that the agents (here, the teachers) have well-defined goals (preferences, objectives), and the main problem is the conflict between those preferences and those of the principal (the educational system as a whole), as mentioned earlier. The central issue is how and to what extent economic incentives can be used to align the interests of the two. In this case, teachers generally hold only unclear and ambiguous goals; they function without a well-defined objective function. There are certainly general goals, such as student learning, but general goals give little operational direction, as Simon (1947, 1991) has stressed for over forty years. The lack of clearly defined objectives on the part of agents (teachers) may be a more basic issue in decentralizing decisions than the conflict between teachers' objectives and those of the system. A central element of the reportedly successful decentralization reforms we studied, for example, is the provision of mechanisms that help teachers define the objectives associated with their work in fairly concrete terms.[3]

A second key assumption in the principal-agent literature is that the agent has more knowledge about the production process than the principal does, and the central objective of decentralization is to allow the agent to make use of that knowledge. By contrast, one of the central objectives of decentralization in the schools we studied was to promote teachers' learning of new and presumably more effective ways to carry out their work—to enhance teachers' understanding of the process of education. This is an important task because the technology associated with teaching and learning is generally very poorly understood; as an economist might put it, there is no clear production function.

A further departure from the standard principal-agent paradigm is that, rather than creating problems of agency, decentralization in education appears to reduce agency problems. In a decentralized arrangement, where teachers are involved in decisions about their work, their professional life is more observable and therefore more open to monitoring and influence by others. At least their views of their work, the way they go about planning for it, and their reports about what goes on in their classrooms are more public than in a traditionally organized school, where individual teachers in their classrooms function in isolation.

A fourth departure from the standard paradigm is that the controls that affect teachers' behavior in education tend to be primarily social and cognitive, rather than monetary (as suggested by economic theories) or based on rules and regulations (as suggested by bureaucratic theories).

Our analysis overall has led us to conclude that teachers in successful decentralized districts work under conditions where organizational controls over their behavior are in fact high relative to what we would expect in traditionally organized schools. Indeed, the discretion of school-level actors in many decentralized systems may be far more restricted than the discretion of school-level actors in traditionally organized systems.

The claim of many analysts (for example, Chubb and Moe, 1990) that excessive regulation is alienating public school teachers from their work and strangling their creativity may be overstated. Teachers in public systems are not overregulated; they are ignored. The system as a whole may be increasingly regulated, but the primary operational effect of central regulation on schools is to turn the attention of critical actors, in particular school and district administrators, away from teaching and learning concerns to other matters (see Hannaway, 1989, for evidence on this point). The result is that public school teachers in traditionally organized systems are likely to work in isolation, where they get exceedingly little direction in focusing their work and exceedingly little support in carrying it out. As a consequence, teachers' efforts often are not well directed, teachers' learning is limited, teachers' good work is not appreciated or supported, and their bad work is not criticized or corrected. In sum, no one pays much attention to teachers and their work in traditionally organized schools. The daily life of teachers and principals in the decentralized systems we studied are quite different. I describe the districts and their management systems in the following section and discuss their effects on the job and work attitudes of school-level actors.

## The Case Studies

### *The Districts*

The two districts we studied are known for their innovative governance practices. Both districts locate significant authority at the school site, but the responsibilities are distributed in very different ways in each of the districts. In District A, the principals are clearly the lead actors; in District B, the lead actors are the teachers. The districts themselves differ in significant ways other than their management approaches, as described here. These differences have both complicated and enriched our research effort, as I shall discuss later.

*District A* is in a well-to-do suburb about thirty miles outside a major urban area in southern California. It is a fast-growing upper-middle-class area. Enrollment in the district has increased from 12,000 in 1975 to 23,232 in 1989 and is projected to approach 33,000 in 1995. In the 1989–90 school year, the district operated twenty-four schools, and two new schools were under construction. The district's population is largely white, upwardly mobile, and very supportive of the schools. The proportion of students in the free- or reduced-lunch program is only 6 percent. The community places a high value on education, and teachers consider the district an attractive place to work. The district is a high performer, as measured by student achievement tests. The results of the 1988–89 California Assessment Program put the district above the 90th percentile in the state on all tests and above the 95th percentile on most of them. One assistant superintendent reported that there are forty to fifty applicants for every open teaching position, and the district has been hiring as many as one hundred people per year. Expenditures per student were $3,753 for the 1989–90 school year, somewhat below average for the state of California. Starting teacher salaries were $26,211, and the average salary was $38,391.

*District B,* in a state that is primarily rural, has an enrollment of 12,556 students, served in twenty-four schools. Its boundaries encompass a city, which is an attractive tourist and cultural center, as well as sparsely populated rural communities as far away as fifty miles. The student body is heterogeneous. The superintendent underscored the socioeconomic heterogeneity of the district by describing one school that was able to raise $17,000 with an auction. An auction at that school, he explained, typically attracts hundreds of people from all over the city because valuable items may be auctioned off, and yet there were other schools in the district that, with considerable effort, could barely raise $150. Forty-five percent of the students in the district are eligible for free or reduced lunches. Expenditures per student in the district for the 1989–90 school year were $2,700. These expenditures are low by national standards, as well as low within the state. Ninety-eight percent of the district's resources are from the state. Teachers' salaries in the district are also low by national standards. The starting salary in the 1989–90 school year was $17,000, and the average salary was $23,493. These salaries are particularly low given the cost of living in the area, which the tourist trade drives up.

To get a better understanding of the governance mechanisms in these districts and their implications for practice, we collected data in a three-stage process. First, we interviewed nearly all the central office administrators in both districts and reviewed relevant district materials and documents. In the next two stages, we collected data in four selected schools in each district. This effort included interviewing the principals in each of the four schools and subsequently collecting from some of them data on how they allocated their time for a one-week period and on the extent of their interaction with district-level actors for a one-month period. In the third stage, we collected information from teachers. This stage included interviews in each school with a small group of teachers as well as surveys of all the teachers (see Hannaway, 1991a, for a full report on this research effort). In this discussion, I am relying mostly on the interview and survey data.

### *The Decentralization Plans*

Because decentralization can take a variety of different forms, it is necessary to describe in some detail the management arrangements in each of the districts. As will be evident, the patterns of decentralization in the two districts are quite different.

***District A.*** The District A superintendent describes his overall management objective as getting school-level actors to "buy in" to district policies and programs and to encourage school-level "entrepreneurship." His strategy for achieving these objectives centers on decentralizing decisions to the schools. While a decentralization strategy characterizes much of the management approach of the district, elements of it are highly centralized. Budget and personnel decisions, for example, are decentralized, but curriculum decisions are highly centralized.

Principals receive a discretionary lump-sum annual budget to cover almost all school costs except salaries and major capital expenses. Textbooks, computer labs, media materials, study trips, some staff development, and minor capital costs, for example, come out of the school budget. The fraction of the total budget that is discretionary is small (perhaps less than 10 percent) but important. The superintendent claims that school-level budget discretion forces a school to rethink its priorities continually. The district has no guidelines on how the money is to be spent or on how budget decisions are to be made. According to the superintendent, "There are twenty-four [the number of schools] different ways it gets done." In some schools, teachers are heavily involved in the decision process; in others, they are not. Schools receive additional funds through internal district grant competitions, open to teachers and site administrators, as well as through PTA fundraising efforts. Principals claim that the flexibility that the budget gives them is critically important in addressing the school-specific problems that they and their teachers define, although the differences among schools in allocation patterns are relatively minor. For example, one school may invest more heavily in establishing math labs; another may address particular staff development needs.

A significant amount of personnel authority also rests with the principals in District A. Each school is given a number of personnel staffing units (PSUs) with which the principal configures a school staff. Different types of personnel (counselors, aides, assistant principals) cost different units in the district's schema. A teacher advisory committee exists at each site, but the involvement of teachers in the process varies by site. Variation in the configuration of personnel across schools is again small, but principals and teachers claim that it gives them important degrees of freedom when they need it. Staff hiring is also the responsibility of the principal. Given the enrollment growth rate in the district, it is a big part of a principal's job, and the principals take it very seriously. According to one principal, principals interview as many as thirty individuals for a teaching position. Some candidates are drawn from the pool of applicants available at the district personnel office, and some are identified through the extensive independent search and recruiting efforts that principals themselves conduct.

In contrast to budget and personnel decisions, curriculum decisions are made at the district level, although principals and teachers are the prime decision makers. There are no district-level curriculum specialists. District-level committees (elementary school language arts, secondary school modern languages, and so on), made up of representative teachers from each of the relevant schools and chaired by principals, make decisions about the district curriculum for each subject, as well as about the textbook that will be used by all schools in the district teaching that subject. According to one principal, "Schools do not have the latitude to reject a district textbook-adoption decision. The district is responsible for delineating and defining the curriculum in terms of text, framework, and philosophy. We will not open that up." Curriculum decision making in the district is therefore centralized, but highly participatory. A representative set of lower-level actors makes the decisions, but the decisions become district policy.

The process of getting a new high school course approved in the district illustrates the participatory and centralized nature of the curriculum process. The process typically starts with an individual teacher, who begins by submitting a course syllabus for review to the relevant department within the school. The proposed course is reviewed next by the district-level committee responsible for that particular subject. This committee includes representative teachers of the same subject from all the high schools in the district. If approved, the decision moves back to each of the schools, to a school-level advisory curriculum council made up of all the department chairs, who make a recommendation to their principal. With the approval of the principal, the proposal goes to a district-level curriculum committee made up of one teacher from each of the subject area curriculum committees, the district-level administrators, and a principal. The district committee then sends its recommendation to the school board for approval. The process is intentionally long and, according to the superintendent, has two important virtues. First, it maintains quality control over the curriculum as a whole and guards against what the superintendent calls a "mishmash" of course offerings. Second, because it involves many individuals at all levels of the system, it promotes districtwide understanding of the educational focus of the district.

The district also has "articulation" committees for each subject area, again composed of teachers and chaired by a principal, that review curriculum areas for coherence and integration across the elementary, middle, and high school levels.

Responsibility for staff development rests with both the district and the individual schools. A district-level committee of teachers (with a principal as chair) organizes staff development activities around newly developed district curricula and newly adopted textbooks, as well as around whatever other specific professional development needs are identified. Teachers in the district, many of whom have piloted the materials for a new textbook adoption, conduct much of the district-level training. Although teachers are not compensated for attending staff development sessions, which are usually in the evening and include a district-sponsored dinner, the sessions are extremely well attended, and the district's program is highly regarded both in and out of the district. Individual schools also carry out their own staff development activities, supported with school discretionary funds and focused on areas they define.

District A's management arrangements have essentially been in place for more than a decade. They are mature and well developed. The superintendent uses the term *loose-tight* to characterize the district's approach, and it appears to capture aptly the district's efforts to delegate significant authority to school-level actors and at the same time maintain coherence and quality control across the educational program of the district.

***District B.*** Unlike in District A, the centerpiece of District B's approach is decentralization of curriculum to teachers within the school. Early in his tenure, the superintendent told the teachers in the district that they were the key to the solutions to educational problems and that he wanted them to be the leaders in the district. He developed no grand scheme into which teacher participation fit as one element; rather, he told teachers to get together, analyze the situation at their schools, and devise solutions and programs they thought were feasible. According to the superintendent, the sky was the limit.

The district's commitment to and faith in teachers is demonstrated in a number of ways, but probably in no way better than by allowing teachers (with the involvement of parents) to select their own principals when openings occur. In fact, teachers in one school have decided not to hire a principal but rather to have a teacher committee manage the school.

An important aspect of District B's story is the steady financial assistance of a foundation and the intensive involvement in the district of a major, nationally recognized education-reform group. The foundation provides financial support for school-based change that is student-centered, teacher-initiated, administrator-supported, board-approved, and parent-involved. Functioning symbiotically in the district is the education-reform group, whose objective is to redesign education in ways that focus school-level attention more directly on student learning. Locating greater decision-making authority in the classroom and in the school is a central part of the strategy that the group proposes for achieving this objective. (I shall discuss the significance of this group's involvement later.)

Each school in the district has a school-improvement program (SIP) committee with at least one teacher representative for every ten teachers. The school-improvement program is the vehicle that the foundation uses to allocate financial support. Teachers, either individually or in groups, develop proposals at the school site, pass them through the respective school SIP committee, and then submit them to the district-level SIP executive committee, which is made up of one teacher from each school-level committee. The proposals are reviewed and signed by (but not necessarily approved by) the school principal. If the executive committee supports the proposal, it goes to the superintendent and then to the executive director of the foundation for funding. Examples of proposals range from a curriculum development project for one subject to a major restructuring and integration of the complete middle school curriculum. Proposals may also include a parent-involvement project or a staff development effort on alternative student assessment strategies. Only proposals that involve major restructuring go to the school board for approval. Decisions about programs that do not need funding are handled within the school.

In contrast to District A, the management arrangements in District B are relatively new and experimental. The superintendent willingly entertains any programs coming up from the schools, as long as there is agreement between teachers and parents. He anticipates a district role in assessment and coordination of school-based reforms sometime in the future, but he has intentionally held off any type of evaluation of school innovations in order to encourage teachers to generate creative alternatives in a relatively risk-free environment and not to squelch good ideas in their infancy.

The central office staff in both districts is lean. In District A, in addition to the superintendent and associate superintendent, there are two assistant superintendents, one concerned with elementary and middle schools and the other with high schools. The assistant superintendents review school budgets, to make sure that they are "in the black," and school PSU plans, to make sure that they are in compliance with state regulations. Assistant superintendents' responsibilities include evaluating principals in terms of the goals that each principal sets for his or her school, as well as serving as staff to the various district-level committees. Central office administrators, along with three principals and a representative of the teachers' union, also serve in the superintendent's strategic planning group, which meets regularly to take a long-term view of the district (for example, to determine what a year-2000 high school graduate should look like in terms of skills and values). Directors of special areas (for example, transportation, maintenance, and categorical programs) also sit at the central office. As mentioned earlier, there are no district-level curriculum specialists; developing curriculum is the job of the teachers. All the central office staff, without exception, define their jobs in terms of support and service to the schools. One assistant superintendent reported, "The whole culture of the district is pitched to the schools. We're here to do whatever has to be done to help those schools be successful." Principals corroborated this view.

Administrators at different levels of the system spend a considerable amount of time together, and one result is a strong understanding throughout the district of "who we are" and "what we do here." Both at the district level and at the school level, for example, administrators invariably refer to the district's six goals and its mission statement when describing their work. Principals in District A spend an average of 17.4 hours per month on district-level issues, such as curriculum and articulation committee work. During the week we collected data, they spent an average of 20 percent of their time interacting in one way or another with at least one other principal. It should probably not be surprising that whenever administrators in the district used the term *we* in interviews, they were referring to the district, not to the school.

The central office in District B is especially lean. The central office staff consists of the superintendent, an associate superintendent, and two assistant superintendents, one for personnel and one for instruction. (The superintendent is considering abolishing the post of assistant superintendent for instruction.) The central office performs mainly bureaucratic functions (for example, payroll and personnel) for the district. With the exception of tremendous symbolic and political support from the superintendent, the schools receive little guidance or support from district-level actors. The work of principals in District B is more schoolbound than that of District A principals. They spend about half as much time with administrators outside the school (11 percent) and about 50 percent more time (30 percent versus 19 percent) working with teachers within the school.

## Similarities: Technical Demands and Social Control

The differences in administrative arrangements between the two districts are great, but the similarities may be far more important for an understanding of decentralization in education. The most significant common element is the extent to which the districts' management arrangements generate interactions for school-level actors around technical demands (issues related to curriculum and staff development). This aspect of the districts' operation is central to this discussion because it is directly related to a clarification of goals for teachers' work and to increased understanding among teachers of the process of teaching and learning. The interactions also reduce problems of agency.

### *Technical Demands and Technical Interactions*

School-level actors in both districts face technical demands from agents or groups outside the school that provide teachers with direction in their work, as well as technical support and professional exchange. As should become evident from the following discussion, the amount of direction and support that teachers receive is undoubtedly greater than the amount that teachers in traditionally organized schools receive.

In District A, technical demands on teachers originate in the decisions of district-level committees, which lay out the curriculum the teacher is to follow and which design training sessions for teachers, to help them acquire the skills and knowledge necessary to deliver the curriculum. District-level activities also have ripple effects within the schools; teachers report high levels of interaction with their colleagues as they react to and interpret district stimuli. Beyond their normal teaching responsibilities, teachers in the district spend 14.7 hours per month, on the average, in activities primarily focused on curriculum and staff development; the ratio of school-based to district-based activity is a little more than 2 to 1.[4]

The high levels of interaction within the schools demonstrate the seriousness with which everyone in the district takes the district curriculum. The interactions are also a consequence of the fact that district curriculum and staff development policies and practices are targeted to well-defined groups within the schools (for example, secondary school English teachers or primary grade teachers). Teachers know, for example, when some district action or policy is relevant to them, and they also know the others to whom it is relevant. As any sociologist knows, similarly affected individuals tend to interact, especially if they are trying to interpret something new, and teachers are no exception.

The strength of the effect of district demands on schools was particularly noticeable in one school with a soon-to-retire principal who, the teachers reported, had actually "retired on the job." The principal had little involvement or interest in school activities, but because the professional world of teachers in the district is not schoolbound, the school was far from "rudderless." District-level activities provide valuable direction, directly as well as indirectly. Teachers in elementary schools, for example, reported interacting regularly with teachers at the same grade level in other schools in the district, and they claimed to be very knowledgeable about how these teachers deal with district curriculum issues. At the high school level, subject-based departmental boundaries, both within and across schools, largely define the network of interactions of high school teachers. In an important sense, district demands shape professional communities in the district.

The possible wrinkle in the District A story, of course, is that the district curriculum restricts the discretion of most individual teachers in the district in significant ways. Only a small minority of teachers actually serve on district decision-making committees at any one time, yet all teachers must follow the district curriculum and use the selected texts. To what extent do teachers find this system oppressive? In interviews, we probed teachers on this issue. Somewhat to our surprise, teachers reported that they do not feel unduly restricted by district curriculum policies; in fact, they strongly approve of the curriculum decision-making process. They claim that a primary advantage of a common district curriculum is the professional exchanges that it facilitates: well-delineated common purposes provide a familiar and relevant basis for interaction. Teachers teaching at the same grade level or teaching the same subject simply have a lot in common. Some teachers, who had taught only in District A, said that they imagined teaching in a district without a common curriculum would be chaotic and lonely. Teachers also stressed that the nature of teaching is such that, even with a standard curriculum, there is always considerable room for discretion in executing it in the classroom.

Interviews with teachers gave us the impression that the right to participate in curriculum decision making is perhaps more important to teachers than actually making the decisions. Teachers know that they have easy access to the decision process through a representative if they want it. They also know that they have the right to volunteer and participate directly if they feel strongly. Teachers who had served on district committees in previous years reported that committee work is rewarding but time-consuming. They might volunteer every few years or so, but continual responsibility for curriculum and staff development programs would be too much; they claim that they would soon burn out. In any case, even if teachers do not serve on decision-making committees, they still have ample occasion for professional interaction through district staff development and the more informal exchanges that it reportedly triggers within schools.

To a large extent, the district curriculum drives the whole system. Delegating school-level personnel and budget decisions, for example, provides highly valued flexibility for dealing with school-specific implementation problems in District A, but curriculum and staff development are the common ground on which professionals in the district regularly interact. Indeed, school-level budget and personnel decisions appear to be framed largely by the demands of the district curriculum.

In District B, each school works fairly independently, developing its own education program, but the nationally based education-reform group plays an important role, giving technical direction and support to teachers at the school level. The reform group provides them with principles to guide the process and with consultants to help them in implementation. The group also sponsors visits to other schools and districts working with the reform group. The task of actually developing the curriculum falls squarely on the teachers themselves, however. Teachers at each school are collectively responsible for developing their own school-specific curriculum. Site administrators also participate actively. The teachers in District B expend significant effort in this direction. On the average, teachers spend 27.7 hours per month in activities,[5] mainly curriculum and staff development, beyond their regular teaching. The amount of time they spend in these activities is about twice what it is in District A. Not surprisingly, most of the difference between teachers in the two districts has to do with the amount of time they spend working with other teachers within their own school. The ratio of school-level to district-level activity[6] for District B is almost 4 to 1.

Teachers in both districts work in settings very different from the typical "egg-crate" world of schools (Lortie, 1975), which fosters isolation and a highly individualistic teacher orientation. In both districts, teachers are stimulated, prodded, and supported to reflect with each other about their work and to act together on ways to make it better. In District A, the district curriculum defines the classroom focus of teachers, and the district staff development effort, as well as the professional exchanges it stimulates, provides mechanisms for teachers to learn how to implement the curriculum. In District B, the education-reform group helps teachers work collaboratively to frame their work more concretely and share their teaching knowledge. Our analysis suggests that the curriculum-focused interaction among teachers is the most important consequence of the way the districts we studied structured themselves.

### *Technical Interaction: Control, Motivation, and Learning*

To the extent that there are beneficial effects of the decentralization arrangements,[7] they may be due more to control, motivation, and learning effects associated with the professional interactions produced by the management arrangements than to efficiency effects typically presumed to flow from the increased discretion that accompanies decentralization to knowledgeable actors.

***Control.*** A major way in which the management arrangements in the districts affect teachers is through increased organizational (district or school) control. Controls of some sort are important in any organization; without them, an organization is only a set of independent actors who work according to their own individual proclivities and preferences. Controls, however, are problematic in education, largely because activities are nonroutine and unpredictable and require initiative and flexibility (Dornbusch and Scott, 1975). For the most part, formal controls that assess outcomes or monitor conformity to rules are inappropriate. They typically engender resentment and resistance from educational professionals, usually for good reasons. As a consequence, however, education operates with very weak controls over the behavior of its actors. Some school-level professionals are undoubtedly highly talented, committed, and effective actors without controls; but, just as undoubtedly, others are not. The question before us is this: Can we devise controls that are more effective and still appropriate to the work of education? The cases described here suggest some ways to devise more effective control mechanisms, but these require an understanding of the dynamics associated with *social* processes of control, not bureaucratic ones.

Social control, by definition, requires interaction. It is the process by which individual behavior is affected by the informational and normative influence of others (Salancik and Pfeffer, 1978; Bandura, 1977). In traditionally organized schools, teachers mostly work isolated in their individual classrooms, with limited regular contact with other professionals. The likelihood that effective social controls will operate in these schools is consequently very small. Both of the districts we studied, by contrast, structure numerous opportunities for individuals to interact with other professionals around their work; indeed, in a sense, the districts demand it. With interaction levels as high as teachers in the two districts report, the emergence over time of some form of social control system, or culture, is highly likely. There is no guarantee, of course, that the culture that emerges will support productive work in the district. Many organizations are plagued by nonproductive cultures. It is not difficult to imagine a highly interactive school district functioning, for example, with a culture of despair, disgruntlement, or apathy. Occasions for interaction, thus, are necessary but not sufficient for producing a productive work culture. The occasions establish the channels of communication, but not necessarily the substance.

The districts we studied go beyond simply providing opportunities for interaction. They structure interactions to focus heavily on specific curriculum and staff development issues. They define the substantive focus of teachers' work; they establish the premises underlying teachers' actions. Grounding social controls in defined technical issues is important because of the generally poorly understood nature of the technology of education, its outcomes, and its boundaries. By contrast with the situation in many other types of work, the technology of teaching only very loosely defines appropriate content for teachers' work interactions. One hears stories, for example, of schools where teachers are empowered, and decisions about the photocopying machines or students' hall behavior dominate teachers' efforts (Carol Weiss, personal communication). While such issues may be important to teachers, their likely effect on what happens in the classroom is remote.

In District A, the district curriculum identifies focused areas that shape professional exchanges of direct relevance to classroom practice. In a sense, the interactions and the curriculum are mutually reinforcing: the curriculum gives direction to the interactions, and the interactions give meaning to the curriculum in the daily work life of teachers. Teachers may talk, for example, about how they are dealing with a particular chapter in the district-selected text, or about how students are reacting to a particular novel. The district curriculum establishes common ground for meaningful exchanges. In District B, areas for discussion are not defined by the district. Teachers at the school level define a school-specific curriculum. Much of the teacher-to-teacher interaction in District B schools focuses on what the curriculum should look like and how it should be integrated across subjects and across grade levels.

Interactions "control" the behavior of school level actors in three ways. The first and probably most important control is cognitive control. Curriculum-based interactions send regular messages to teachers about how to think about the focus of their work; they affect the premises that guide teachers' actions in the classroom. Teachers presumably enter their separate classrooms and confront specific challenges with a framework defining what they are trying to accomplish and a set of strategies for accomplishing it.

The second way in which technical interactions control the behavior of teachers is by defining the boundaries and the dimensions of school-level jobs. Developing curricula, engaging in staff development activities, coordinating practice across schools, working with colleagues to incorporate district policies into school practice—these are all expected elements of the jobs of principals and teachers in District A. The district curriculum and staff development programs have been in operation for a number of years and are embedded in the professional life of the district. Teachers interact regularly with one another around these concerns; the normative climate in the district encourages regular interaction. It is simply what teachers in the district do.

In District B, the controls are more intense, more direct, and more observable. A large portion of activity takes place within the school, and everyone is expected to take part. Teachers put considerable peer pressure on one another to be involved and do their share. In one school, the pressure was so great that some teachers requested transfers to other schools. The data show, for example, not only that the average level of involvement is higher in District B schools but also that within-school variance is considerably smaller (Hannaway, 1991b). The reforms in District B are still relatively new, and the involvement of teachers in activities outside teaching is not yet taken for granted. Some teachers, for example, grumble about the new definitions of teachers' responsibilities that are emerging.

Technical interactions also "control" the behavior of school-level actors through peer pressure and peer monitoring of quality. In both districts, professional interactions make teachers more aware of the professional views (and, to some extent, the classroom practice) of other teachers. The public nature of much of teachers' professional lives in these two districts undoubtedly affects the behavior and the seriousness of purpose with which teachers attend to their work (O'Reilly, 1989). For this reason, it might be argued that high levels of technical interaction among teachers reduce the agency problems, mentioned at the beginning of this chapter, that are commonly assumed to accompany decentralization.

***Motivation.*** The management arrangements in both districts involve school-level actors in the decision-making process in consequential ways; either directly or through representatives, they make decisions. Research suggests that this type of involvement is likely to have motivational benefits for the individuals involved (see Locke and Schweiger, 1979, for a review). The most widely discussed motivational effects are increased commitment to decisions that are made (Janis and Mann, 1977) and a related effect—decreased resistance to change (Coch and French, 1948; Lawler, 1975;

Lammers, 1967). These effects are generally assumed to result from psychological mechanisms associated, for example, with ego involvement and feelings of responsibility (Hackman and Lawler, 1971; Hackman and Oldham, 1980). As a consequence, agency problems again may be reduced.

Social mechanisms are probably also at work, linking decision-making arrangements in the district with motivation (Salancik and Pfeffer, 1978). Involving teachers in decision-making roles that determine what is to be taught and what training the staff needs sends the message that teachers' views about their work are highly valued. In District A, both the teacher-designed district curriculum and the district staff development program provide evidence that the district pays attention to what teachers say. The district-structured interactions also convey the clear message that the substance of teachers' work is important enough for the district to direct the serious attention of teachers and administrators to it and to support this attention symbolically and financially. District B's decision-making arrangements obviously show at least as high regard for teachers and their work.

We have no data to assess the effects of increased motivation on teachers' effort in the classroom. Nevertheless, the strong focus in both districts on issues directly related to classroom practice would lead one to expect effects to show up in the classroom. For example, teachers are likely to feel more committed to a program of study that they have helped design and that others think is important, and this commitment is likely to affect the level of effort that teachers expend in teaching the curriculum in the classroom. Any divergence of interest between the school district and individual teachers is presumably lessened as a consequence.

***Learning.*** In addition to control and motivational consequences, professional interactions no doubt also have significant cognitive consequences, in terms of learning, as teachers exchange ideas and discuss their work. Thus, the structural arrangements in the district have important knowledge-generating effects. In traditional schools, teachers learn from their own experience, while learning from the experience of others is limited. In settings where professionally oriented interactions occur, the learning of individual teachers can be shared, so that teachers become aware of new possibilities in classroom practice; private learning becomes a public good. Thus, a major likely consequence of professional interactions such as these promoted by the two districts' structural arrangements is a more knowledgeable faculty.

## Differences and Complications

The similarities between the two districts are more important for the purposes of this chapter than the differences are, but the differences are also instructive. The arrangements operating in District B are considerably more work-intensive for school-level actors than those operating in District A. The school is the locus of reform, as already noted, and the management design presumes the involvement of all school-level actors, not just a representative set. Teachers are expected to define and develop the curriculum, as well as to determine the best ways of implementing it. I shall speculate here not only about some of the conditions that may make more intensive work of this sort at the school level more appropriate, but also about some of the likely effects and cautions associated with it.

In interviews, teachers in District B expressed both greater enthusiasm and greater frustration with the decentralization reforms than teachers in District A did. Part of this difference is no doubt due to the early stage of the reforms in District B. In surveys, the teachers in District B reported, on the average, significantly greater influence over school policy, greater control over classroom practices, better administrator-teacher relationships, greater support for innovation, and a more personalized school environment than did their District A counterparts.[8] In interviews, however, the teachers reported that they were tired and might be "doing too much." Despite the greater influence of teachers, more support for innovation, better relations with administrators, and higher rates of interaction with their colleagues, the teachers in District B reported significantly lower levels of job satisfaction, as well as lower average levels of efficacy in teaching, than the teachers in District A did. What do these findings mean?

The differences between the districts indicate some of the complexities involved in school reform. Multiple factors affect how schools work and how teachers are engaged as professionals in the schools. One major difference between the districts involves the types of students they serve. As noted earlier, the students in District A are advantaged, for the most part, and student performance in the district is high; a large proportion of the students in District B are "at risk." Almost any educational professional would probably agree that the teachers in District B have a more difficult job than the teachers in District A do. It is no wonder that their feelings about their teaching efficacy are lower than those of teachers in District A (see Ashton and Webb, 1986; Rosenholtz, 1989; Pallas, 1988; Hannaway, 1991a; these sources offer discussion of teacher efficacy and student achievement). Tougher jobs may require different types or different levels of professional exchange and technical support. More intensive school-based reforms, such as those operating in District B, may indeed be better suited to "at risk" situations than to "advantaged" situations. Nevertheless, engaging in professional interactions requires time and energy that may be in shorter supply in schools with the pressing educational problems of "at risk" students than in schools with more advantaged students.

The job satisfaction ratings in District B are probably related to some of the same factors that affect efficacy ratings, but job satisfaction is also affected by other factors. The reform process, for example, was clearly affected by the limited resources of the district; teachers' attitudes about their expenditures of effort were clouded by the low salaries they received; one principal thought that low teacher salaries were going to be the eventual downfall of the reforms.

We do not have the data to assess the effect of management arrangements on changes in job attitudes, but experiences in District B suggest some words of caution. The costs of reforms that promote teachers' involvement in activities outside the classroom need to be carefully identified and assessed alongside the benefits. Although the involvement of teachers in activities outside classroom teaching is, for the most part, directly related to their teaching, the management design in District B requires high levels of involvement. The District B design is considerably more "bottom heavy" than the design in District A; school-developed curricula demand broad participation and high levels of teacher effort. Since there seems to be no perfect curriculum (if there is one, the criteria for recognizing it have not yet been established), there is no natural limit to work on curriculum development. When is "enough" enough? "Wheel spinning" is a real danger in the absence of some authority to set a deadline or a standard, or in the absence of some feedback mechanism to mark progress. Many current reforms in education are calling for greater involvement of teachers in decision making—and I agree in principle with these calls—but there are necessarily limits to teachers' involvement. At some point, it can simply become too much and, indeed, do more harm than good. I am not saying that the teachers in District B have reached this point, but there are worrisome signs that suggest that teachers may not be able to sustain their currently high levels of effort, at least not without serious effects on the level of energy that they have left for the classroom. The District B superintendent is well aware of the challenges. In an interview, he stressed that it is easy to generate a high level of energy and optimism, and maybe even some productivity gains, at the beginning of new reforms, especially with teachers who have been ignored for so long; the hard part, he says, is sustaining it. If discouragement sets in, mobilizing teachers' energies for another round will be truly difficult.

## Conclusion

In this chapter, I have argued that standard thinking about decentralization, particularly as it takes a principal-agent approach, has limited applicability to education. This does not mean, however, that changes in the structure of education do not have important effects on the behavior of those involved in the education process and therefore on the performance of educational systems. Nevertheless, if decentralization seems, in some instances, to have beneficial effects, we need to know why. Is actual decision-making authority necessary, or is regular professional involvement with others sufficient? Are different structures more appropriate to some settings (for example, those with disadvantaged students) than to others (for example, those with "at-risk" students)? Are strategies that are effective in the short run also viable in the long run?

This chapter has offered a framework for thinking about

how decentralization may affect educational performance and about some of the conditions necessary for it to have beneficial effects. I have argued that thinking about the implications of decentralization strategies—in terms of clarifying teachers' objectives and expanding teachers' understanding of the instructional process—may be particularly worthwhile. The explicit structuring of teachers' interactions around technical demands (issues of curriculum and teaching) appears to be a critical element of successful decentralization. I have argued that technical interactions among teachers form the basis of effective processes of social control, motivation, and learning that are necessary in a well-run decentralized system. In short, what should be obvious is that structural reforms that direct teachers' attention to their central functions, that stimulate them to interact professionally around defined common objectives, and that give them a sense of the importance of their mission are nearly certain to result in more effective schools than the traditional "egg-crate" structures do. What is not obvious, and what requires systematic analysis, is the relative merit and cost associated with alternative structures designed to direct the attention of school-level actors. The research reported here is a first step in that direction.

## Notes

1. Although not germane to this discussion, there are also issues that concern the relationship between decentralization and political representation; see Chapters Three and Five for discussion.
2. We do not know the standard that respondents were using, but teachers themselves in the High School and Beyond survey report high levels of control over what goes on in their classrooms. On a 6-point scale, where 6 denotes "total control," 92 percent report 5 or 6 for teaching techniques, 72 percent for content and skills taught in class, 68 percent for discipline, and 65 percent for textbooks and materials (Rowan, 1990).
3. This process of delineating and clarifying objectives is distinct from what Simon (1991) and others have emphasized: inducing an identification of the interests of the agent with those of the organization.

4. Teachers receive monetary compensation for 14 percent of this work and release time for 25 percent of it. An additional 14 percent is during planning periods, and the remainder is on personal time.
5. Teachers receive release time for 53 percent of this time and monetary compensation for 8 percent; 15 percent is during planning periods, and the remainder is on personal time.
6. District-level activity would include conferences and workshops organized by the reform group, as well as district-sponsored fairs where teachers in each school describe their programs.
7. We have no information, for example, on improvements in student achievement.
8. There were differences from school to school on these measures. In almost all cases, however, the averages for the schools in District B were higher than the averages in District A. See Hannaway (1991b) for details.

## References

Ashton, P. T., and Webb, R. B. *Making a Difference: Teachers' Sense of Efficacy and Student Achievement.* White Plains, N.Y.: Longman, 1986.

Bandura, A. *Social Learning Theory.* Englewood Cliffs, N.J.: Prentice-Hall, 1977.

Bidwell, C. "The School as a Formal Organization." In J. G. March (ed.), *Handbook of Organizations.* Skokie, Ill.: Rand McNally, 1965.

Blau, P., and Schoenherr, R. A. *The Structure of Organizations.* New York: Basic Books, 1971.

Child, J. "Predicting and Understanding Organization Structure." *Administrative Science Quarterly,* 1973, *18,* 168–185.

Chubb, J. E., and Moe, T. M. *Politics, Markets, and America's Schools.* Washington, D.C.: Brookings Institution, 1990.

Coch, L., and French, R. P. "Overcoming Resistance to Change." *Human Organization,* 1948, *1,* 512–532.

Dornsbusch, S. M., and Scott, W. R. *Evaluation and the Exercise of*

*Authority: A Theory of Control Applied to Diverse Organizations.* San Francisco: Jossey-Bass, 1975.

Galbraith, J. R. *Organization Design.* Reading, Mass.: Addison-Wesley, 1977.

Hackman, J. R., and Lawler, E. E. "Employee Reactions to Job Characteristics." *Journal of Applied Psychology,* 1971, *55,* 259-286.

Hackman, J. R., and Oldham, G. R. *Work Design.* Reading, Mass.: Addison-Wesley, 1980.

Hannaway, J. *Managers Managing: The Workings of An Administrative System.* New York: Oxford University Press, 1989.

Hannaway, J. *Breaking the Cycle: Instructional Efficacy and Teachers of "At-Risk" Students.* Stanford, Calif.: Teacher Context Center, 1991a.

Hannaway, J. *Restructuring: The Tale of Two Districts.* Report submitted to Consortium for Policy Research in Education, February, 1991b.

Hannaway, J., and Sproull, L. "Who's Running the Show? Coordination and Control in Educational Organizations." In J. Hannaway and L. Sproull, *Administrators' Notebook.* Chicago: Midwest Administration Center, University of Chicago, 1979.

Hinings, C. R., and Lee, G. "Dimensions of Organization Structure and Their Context: A Replication." *Sociology,* 1971, *5,* 83–93.

Janis, I., and Mann, L. *Decision Making.* New York: Free Press, 1977.

Jennergren, L. P. "Decentralization in Organizations." In P. C. Nystrom and W. H. Starbuck (eds.), *Handbook of Organizational Design.* Vol. 2. Oxford, England: Oxford University Press, 1981.

Khandwalla, P. "Mass Orientation of Operations Technology and Organizational Structure." *Administrative Science Quarterly,* 1974, *19,* 74–97.

Lammers, C. J. "Power and Participation in Decision Making in Formal Organizations." *American Journal of Sociology,* 1967, *73,* 201–216.

Lawler, E. E. "Pay, Participation and Organizational Change." In E. L. Cass and F. G. Zimmer (eds.), *Man and Work in Society.* New York: Van Nostrand Reinhold, 1975.

Locke, E. A., and Schweiger, D. M. "Participation in Decision-

Making: One More Look." In B. M. Staw (ed.), *Research in Organizational Behavior.* Greenwich, Conn.: JAI Press, 1979.

Lortie, D. *Schoolteacher.* Chicago: University of Chicago Press, 1975.

March, J. G., and Olsen, J. P. *Ambiguity and Choice in Organizations.* Bergen, Norway: Universitetforlaget, 1976.

Meyer, J. W., and Rowan, B. "Institutionalized Organizations: Formal Structure as Myth and Ceremony." *American Journal of Sociology,* 1977, *83,* 340–363.

Meyer, J., and Scott, W. R. *Organizational Environments: Ritual and Rationality.* Newbury Park, Calif.: Sage, 1983.

O'Reilly, C. "Corporations, Culture, and Commitment: Motivation and Social Control in Organizations." *California Management Review,* 1989, *31,* 9–25.

Pallas, A. "School Climate in American High School." *Teachers College Record,* 1988, *89,* 541–553.

Pugh, D., and others. "The Context of Organization Structures."*Administrative Science Quarterly,* 1969, *14,* 91–114.

Rosenholtz, S. *Teachers' Workplace: The Social Organization of Schools.* White Plains, N.Y.: Longman, 1989.

Rowan, B. "Commitment and Control: Alternative Strategies for the Organizational Design of Schools." In C. C. Cazden (ed.), *Review of Research in Education.* Vol. 16. Washington, D.C.: American Educational Research Association, 1990.

Salancik, G., and Pfeffer, J., "A Social Information Processing Approach to Job Attitudes and Task Design." *Administrative Science Quarterly,* 1978, *23,* 224–253.

Simon, H. A. *Administrative Behavior.* New York: Macmillan, 1947.

Simon, H. A. "Organizations and Markets." *Journal of Economic Perspectives,* 1991, *5,* 25–44.

Weick, K. "Educational Organizations as Loosely-Coupled Systems." *Administrative Science Quarterly,* 1976, *21,* 1–19.

# 7

# School Improvement: Is Privatization the Answer?

**Martin Carnoy**

America's public schools are in trouble, just when the country needs a better-educated populace to confront a world economy gone high tech. In this era of budget deficits and deregulation, the discussion on how to improve schools has inevitably come to focus on management and organization, with a wide range of decentralization (or "restructuring") schemes at center stage. The major issues are whether any of these decentralization proposals can make a difference in educational quality and whether successful decentralization and improvement can be achieved through the present public school system.

This is not the first time that public education has faced the firing squad. Since World War II alone, there have been several waves of criticism and reform. These attacked and responded to whatever the "crisis" seemed to be at the time: to the apparent lag of American space science and technology in the 1950s, to racial segregation in the 1950s and 1960s, to corporate conformity in the 1950s (Goodman, 1956), then (after the permissive 1960s) to the *lack* of conformity and standards in the 1970s and early 1980s (the back-to-basics movement), and, in the late 1980s and early 1990s, to declining test scores, overcentralization, and bureaucratization.

There is, however, a distinctly new feature of this last round of critiques: after a decade of limited and generally unsuccessful efforts to improve high school academic standards at the state level and overall academic achievement at the district level, the most vocal criticisms have begun to call for the privatization of public schooling, particularly of its management.[1] In this context, *privatization* means that individual schools—whether publicly owned, privately owned and secular, or privately owned and religious—would operate with equal access to public resources, and largely independently of public controls, in a free market for educational services. There are many different versions of such educational market proposals, from parental "choice" among existing public schools to competition among all schools, public and private, for publicly provided educational vouchers (see Levin, 1990). But the proposals all have in common the concept of making schools individual administrative units,[2] geared to attracting a fee-paying (even if the fees are publicly funded vouchers or district transfers) student clientele.

The basis of the argument for privatization is not only the allegedly greater efficiency in delivering school services but also the purportedly high value attached by families to choosing freely the kind of education their children should have. Even though this choice now exists (private schooling is a possibility for everyone willing to pay the price), most advocates of privatizing public schooling argue that parents should also have their tax dollars available for public and private choices; this would put all school consumption and production squarely in the marketplace and would give parents a truly "free" selection of educational alternatives for their children (Coleman, 1990). Privatization thus presumes to decentralize decision making about children's learning, to the point where each school is competing for customers among a diverse set of parental tastes and incomes, and parents face a wide range of available schooling choices for their children. The end result, it is claimed, would be increased economic welfare for individual families (they get to choose schooling for their children and get more schooling output per dollar spent) and for society as a whole (the market would do a better job than the government).

In this chapter, I analyze the underlying economics of these arguments. The main case for public schooling rests on its inherent consistency with democratic ideals—the antithesis of the private provision of educational services—but it is important to understand the public-private debate as it is now being framed. In that framework, I find that the most logical and consistent empirical explanation for higher-quality education, whether public or private, lies primarily in differential demand, not in cost differences. But such differential demand appears to result as much from variation in expressed values of schools themselves as from parents. My analysis not only takes issue with privatization's main premise—that a large "unmet demand" by parents for higher-quality schooling and private schools' lower costs per unit of educational quality together form the basis of significant improvements in American education—but also suggests that working with individual schools and school districts within the public system to raise pupils' achievement still holds out promise for better education (Levin, 1990; Witte, 1990, 1991). The very "publicness" of public schooling may make it possible to mobilize the time and effort needed to raise demand for quality education. I conclude that, despite the real problems of reforming its management, public schooling is still our best bet for improving the delivery of educational services to the wide range of children currently served by the system.

An enormous amount has already been written on this subject, and I do not intend to cover all the arguments for and against choice and decentralization (for an excellent symposium on choice, see Clune and Witte, 1990). There is an ideological and historical tension between the democratic ideal of public schooling and the family's desire for expressing private tastes in its children's education (Levin, 1990). There are also serious issues of control underlying the education-reform debate (Weiss, 1990; Witte, 1990), and a lively debate is under way about the validity of the claim that private delivery of public services (such as health and education) is more efficient than public delivery (Elmore, 1990; Shanker, 1991).

As a complement to the existing discussion, I focus on three main issues: What is the source of achievement gains in the decentralization argument, and are its claims valid? How would market decentralization versus "public" decentralization affect parental choices for children's educational gains? What are the implications of the answers to these questions for improving public schooling?

## Rationales for Public Education

As a starting point for the analysis, let me restate the underlying economic and political rationales for public education in free-market economies and the principal critiques of those rationales in the present historical context. They are both important to understanding the decentralization debate.

### *Rationales*

Put simply, the claim is that society benefits economically from an educated population, beyond the gains from education captured by individuals and their families. These social gains—called *economic externalities*—accrue through the lower costs of social and economic infrastructure, a better social environment (higher public consumption), a more effective political system, and even, under certain organizational arrangements, higher productivity (on this last point, see Levin, 1987). Because of externalities, if investment in education were left entirely to families' private economic decisions, they would *under*invest (Weisbrod, 1964). By taking public education, children receive a common set of experiences and engage in a shared discourse that serves to benefit the economy and the polity as a whole. Publicly financed and administered education effectively subsidizes schooling, so that children will take a socially optimum amount and will obtain a sufficient amount of this common experience.

The second argument for public financing of education is that with the laws against chattel slavery making it impossible to pledge future labor as collateral for human capital investment loans, the cost of borrowing for education is much higher than for other forms of investment. Again, relying purely on the private capital market would hold spending on education below its socially optimal level.

It is this second argument that privatization advocates focus on when pushing for public financing and private administration of education; but the externalities rationale for public schooling has implications that go far beyond solving capital market imperfections. If there are large externalities from having a well-educated population, how much of the decision about investing in schooling should be left to parents, teenagers, and the (private) labor market, even if capital were available for education under the same conditions as for other investments?

Most societies eventually end up legislating against child labor and for compulsory schooling. Parents are legally bound by the state to send their children to school. At some point, "the public" decides that the best way to resolve varying preferences for schooling among families is to require all parents to consume (or invest in) a certain amount of it for their children, primarily by eliminating alternative income-earning opportunities and enforcing truancy laws. There are ways around this: no one can compel children to learn what is taught in school or compel parents to devote the time and energy usually needed to ensure that such learning takes place. But the intervention of publicly administered education in the family decision-making process aims to regularize at least a minimum demand for schooling, in ways that go beyond its public financing.

In addition, the state, or the public sector, as representative of the collectivity of individuals' social demands, translates its vision of externalities into what should be called the "common experience" of schooling. A public school in Iowa creates approximately the same social experience for its pupils as a school in Massachusetts. This experience, for all its hypocrisies and problems, has in the past been fairly successful in conveying a set of common values to many generations of young people. It is probably the only unifying and democratizing process that young people undergo in a highly diversified society with no compulsory military service.[3]

The essence of this democratizing process is symbolized by the neighborhood school, the local high school, and the *absence* of individualized, private choice in public goods. It is the conscious giving up of privilege and difference by the citizenry that forms the underpinnings of the democratic ideal. The legal, political, and educational systems of modern democratic societies are the expression of this commitment to leveling differences among individuals, even as the market tends to extol and exercerbate them. Although recent critiques argue that such collectivity ultimately places too much power into the hands of the state bureaucracy, it is precisely the democratic ideal of public accountability—developed in the public school experience—that is supposed to force the state to respond to the collective will.

### *Critique*

One of the most profound arguments leveled against public schooling has been made by Coleman (1990). He claims that, given access to capital, parents today would invest the socially optimal amount in schooling without public intervention on the demand side.[4] Such intervention may have been necessary in the unschooled, agricultural society of a century ago, he argues, when a parent was less interested in his or her children's schooling than in their labor, but now—living in a postindustrial, urban-suburban, media-saturated, and relatively well-schooled environment—families are well aware of schooling's value (and of the inadequacy of the public educational system). Coleman contends that in such an environment, the bureaucratic public school system, with its professional educators "deciding" for families what education should be and how much children should take, is an anachronism that the country cannot afford. Worse, he argues, the public school has become least effective for the urban poor, for whom, because of its low quality, the externalities of public schooling are probably negative. The educational focus should therefore change to efficient educational delivery, regardless of school "ownership." In the Coleman vision, the public sector's role would be mainly financial, allowing private and public schools to compete for public funds on the basis of parent demand. Although not quite specified in this way, the concept that consumers (parents and teenagers) have sufficient information about schooling and have an accurate assessment of schooling's value underlies much of the current argument for privatization.

A second general critique of public education is that the public sector is such an inefficient producer of any good, including education, that society would be better off by privatizing as much of its production as possible. Further, proponents claim, teachers' unions and the school bureaucracy have been instrumental in preventing any real educational reforms and in keeping the cost of education rising. Without privatization and greater competition among schools vying for clients, these monopolistic elements will continue to impede educational improvement.

At the heart of the second critique is a deep distrust of and antipathy to public management. Public school administration, from the principal at the school site to the school district up to the state, is blamed for declining student achievement because of its resistance to change, its overcentralization, its inflexibility, and its overstaffing. The other element of this bureaucracy is teachers' unionization—also inflexible, also a barrier to change, also a key reason for the lack of innovation in the classroom and instrumental in driving the cost of schooling up, without any corresponding increase in quality of outcomes.[5]

In the most recent critique of this type, Chubb and Moe (1990) argue that schools with greater control over school policies and personnel are more effectively organized than schools that have less organizational autonomy: "The specific reasons for concern about school control in the public sector are that, all things being equal, public schools are substantially less likely to be granted autonomy from authoritative external control (i.e., from superintendents, district offices, and boards) than are private schools; and as important, schools in urban systems—where the problems of school performance are most grave and where the efforts to solve them have been the most bureaucratic—are much less likely, all else being equal, to enjoy autonomy" (p. 233).

These criticisms are (and should be) taken seriously, especially in the context of twelve full years of unabashed deprecation of everything public except the military.[6] Coleman's point implies that demand for good education is equal among all parents, and that it is the (public) schools in low-income neighborhoods that have shortchanged children and their parents by delivering low-quality education, even in the face of high demand.[7] Chubb and Moe make the same point in a different way by arguing that the greatest inefficiencies (bureaucracies) are in low-income neighborhoods because urban school districts are subject to the most external control. In both cases, the arguments imply that the present system of public schooling is structurally incapable of correcting these deficiencies. Chubb and Moe end up proposing increased competition for vouchers among public schools. Coleman is even less sanguine about public education and argues for increased reliance on private schools, again through a voucher system.

## Modeling the Arguments

We can break these arguments down into two parts: the issue of parental demand for educational quality and the relationship between the demand for high-quality schooling (from all sources) and its supply (from all sources).[8]

### *Parental Demand for Educational Quality*

All parents, regardless of social class, want the best education for their children. All things being equal, the latent demand for education by parents of different social classes would therefore be the same. Logic and surveys suggest that this is so. But the issue in the marketplace is not what people say but how they behave. Since education is partially provided directly by families to their children and, when acquired outside the family, is partly a public good, then how much education (quality and quantity) individual children get is at least partly determined by parents' "voice" (Hirschman, 1970)—parents *revealed* willingness and ability to influence their children's education, either through direct efforts at home or by pressuring the system in favor of their children.

The greater voice of higher-educated, education-wise families expresses itself in three important forms: in the greater school-relevant experience that families provide to their children *before* they enter school; in the greater school-relevant support they provide their children once the children are in school; and in the greater weight they bring to bear on decisions about their children by school authorities.

Yet, since education is delivered unequally even as a public good (Carnoy and Levin, 1985) and is provided privately (under public scrutiny), how much children get is also a function of income and price. Higher-income parents have greater possibility, in Hirschman's terms, of "exit" into alternative (higher-quality) educational situations, either by moving to higher-priced neighborhoods or by buying higher-priced private schooling.

We can break this problem down into two parts: how the family allocates its time among activities producing material consumption ($C$), leisure ($L$), and children's school-relevant achievement gain[9] ($Q$) and how the family allocates its consumption between material goods and increased achievement for its children. This choice among activities takes place before the child goes to school and while the child is in school.

The family earning unit maximizes the utility function:

$$U = f\,[C, (L + Q)],$$

subject to the budget constraint

$$Pc{*}C = W{*}\,(T - L - Q),$$

where $T$ = total time available for work, leisure, and achievement-producing activities, $W$ = wages, and $PC$ = prices of consumption goods.

In this formulation, voice would only be a function of $Q$, but we know that it is also a function of parents' educational "wisdom," highly correlated with parents' education. For the moment, however, let us assume that it is only a question of time spent on achievement-enhancing activities.

The voice function is complex and highly nonlinear. Figure 7.1 shows that $Tw$ bends backwards as a function of wages, and Figure 7.2 shows that over the last fifteen years, as women's wages have risen and men's fallen, women have increased the average hours they work. In addition, the women's curve has shifted to the right as families attempt to maintain real income and the percentage of single-head-of-household females increases. Under quite usual assumptions about the trade-off between leisure ($L$) and time spent with children on school-related activities ($Q$),[10] the time available for educational functions in the parents' day is greater among low-wage earners than among middle-wage earners, at least when we compare two-parent families and one-parent families as separate categories (Figure 7.3). Once we account for the higher incidence of female-headed households among the low-income families, however, and for the possibility that low-income fathers may be less likely to substitute for traditional female roles, this shifts the low end of the $Ts$ curve to the left (Figure 7.4). Finally, in both Figures

Figure 7.1. Supply of Labor, White Males.

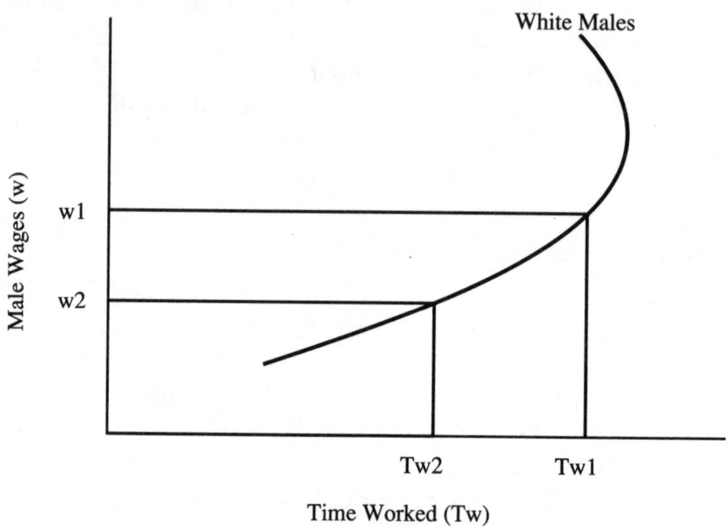


Figure 7.2. Supply of Labor, Females.

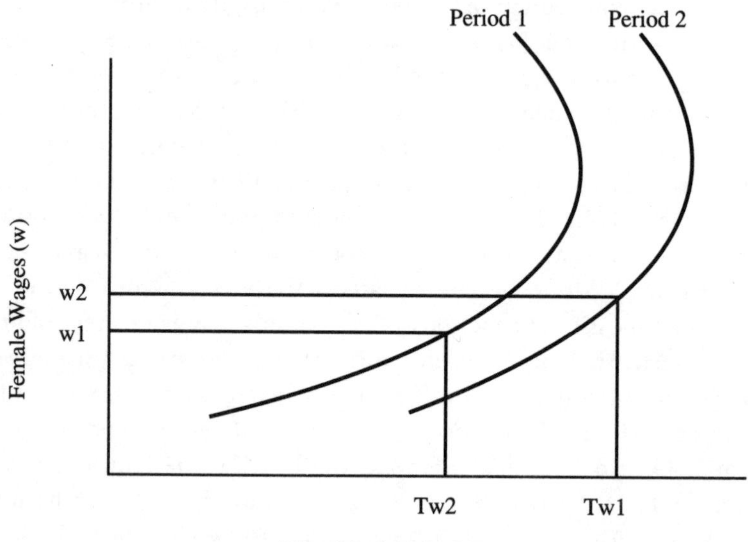

**Figure 7.3. Supply of Parent Time for Child's Intellectual Development.**

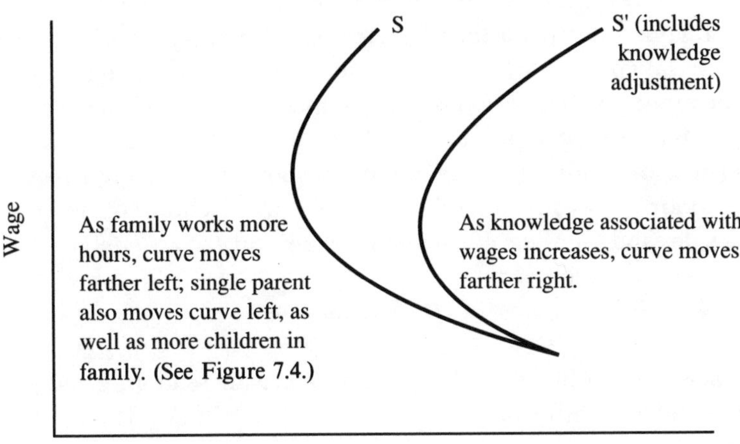


**Figure 7.4. Adjusted Supply of Parent Time for Child Development.**

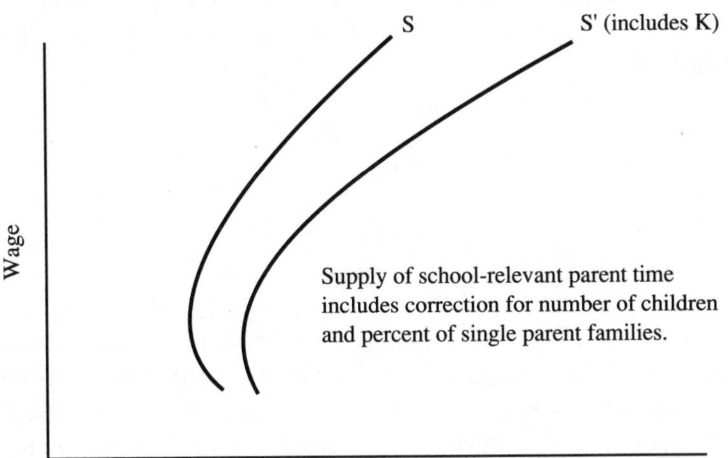

7.3 and 7.4, when we add parents' educational wisdom ($K$) into the curve, the upper end shifts far to the right.[11]

Once children are old enough to go to school, parents can also choose to spend their income on schooling of children or on material goods. In this case, they maximize the utility derived from consuming material goods and the increased quality they get from purchasing better public schooling (higher taxes and home payments, or, under a choice program, more distant, higher-quality schooling) or private schooling for their children. Following Gertler and Glewwe (1989) and Glewwe and Jacoby (1991),

$$U = g(C, Su, Sv),$$

where $Su$ = public schooling and $Sv$ = private schooling, subject to the budget constraint

$$Pc{*}C + Pu{*}Su + Pv{*}Sv = Y,$$

where $Pu$ = the cost of public schooling and $Pv$ = the cost of private schooling.

Since parents are assumed to be buying additional quality of schooling, we can express schooling as some function of a vector of school-quality factors: $Xu$ in public school, and $Xv$ in private school. Thus,

$$Su = AuXu,$$

and

$$Sv = AvXv.$$

The school-quality choice function subject to the budget constraint yields demand curves for school quality. Even assuming that all parents have the same utility function for schooling quality and other goods, higher-income parents could purchase more schooling quality with their higher income and would have more "exit" potential because of the availability of more income to spend on schooling, even if they did not exercise "exit."

Put together, the equations suggest that both voice and the income available for buying higher-quality schooling—hence, the demand for educational quality—are considerably higher among higher-educated parents and that two-parent families (with more income and/or more time) are more likely to have a higher demand for educational quality than single parents, all other factors being equal. Higher-income parents also have the greatest possibility to substitute the purchase of higher-quality schooling for time spent with their children, although it is likely that, on the average, voice and spending on school quality are higher among higher-income parents.

All this is hypothetical but measurable. If I am right about the voice curve, the demand for educational quality is lower among low- and middle-educated low-income parents on two counts: they are likely to have less expressed voice and certainly have less "exit" than higher-educated, higher-income parents. They are also likely to invest less in their children before the children enter elementary school. Therefore, as I shall emphasize, children from higher-educated, schoolwise homes may come to school "easier to teach,"[12] increasing institutional demand for higher achievement gains through the higher academic expectations of teachers and parents.

The more recent voucher plans propose larger vouchers for low-income (less schooled) families, to compensate for these families' lower income and consequent fewer options in the marketplace. But, according to the analysis presented here, larger vouchers for less-educated parents would have to compensate for more than just current income differences. They would have to compensate for lower preschool, school-relevant investment (the result of lower voice and lower income in a period of completely private decisions about education) and for lower voice during the school years (the lesser ability to influence children's education while they are in school).

### *Supply of Schooling*

The second part of the debate concerns the delivery of schooling. The critique of public schools' inefficiency is often tied, implicitly or explicitly, to arguments that private schools are relatively efficient. The reasons vary, but the two main ones given are that public schools have become a monopoly and, as such, have no incentive to improve efficiency of production (see, for example, Peterson, 1990), and that public schools are dominated by a large public bureaucracy focused on bureaucratic control, rather than on student achievement, and hence are unable—because of this very structure—to improve educational delivery (Chubb and Moe, 1990). Chubb and Moe also argue that the bureaucratic control function of schooling has its greatest effect on schools in low-income neighborhoods, significantly raising costs per unit of quality produced. Because of the lack of local resources in such neighborhoods, state public bureaucracies are likely to supply a high fraction of educational funding in the form of categorical grants and to demand considerable bureaucratic accountability. This, according to Chubb and Moe, would contribute to greater bureaucracy at the local level and to increased inefficiency.

Figure 7.5 summarizes the monopoly argument. In the figure, I make the typical assumption that the monopoly (public schooling, in this case) faces a downward-sloping demand curve and, were it a profit-making firm, would restrict output (educational quality) to the point where marginal cost equals marginal revenue (*A1* and *A2*). Educational quality is defined as the change in, or value added to, achievement delivered by schools. Since the demand for educational quality is lower (and, I assume, more inelastic, because of fewer alternatives) in low-income neighborhoods, the monopoly provides *A1* amount of educational quality to pupils of low socioeconomic status (SES) and *A2* to high-SES pupils. If the monopoly were permitted to engage in discriminatory pricing, it would "charge" low-income families *P1* for educational services and charge high-SES families *P2*. The "monopoly rent"—represented by *P1CDPo* in the low-SES case and *P2EFPo* in the high-SES case—would presumably be absorbed by the salaries of a bloated public school bureaucracy.

Making schools competitive would, in this analysis, increase output to the point where supply (the sum of marginal cost curves of individual schools providing education in each neighborhood) equals demand. If schools in the low- and high-SES neighborhoods face the same supply curve (*MC*), educational quality for low-SES

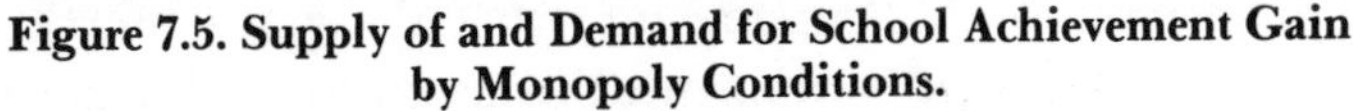

**Figure 7.5. Supply of and Demand for School Achievement Gain by Monopoly Conditions.**

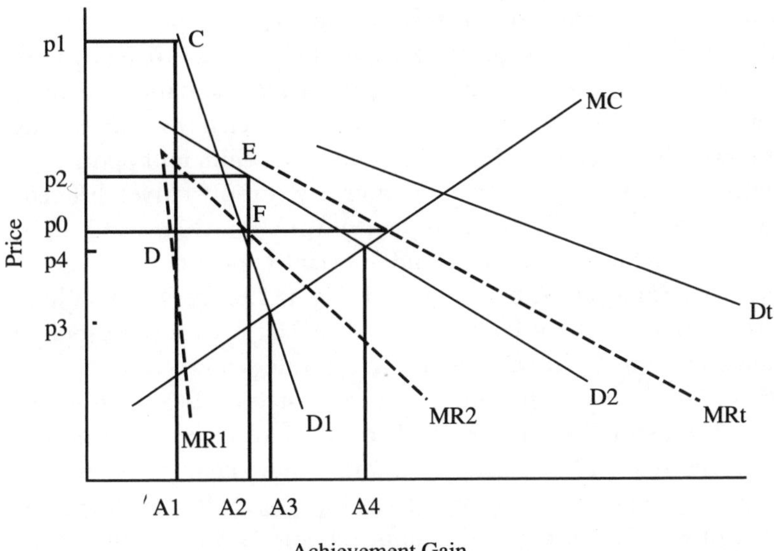


schools would increase to *A3* and for high-SES schools to *A4*. The price of value-added achievement for low-SES families would fall from *P1* to *P3;* for high-SES families, from *P2* to *P4,* or (if the monopoly did not engage in discriminatory pricing) from *Po* to *P3* and *P4.*

There are problems with the argument that public schools are monopolies. It requires public education to be restricting achievement gains in order to maximize revenue—in this case, to maximize bureaucratic salaries. Although a good case can be made that public schools are overbureaucratized, the monopoly argument claims that the bureaucratic payroll *derives* from public education's monopoly power to restrict achievement gains. This is not a particularly good model of public agency behavior. In addition, the cost (price) of the lower achievement gains in low-SES neighborhoods is generally lower, not higher, than the price of gains in high-SES neighborhoods, which suggests that public education does not exercise monopoly power.

The more logical argument is that the value function of public education includes an intrinsic value placed on bureaucratic control, that this competes with the value placed on achievement gains (I shall deal with this issue shortly), and/or that public schools in low-SES neighborhoods are indeed less efficient (more bureaucratized) than in high-SES neighborhoods and therefore have higher supply (cost) curves. This latter inefficiency argument, as expressed by Chubb and Moe (1990), does not claim monopoly-type output restriction, but rather an efficiency (supply curve) differential between low-SES, low-achievement (public) schools and high-SES, high achievement public and (especially) private schools.

The analysis is characterized in Figure 7.6. I assume that low-income public school consumers are on *D1,* high-income public school consumers on *D2,* low-income private school consumers on *D3,* and high-income private school consumers on *D4,* according to the previous analysis of parental demand. Here, price represents the resources required per unit of pupil achievement *added* by the school during the school year.[13] The supply curve for low-SES public schools is *S1,* for high-SES public schools *S2,* and for private (or independent and competitive public) schools *S3.* I have drawn *S1* and *S2* as relatively inelastic because Chubb and Moe claim that public school bureaucracy is highly inflexible, implying that "externally controlled" public schools cannot adjust factors of production as demand for output (greater achievement gains) increases over time. Given this characterization, consumers of educational quality will achieve higher amounts of educational quality at lower cost per unit of gain (but not lower cost to them) by sending their children to private (or independent and competitive public) schools (*A3* and *A4*).

What evidence is there that the differential efficiency model is an accurate characterization of the way schooling is produced publicly and privately (in its currently most centralized form)? To begin with, most of the available data suggest that private schools in the United States do not produce significantly greater achievement gains than public schools do, especially among students with higher-educated parents. For example, National Assessment of Educational Progress (NAEP) math achievement scores among high school seniors show a 6–8-point higher score for private over public

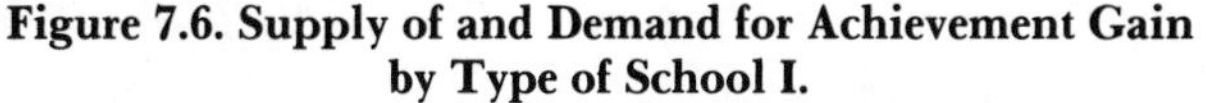

**Figure 7.6. Supply of and Demand for Achievement Gain by Type of School I.**

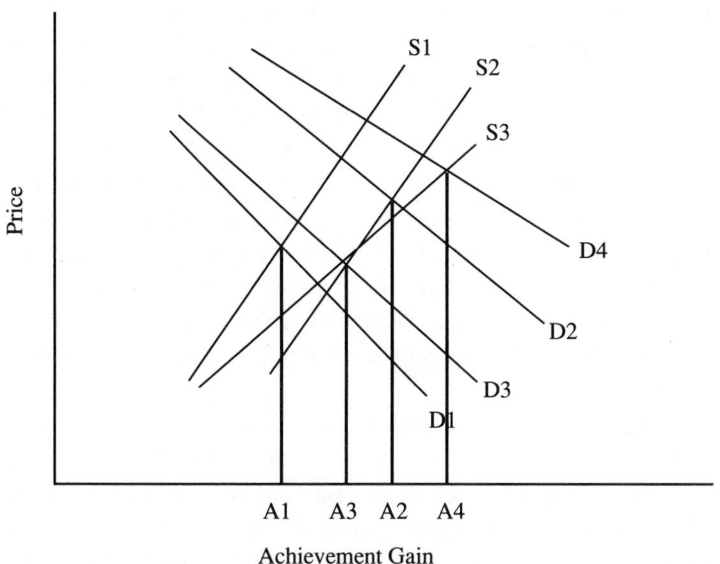


school students when parents have high school or less education, and no difference when parents have some college or more.[14] The results of Coleman's own study (1990), often cited as an argument for private schools, also suggest that achievement differences between students in private and public schools are not large. If we take the Chubb and Moe results (1990) and place them alongside the NAEP math results, the strongest argument that can be made is that private schools produce better results among children of less educated parents, and they do so primarily by moving students into more academically oriented courses.[15]

To reflect such empirical results, we can modify Figure 7.6 in the following way: we assume that parochial private schools are, on the average, less costly than public schools. This is already a heroic assumption because the output mix of parochial and public schools is different: parochial private schools do not usually take much more costly special education students, whereas public schools must take all students, regardless of their ability or emotional or physical problems.[16]

There is another category of private schools—call them high-SES private schools—that are much more costly than public schools, even though they too do not take special education students. Call their supply curve *S4* (see Figure 7.7). Rather than buying the higher *A4* gains in Figure 7.6, as originally claimed, higher-income parents pay more in private schools but get the same achievement gain as in public schools (*A4* equals *A2* in Figure 7.7 but is purchased at a higher price). Apparently, achievement scores are not closely tied to how much parents spend on schooling, and parents are willing to pay more for private education for reasons other than higher added achievement—for example, a better chance for their children to get into better colleges with the same achievement attainment.

This is not a minor point: all schools produce a variety of outputs, including but not limited to achievement. Independent private schools specialize in preparing students for college ("preparatory" schools) or discipline (military academies), and higher-income parents pay for these special outputs. Achievement gains at different *levels* of achievement may also be indirectly valued differentially in the labor market (I discuss this in a moment), so that higher-income parents want to reduce risk by buying "guarantees" of higher achievement gains through private education.

The second set of empirical data to consider is the NAEP tests over time. They suggest that low-SES minority pupils made large gains in 1975–1989, relative to higher-SES whites (Smith and O'Day, 1991a). The evidence further indicates that much of this minority gain was due in part to the rapid decline of poverty in the late 1960s and early 1970s, when the pupils taking these tests were young children, and in part to the increased spending on minority schooling during the same period, especially in the South.[17] Since these were public sector interventions, the data imply that it is possible for the public sector to increase the demand for better education, both through increased family income (an income policy that reduces poverty) and increased voice, and for the public sector to affect the supply of achievement by increasing the income of public schools and their ability to deliver higher achievement gains.

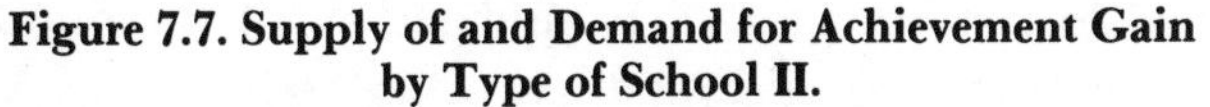

**Figure 7.7. Supply of and Demand for Achievement Gain by Type of School II.**

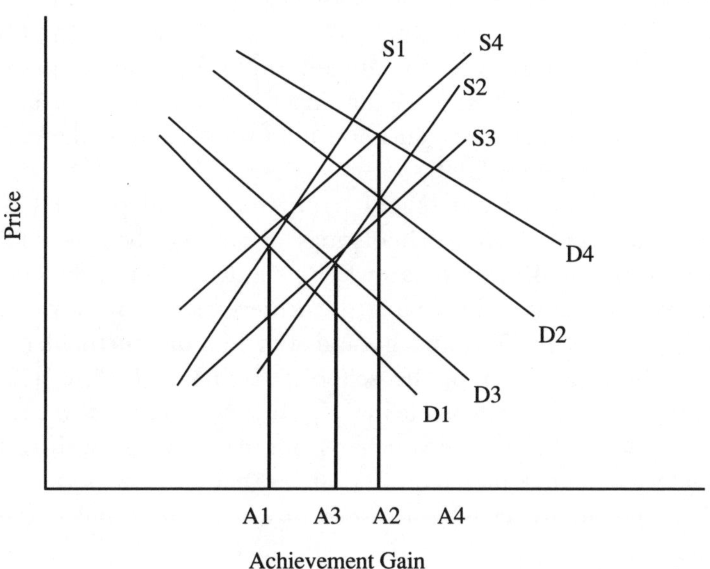


All this suggests that among lower-income students, the small percentage of students in private schools do better than those in public schools, even though the differences do not appear large. Chubb and Moe (1990) claim, for example, that lower-SES students do better in magnet public schools. When costs are measured correctly, it is likely that private Catholic parochial schools are less costly (have a lower supply curve) than public schools, although it is difficult to measure all the "free" cost of capital and free services provided by the Catholic Church—and, again, parochial schools do not produce the full range of services required of public schools.

Nevertheless, higher achievement gains in such schools—if they exist—are as much the result of higher demand for achievement as of greater "efficiency" in production. Where greater efficiency exists, it probably does come from much lower bureaucratic costs per student—unusually high in urban public school districts. Moreover, the output mix in both magnet schools and parochial schools is different from that in "average" public schools, because the former do not have to accept and retain all the pupils who present themselves. Magnet and parochial schools (as well as independent, high-SES private schools) can pick the student body (and their parents) and can expel ("cool out," in the case of public magnet schools) those who do not conform to the demands placed on them. There is also evidence that black Catholics have a significantly greater demand for education than non-Catholic blacks do (Lachman and Kosmin, 1991).

This "fit" between school requirements and parental demand in private parochial schools may or may not be extendable to the population of parents as a whole. Yet, whether it is or is not, we know that it is possible to increase achievement gains in public schools, even for low-SES students and even with unstructured, centralized, bureaucratized public schools. Chubb and Moe (1990) claim that change is impossible in the public system as it now exists (that is, without "choice" or vouchers), but that claim is empirically wrong. Such change may require policies that are now politically unlikely, but many have been shown to work (Smith and O'Day, 1991b).

### *Increasing Demand Through Institutional Commitment*

So far, I have not considered that both private and public schools are nonprofit institutions, which do not behave as profit-maximizing firms. Nonprofits place intrinsic value on their activities. Their institutional values affect the demand for students' academic gains. This should add to the demand for high-quality education. It makes sense that "good schools" are those that place high intrinsic value on academic achievement, even if, in either money or staff time and energy, it costs more to produce it. Figure 7.8 compares the effect of intrinsic demand for greater achievement in "good" and "bad" schools.[18]

Unfortunately, we do not know whether the higher demand for achievement gains among low-SES students in magnet public schools and in private parochial schools comes from the selected families who send their children to such schools or from the intrinsic value placed on higher achievement gains by these schools' teachers and administrators. Chubb and Moe's results (1990) suggest

**Figure 7.8. Institutional Supply of and Demand for Achievement Gain.**

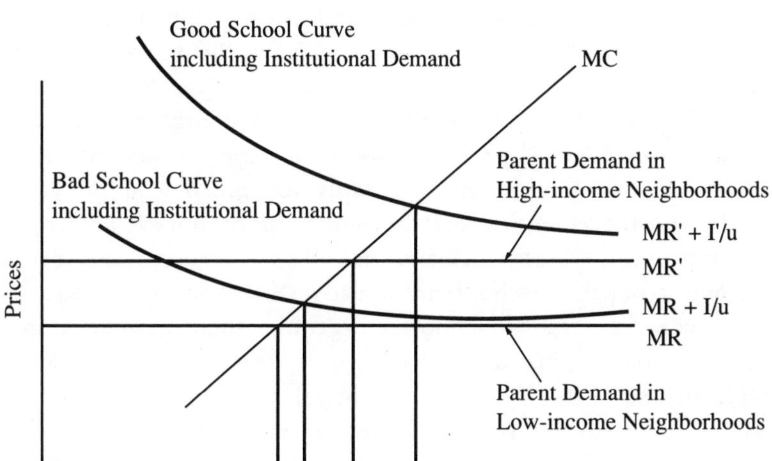


that higher gains from the organizational (supply) side turn out to be largely the result of expecting more from students and enabling them to do more demanding coursework. This may very well be an institutional demand effect, not a lower marginal cost.[19] It is also likely that both parents and students, on the one hand, and the school, on the other, are behind such behavior. Thus, in Figure 7.8, I show the higher demand for academic achievement in "good" schools to be the result of a higher parent demand (*MR′*) and a higher instrinsic value placed on achievement gains by the school (administrators and teachers) itself.

If parochial schools do better in terms of achievement, they are only somewhat more successful than public schools; and, whatever their success, it is due primarily to demanding more achievement from lower-income students and getting it. Since such schools do not generally accept students who require special educational services, do select only those students whose families are aware of the greater achievement demands (and are willing to pay to get access to them), and can expel those students who do not meet the greater demands, it is difficult to separate greater student or parental demand for higher academic quality from the schools' greater demand.

Despite similar self-selection and possibly higher demand for academic excellence, private schools catering to students from *higher* SES backgrounds are apparently not able to do significantly better on achievement gains than public schools do, even at higher cost per pupil. But, by focusing on college entrance, a number of the high-cost private schools are able to do much better than equally high-achieving public schools in getting their graduates into "good" colleges. They also deliver other services, such as providing high-income peers or the "right" social atmosphere. Parents are apparently willing to pay a great deal for these services.

Put another way, a school's value function may include a number of objectives—one of them being higher achievement gains. Public schools, by their very nature, place greater intrinsic weight on imparting democratic values and on delivering educational services to all students, regardless of their or their parents' demand for high achievement gains. Many public schools, it is argued, also place high value on bureaucracy and on bloated, highly paid district administrations that detract from higher achievement gains. Higher-quality public schools and districts, especially in marginal neighborhoods, often stress safety for their pupils as much as academic achievement. Greater security may be possible only with larger and more centralized administrative apparatuses. Private schools, by their very nature, can place higher intrinsic value on higher achievement gains and select those students and their families who *in practice* also demand more achievement. Private schools place less weight on imparting democratic values and less weight on providing educational services for difficult-to-school students. Many private schools also place a high value on creating a particular social atmosphere and on delivering places in "good" colleges to their graduates.

In terms of the intrinsic value placed on any of these outputs—the $I(X)$ discussed in note 18—the institutional demand for that output will increase (or decrease) total demand and the amount produced. The choice argument claims that if a better match is allowed for between parents and schools that want greater achievement gains, both gains and welfare will be maximized; but, to a large extent, that may already be true. It may also be true that shifting the institutional demand function in public institutions is a more effective route to increasing overall demand for achievement than relying on market mechanisms is.

### *The Differential Value of Lower and Higher Achievement*

One of the most important assumptions made in the analysis of educational quality is that the demand for improved quality of education (achievement gains) *should be* the same at all levels of initial achievement. This would mean that the perceived economic or social returns of achievement gain are the same whether students are low or high achievers to begin with. This is a questionable assumption, for two reasons. First, the private economic return to higher achievement has fallen significantly in the 1980s for those students who are not at a college-bound achievement level by the time they reach junior high school, relative to those students who are "college material" (Carnoy, Daley, and Hinojosa, 1990). Second, American society has consistently been willing to provide greater public subsidies for the education of higher-achieving students than for lower achievers, primarily through higher-cost public schools and universities for higher achievers and through the willingness to increase subsidies the farther a student goes in school (Hansen and Weisbrod, 1969); thus, higher-achieving, higher SES students get much more subsidized education because they get more years of schooling and take it in higher-cost institutions.

From the standpoint of a *private* decision, the rate of return on investment in an initially low-achieving pupil could be substantially less—even if cost and equal achievement gain were equal to those for a higher-achieving pupil—if the total value added in achievement would not raise the student high enough to have a good chance at college success. The incentive for families to spend private funds on such pupils may not be very great. Raising achievement gains for initially low-achieving pupils to the level that would push them into the college success category could therefore require considerably higher *public* subsidies than for initially higher-achieving pupils (Witte, 1991). Voucher proponents have recognized this problem and have argued for voucher amounts to be inversely correlated with income (see Coons and Sugarman, 1978; Friedman, 1955, 1962; Chubb and Moe, 1990).

This brings up the second point, however. Americans historically have not been avid to provide larger subsidies for the children of the poor than for the children of the middle and even upper middle classes. In recent years, opposition to expanding such programs as Head Start or to spending more on urban schools has increased as part of the general decline in support for social programs that help lower-income families and children.[20]

Where is the political support for an inverse voucher scheme? The answer is that there is about as much support for need-based vouchers as for sharply increased public spending on the schooling of the poor. We have to assume, realistically, that any voucher plan would provide equal vouchers for all children, regardless of parents' income.

## The Case for Improving Demand for Achievement Through Public Schools

Market-solution proponents assume that there is a large, unmet demand for achievement among parents whose children are currently in public schools and that private or "choice" schools would supply greater achievement to all pupils through more efficient educational delivery (lower marginal cost of achievement gains). The available data, I have argued, suggest something different. In the present configuration of U.S. private and public schools, in which private schools enroll about 13 percent of all students and a smaller percentage of low-income students, there are definitely arguments for increasing access to magnet (or "choice") public and private schools for those pupils from low-SES families who do not necessarily have the income but do have the "voice demand"—the time, the willingness to spend the time, and the ability to raise achievement gains. There is no hard evidence that either private or magnet schools produce higher achievement gains for pupils from "low-voice" families.

Neither is there evidence of a large unmet "voice demand" for higher achievement. To the contrary, results in Minnesota's choice program show that few parents transferred their children to other districts (Bennett, 1990);[21] and, in a recent study of three Sacramento schools, parents in the "choice" school chose it for safety reasons, not for its higher academic achievement record (Smreker, 1991). Elmore's work (1990) on health plans also suggests that most people choose health care providers because of convenience (distance), rather than because of extensive differences in quality. Thus, available information indicates that a relatively small percentage of parents—primarily low-income, "high-voice" parents or middle- and high-income, "high-voice" parents—would take advantage, through choice, of high-achievement private or magnet schools unless the schools were in their own neighborhoods. For those students and their families, it can be argued that positive gains would probably result, if only from the greater freedom to choose.

What about the mass of students who come from low- and middle-income, "low-voice" families? For them, the freedom to choose may actually lower their welfare. If the entire system were privatized (with existing public school buildings leased to private companies or parochial schools and all pupils given equal vouchers) and schools competed for pupils, the probable results would be, first, that most families would opt to send their children to local schools, not necessarily to the highest-quality schools available in a larger surrounding area (Archibald, 1988); and, second, that variation in quality (achievement gains) would probably increase as pupils were grouped more than they are now in separate schools by parents' demand (voice). The best schools would strive to pick up the best students, charge them more to be in those schools, and demand more time and energy from their parents. In this kind of educational marketplace, parents with the most problematic or even average children, unwilling to pay more and unwilling or unable to put out increased effort (low-voice), might end up having to send their children to schools that would be defined as those where such children ought to go because their parents do not care. The market would tend to privatize the responsibility for failure as much as it would privatize the responsibility for success.[22]

A similar result would obtain with "choice" limited to the public sector. In either case, there would be no logical incentive for low-performing schools to compete with high-performing schools, when these two kinds of schools would be competing in different niches of the market, much as Saks and K-Mart do. It is more likely that high-performing schools in one part of town would compete for the same high-demand (high-voice *and* high-income) clientele with high-performing schools in another part of town. The high-performing schools would have the most extensive market because their clientele would be the highest-income and highest-voice families, willing to spend the most on their children and able to shoulder the transportation costs of sending them the farthest for good schooling. Low-performing schools under a "choice" or privatized system would look like today's low-performing public schools (highly local and not competing for students) except that there would be even less public mandate to make them better. Most schools would still be neighborhood schools.[23]

This analysis suggests that higher achievement boils down mainly to a *demand* problem, where the issue is not providing high-quality education at lower cost but raising the demand for high achievement gains. Furthermore, higher achievement can be realized only if the demand for it is raised in schools and families simultaneously. Coleman (1990) may be right that there is no need in late-twentieth-century, urban, postindustrial America to convince parents of the advantages of sending their children to school; but that does not mean that parents have the optimum level of achievement demand for a society struggling to make the right decisions in the information age. Public efforts to increase achievement gains are therefore as necessary now as requiring attendance in public schools was in the nineteenth and early twentieth centuries.

Given that demand for higher achievement currently varies greatly, privatization or choice among public schools alone, according to my argument, would increase the variance in achievement more than it would raise its average level. Since there is no provision in the "choice" argument for increasing "voice demand" for higher achievement, there is no reason for overall demand to increase. Proponents of free-market delivery of schooling services contend that the problem could be solved by issuing larger vouchers for the poor. This is a pipe dream. But it is highly probable that private spending would be allowed on top of vouchers—why would this be prohibited in a "free-market" solution?—and that private spending would increase somewhat. If so, then competition would drive up the price of the small percentage of "good" private schools and keep the price of "bad" schools about where it is now.[24] Nevertheless, experience in health care suggests that even the price of "bad" schools could rise with publicly financed decentralization and privatization (Levin, 1991b; Elmore, 1990).

The best that could be hoped for in the voucher/free-market scheme is that some children, by dint of more choice and high family demand for better schooling, might get better schooling by moving from "bad" public schools to better public or private schools. Yet most children would not find themselves in a situation very different from the present one.

In the free-market solution, there would also be a social cost: private, market-oriented organizations would not be particularly interested in socializing pupils into a sense of national citizenship and the common values of democracy and equal opportunity. Indeed, their very institutional nature would require them to develop pride in uniqueness and separateness, much as colleges do now.[25] "Choice" public schools would be less likely to do that, but a voucher plan would move the children of many upper-middle-class parents beyond "choice" schools and into private education. The percentage of American families sending their children to private schools would rise, and the democratic ideal in American education would deteriorate.

The socialization into common values is a compelling argument for public, neighborhood, and equal education, monitored from a public viewpoint. Nevertheless, I want to make my case for the present system of public education in terms of its superior ability to raise demand for higher achievement gains. This may seem strange, given the harsh criticisms of the public system currently in vogue. I do not necessarily disagree with the idea that public school administrators and teachers are less effective than they might be, particularly in the achievement standards that they demand of students in their schools; there is a lot of prejudgment, stereotyping, and just plain bureaucratic laziness. Yet, that said, I have found that many if not most public school personnel seem to want their pupils to do well and often work under difficult conditions to provide decent education. A number of school districts are doing better today than ten years ago, even though they are publicly administered (Clune and Witte, 1990). There are even state educational bureaucracies that are innovating and promoting change, with some success (Smith and O'Day, 1991b). Test scores for minority children, especially black children, have also risen sharply in the past fifteen years, even though they remain abysmally lower than they should be. The question, then, is how to reform public schools so that the same teachers and administrators are a source of increased demand for higher achievement, under the (realistic) assumption that family demand is not high enough to achieve a socially optimum achievement gain.

A number of suggestions have been made and some are being implemented:

1. Increase teachers' decision making and mission definition at the school level (Johnson, 1990; Levin, 1991a).
2. Let teachers in a school define their mission as higher achievement and work out concretely (with technical assistance and with the administration's commitment) how to achieve that goal. Raise teachers' expectations (Levin, 1991a).
3. Tie in-service teacher training to the implementation of teacher-defined achievement-enhancing programs (Smith and O'Day, 1991b).
4. Set higher state curriculum standards, beginning at the elementary level, and work with individual schools to implement them (Smith and O'Day, 1991b).
5. Provide and work with counseling personnel to develop greater and more effective parent involvement at the elementary level (Levin, 1991a).
6. Increase early resources (such as Head Start and high-quality day care, for example) and add after-school programs for latchkey children (Schorr, 1988).

In all these examples, the key is that demand for higher achievement is increased in the school or school district by the public administration or the public school teachers. The bulk of parents in lower- and middle-income school districts are simultaneously incorporated into the school project, but the lead is taken by the school. In effect, the concept is to raise expectations in school personnel to match parents' and children's aspirations, and then to raise school wisdom (*K*) and time spent on school-related activities (*Ts*) so that "voice demand" (*V*) increases. It is the *combination* of higher demand by school personnel and raised "voice demand" that makes increased achievement possible in the democratic public model.

Once this process begins to work, it reaches far deeper than the free-market model can. That relies on existing levels of parental *K* and *Ts*. It is the very *public* nature of the public school system's attempts to increase achievement that raises the possibility of large changes in demand across the population. It is also the public nature of such attempts that allows the changes to take place without sacrifice of the democratic goals of public education.

There are other important ways to increase parental demand for achievement gains through public policy. If my model of parental demand is correct, then board-based family real income and individual wage gains, especially at lower- and middle-income levels, would increase the time and energy that families have available to devote to school matters. Increasing the quality of day care, of health information, and of direct health and nutritional interventions for mothers and expectant mothers would all represent the kinds of social wage transfers that could have large effects on children's achievement in school. Real family income rose about 9 percent in the 1980s (1982–1989), but this still leaves it at about the same level as its 1973 high, despite the increase in the average family's number of wage earners and in total time worked.[26]

Both factors are related and have almost certainly had a negative impact on pupils' achievement. These factors are also associated with a macroeconomic policy that has stressed cheap labor and severe cuts in social spending at the federal and now the state level. Ironically, stagnant family purchasing power and increased family time at work are also closely tied to the Reagan free-market policies now recommended for solving the achievement problem in the schools.

## Notes

1. Again, this is not new, since conservatives have been pushing for privatizing education since the 1950s.
2. The use of individual units does not mean that the units could not be connected by a particular philosophy. For example, public schools operating as individual units could share a "public" mission; religious schools of a particular faith could certainly project a philosophy; and a new concept—private, secular, corporate chain schools—could emerge if a voucher system began to function on a large enough scale. It is not difficult to imagine a nationwide chain of for-profit, test-teaching, top-grade schools, run as a large corporation with highly supervised, nonunionized teachers. This chain would also have a unified philosophy.
3. Part of the schools' crisis is that they are *not* achieving their fundamental democratic charge in key groups—those schools dominated by a low-income, minority clientele are generally not successful at creating the middle-class American school experience.
4. Coleman speaks only indirectly to the issue of externalities and the optimal *type* of education (public versus private). He implicitly assumes that the main issue in type of education is the efficiency of achievement delivery, not common discourse and experience, and the main source of externalities is the optimum amount of schooling, not the common experience of public schooling. His implicit argument is that public schooling does not provide this common experience anyway, since public schools for the poor are such a different place from public schools for the middle class.
5. A strong institutional case for dismantling public schools—and, I believe, one that clandestinely underlies much of the present push for privatization—is that such action would destroy teachers' unions, hence reducing wage pressures and providing more leverage for administrators to institute reforms

and restructure the work force. Without unions, it would be easier to get teachers to put in longer hours, take on new tasks, and be forced to perform or change schools. In theory, at least, a nonunionized teacher force would work longer and have less ability to raise wages. Whether it would perform better is a much more disputable issue. Even at present salaries, it is difficult to recruit well-qualified teachers, especially those needed to teach in low-income neighborhoods.

6. Ironically, progressives have been making many of these same criticisms of public education for years (see Dewey, 1919; Goodman, 1956; Kozol, 1967; Sennett and Cobb, 1973; Carnoy, 1974; Bowles and Gintis, 1975; Apple, 1979; Carnoy and Levin, 1985). Their analysis, however, is very different from the current privatization arguments. From a progressive standpoint, state bureaucratic behavior reflects society's configuration of political power. If public schools in low-income neighborhoods are ineffective, this fact reflects the value that society's configuration of political (and economic) power places on the education of the poor. This is a significant departure from the assumption that the bureaucracy has autonomous control of the school system.
7. As I shall suggest, a better way to express Coleman's argument is that public schools themselves effectively *lower* parents' demand for achievement.
8. I have restricted the discussion here to the demand for educational quality. A similar argument can be made for the quantity of education (years of schooling). Indeed, the two are probably highly correlated in that demand for educational quality is related to demand for educational quantity: those parents who want their children to go farther in school (to college or professional school, for example) demand a higher quality of schooling at lower levels of education.
9. The difficulty of defining "quality" as student achievement is compounded by the usual use of normative tests in measuring such achievement. In such tests, if everyone increases his or her performance, 50 percent still do less well than the mean, whether this is measured in percentile position or grade level. If possible, I would restrict the measure of achievement gain

in the models presented here to an *absolute* gain in achievement in each school year or group of school years. One way to measure such gain net of parents' contribution would be to estimate achievement in a given school year as a function of achievement in an earlier year and as a function of the student's socioeconomic level (if the school were the unit of observation, the relevant variables would be average achievement and average socioeconomic level of students in the school). The measured achievement versus the "predicted" achievement of students of similar socioeconomic background could be interpreted as the gain resulting from school contribution.

10. Namely, that the marginal utility of leisure equals the marginal utility of time spent on school-related activities. We also assume that the marginal utility of $L$ with respect to time declines more rapidly than the marginal utility of $Q$ with respect to time.

11. A good example of the power of $K$ is that college-educated female heads of households—even where the father has been absent from a child's early age—may have more voice (influence over their children's education) than lower-educated, often higher-income two-parent families with more time to devote to schooling matters.

12. The difference in school-relevant investment for children coming from less and more educated households comes from three sources: the greater $V$ in higher-educated households ($Ts \times K$); better nutrition in the crucial early childhood years; and more school-relevant resources at home. The latter two are a function of income, as well as of parents' education and school wisdom.

13. The usual measure in production-function estimates is the achievement added by the school, where the production function holds socioeconomic background "constant" to account for parents' contribution. There is a serious question, however, about whether the full impact of parents' contribution, as it interacts with school contribution, can be separated out.

14. Shanker (1991), p. E7. The scores are listed in Table 7.1.

15. Although we have assumed, on the basis of Chubb and Moe's results, that the achievement *gains* are higher among high-

**Table 7.1. NAEP Math Achievement Score.**

| *Parent Education* | *Public* | *Private* |
|---|---|---|
| Mother—some high school | 277 | 283 |
| Mother—high school graduate | 290 | 297 |
| Mother—some postsecondary education | 300 | 300 |
| Mother—college graduate | 310 | 310 |
| Father—some high school | 278 | 286 |
| Father—high school graduate | 286 | 294 |
| Father—some postsecondary education | 301 | 300 |
| Father—college graduate | 311 | 309 |

SES students, neither the NAEP data nor most achievement data provide evidence that the *value added* by either public or private schools for students from lower educated, lower-income homes is lower than that added for students from higher-educated, higher-income homes.

16. See Levin (1991b). Levin correctly points out that private schools produce a much narrower range of outputs than public schools, since they target a particular clientele with a particular product or products. Public schools must meet the needs of a full range of clients (as required by law). He also suggests that private schools, as a result, can reach efficient levels of production at smaller size.
17. Recent National Assessment of Educational Progress data (Mullis and others, 1991) show that the reading test score gains for blacks were reversed in 1990, especially for children who grew up in the 1980s. Greater poverty rates in the 1980s are probably the single most important explanation of the reversal.
18. See Hopkins and Massy (1981, p. 92) for a graphical analysis of the effect of intrinsic demand for outputs on the quantity and price of such outputs. Hopkins and Massy define an institutional value function, $V(X)$, which, when constrained by the institutional production and cost functions, yields the following equilibrium: Marginal Factor Cost ($MC$) = Dollar Value of Marginal Product ($MR$) + Effective Intrinsic Value of Marginal Product, Normalized to Dollar Terms ($V/u$).

    It is the second term ($V/u$) that represents the intrinsic

institutional demand for output *X* (in this case, achievement). In order not to confuse it with the voice function, already defined, I will refer to the intrinsic value function as *I*(*X*).

19. Chubb and Moe's study is on achievement gains in high school, where students' role in the demand function is more important, relative to parents' role, than at the primary level. The school's ability to motivate students to "demand" higher achievement must also be important. Coleman seems to think that private religious schools are particularly successful at achieving such higher demand for achievement among lower-income pupils.
20. See Ellwood (1988). In fact, gains for low-SES pupils have been relatively high since 1975, as measured both by NAEP and SAT results (see Smith and O'Day, 1991a). In the recent flurry over declining SAT verbal scores, for example, the longer-term trends (1975–1991) showed a 50 percent gain for blacks, a 25 percent gain for Latinos, and a 14 percent decline for whites. This is consistent with the gains on the NAEP language-skills test. Since a very high percentage of blacks and Latinos attend public schools, the data suggest that although the gap between whites (higher average SES) and minorities (lower average SES) is still large, it has closed significantly since the mid 1970s.
21. After two years of a statewide choice initiative in Minnesota, fewer than 500 students from over 700,000 in the public school systems participated in the choice process. This number does not include students who transferred to other school systems under interdistrict agreements predating open enrollment (13,000 students). Bennett also points out that no additional funding was provided to school districts to implement this program, nor was funding appropriated to the state to provide information to parents about the program. Therefore, many parents have not even received information about the program, and school districts do not do any marketing (Bennett, 1990, p. 146).
22. It is also likely that parents will insist on a state bureaucracy that would safeguard them against school fraud or low-quality private education. Private schools could well end up

with much more paperwork than many public schools now have if public monies were going for private school tuition.

23. Recent efforts establishing all-black male public schools in Minneapolis reflect an attempt by the black *community* to reach higher school achievement and resolve other problems among black male teenagers. This poses an interesting example of *local* public efforts to raise demand for improved education, as a response to the failure of state and national efforts to do so in a way that benefits that particular community. Local moves to raise demand for educational quality are perfectly consistent with the historical tradition of community schooling; but in this and many other cases, such efforts do conflict with the American integrative ideal. There is a social cost (externality) to such schools, even though no one in either the black or the white community may regard the cost as very high.

24. One possible solution to the limitation on individual school growth is the "franchising" of an effective private school model, much as in the case of chain stores or parochial schools. Thus, rather than expanding a school's size, corporations operating in different market niches could package effective school models for those niches. Again, however, since the product is highly teacher- and principal-dependent, one school may not be nearly as effective as another, even in the same chain. The secret of success would be a clearly defined "corporate" mission, such as in parochial schools, that unifies teachers and principals around common, well-delineated goals and enough teachers who would accept and could be trained into that mission and those goals.

It could be argued that the good schools could expand to take advantage of higher prices, yet there are certain limitations to such expansion in the education business. The very "goodness" of a school often depends on the principal of the school or on the close cooperation and mission orientation of the teachers, and expansion beyond a certain size can quickly reduce these two sources of effectiveness. In fact, the top independent private schools have hardly grown in the past generation, despite increased demand.

25. Levin (1991b) argues that vouchers would present incentives for product differentiation among schools, where schools would aim for particular market niches, attempting to distinguish themselves from other schools.
26. Poverty in the past two years has climbed sharply again and obliterated many of the gains of the mid 1980s, gains that still did not bring poverty down to the levels of the early 1970s.

## References

Apple, M. W. *Ideology and Curriculum.* New York: Routledge & Kegan Paul, 1979.

Archibald, D. A. "Magnet Schools, Voluntary Desegregation, and Public Choice Theory; Limits and Possibilities in a Big-City School System." Unpublished Ph.D. dissertation, School of Education, University of Wisconsin, Madison, 1988.

Bennett, D. "Choice and Desegregation." In W. H. Clune and J. F. Witte (eds.), *Choice and Control in American Education.* Vol. 2: *The Practice of Choice, Decentralization, and School Restructuring.* New York: Falmer Press, 1990.

Bowles, S., and Gintis, H. *Schooling in Capitalist America.* New York: Basic Books, 1975.

Carnoy, M. *Education as Cultural Imperialism.* White Plains, N.Y.: Longmans, 1974.

Carnoy, M., Daley, H. and Hinojosa, R. *Latinos in a Changing U.S. Economy.* New York: Puerto Rican Center, City University of New York, 1990.

Carnoy, M., and Levin, H. M. *Schooling and Work in the Democratic State.* Stanford, Calif.: Stanford University Press, 1985.

Chubb, J. E. "Political Institutions and School Organization." In W. H. Clune and J. F. Witte (eds.), *Choice and Control in American Education.* Vol. 1: *The Theory of Choice and Control in American Education.* New York: Falmer Press, 1990.

Chubb, J. E., and Moe, T. M. *Politics, Markets, and America's Schools.* Washington, D.C.: Brookings Institution, 1990.

Clune, W. H., and Witte, J. F. (eds.). *Choice and Control in American Education.* Vol. 2: *The Practice of Choice, Decentralization, and School Restructuring.* New York: Falmer Press, 1990.

Coleman, J. S. "Choice, Community, and Future Schools." In W. H. Clune and J. F. Witte (eds.), *Choice and Control in American Education.* Vol. 1: *The Theory of Choice and Control in American Education.* New York: Falmer Press, 1990.

Coons, J., and Sugarman, S. *Education by Choice: The Case for Family Control.* Berkeley: University of California Press, 1978.

Dewey, J. *Democracy and Education.* New York: Free Press, 1966.

Ellwood, D. T. *Poor Support.* New York: Basic Books, 1988.

Elmore, R. F. "Choice as an Instrument of Public Policy: Evidence from Education and Health Care." In W. H. Clune and J. F. Witte (eds.), *Choice and Control in American Education.* Vol. 1: *The Theory of Choice and Control in American Education.* New York: Falmer Press, 1990.

Friedman, M. "The Role of Government in Education." In R. A. Solo (ed.), *Economics and the Public Interest.* New Brunswick, N.J.: Rutgers University Press, 1955.

Friedman, M. *Capitalism and Freedom.* Chicago: University of Chicago Press, 1962.

Gertler, P., and Glewwe, P. *The Willingness to Pay for Education in Developing Countries: Evidence from Rural Peru.* World Bank Living Standards Measurement Study, Working Paper no. 54. Washington, D.C.: World Bank, 1989.

Glewwe, P., and Jacoby, H. *Estimating the Determinants of Cognitive Achievement in Low Income Countries: The Case of Ghana.* Washington, D.C.: World Bank, 1991 (mimeographed).

Goodman, P. *Growing Up Absurd.* New York: Random House, 1956.

Hansen, L., and Weisbrod, B. *Benefits, Costs, and Finance of Higher Education.* New York: Markham, 1969.

Hirschman, A. O. *Exit, Voice, and Loyalty: Responses to Decline in Firms, Organizations, and States.* Cambridge, Mass.: Harvard University Press, 1970.

Hopkins, D., and Massy, W. *Planning Models for Colleges and Universities.* Stanford, Calif.: Stanford University Press, 1981.

Johnson, S. M. "Teachers, Power and School Change." In W. H. Clune and J. F. Witte (eds.), *Choice and Control in American Education.* Vol. 2: *The Practice of Choice, Decentralization, and School Restructuring.* New York: Falmer Press, 1990.

Kozol, J. *Death at an Early Age.* Boston: Houghton Mifflin, 1967.

Lachman, S. P., and Kosmin, B. "Black Catholics Get Ahead." *New York Times,* Sept. 14, 1991, p. 15.

Levin, H. M. "Improving Productivity Through Education and Technology." In G. Burke and R. Rumberger (eds.), *The Future Impact of Technology on Work and Education.* New York: Falmer Press, 1987.

Levin, H. M. "The Theory of Choice Applied to Education." In W. H. Clune and J. F. Witte (eds.), *Choice and Control in American Education.* Vol. 1: *The Theory of Choice and Control in American Education.* New York: Falmer Press, 1990.

Levin, H. M. *Building School Capacity for Effective Teacher Empowerment: Applications to Elementary Schools with At-Risk Students.* New Brunswick, N.J.: Center for Policy Research in Education, Rutgers University, 1991a.

Levin, H. M. "The Economics of Educational Choice." *Economics of Education Review,* 1991b, *10*(2), 137–158.

Mullis, I.V.V., and others. *Trends in Academic Progress: Achievement of U.S. Students, in Science, 1969–70 to 1990; Mathematics, 1973–1990; Reading, 1971–1990; and Writing, 1984–1990.* Report no. 21-T-01, prepared by the Educational Testing Service for the National Center for Education Statistics, U.S. Department of Education. Washington, D.C.: U.S. Government Printing Office, 1991.

Peterson, P. "Monopoly and Competition in American Education." In W. H. Clune and J. F. Witte (eds.), *Choice and Control in American Education.* Vol. 1: *The Theory of Choice and Control in American Education.* New York: Falmer Press, 1990.

Schorr, L. *Within Our Reach.* New York: Doubleday, 1988.

Sennett, R., and Cobb, J. *The Hidden Injuries of Class.* New York: Vintage Books, 1973.

Shanker, A. "What's the Real Score?" *New York Times,* Sept. 8, 1991, p. E7.

Smith, M. S., and O'Day, J. "Educational Equality: 1966 and Now." In D. Verstegen (ed.), *Spheres of Justice in American Schools.* New York: HarperCollins, 1991a

Smith, M. S., and O'Day, J. "Systemic School Reform." In S. Fuhrman and B. Malen (eds.) *The Politics of Curriculum and Testing*. New York: Falmer Press, 1991b.

Smreker, C. "Building Community: The Influence of School Organization on Family-School Interactions." Unpublished Ph.D. dissertation, School of Education, Stanford University, 1991.

Weisbrod, B. *External Benefits of Education: An Economic Analysis*. Research report no. 105. Princeton, N.J.: Industrial Relations Section, Department of Economics, Princeton University, 1964.

Weiss, J. "Control in School Organizations: Theoretical Perspectives." In W. H. Clune and J. F. Witte (eds.), *Choice and Control in American Education*. Vol. 1: *The Theory of Choice and Control in American Education*. New York: Falmer Press, 1990.

Witte, J. "Choice and Control: An Analytical Overview." In W. H. Clune and J. F. Witte (eds.), *Choice and Control in American Education*. Vol. 2: *The Practice of Choice, Decentralization, and School Restructuring*. New York: Falmer Press, 1990.

Witte, J. *Market Versus State-Centered Approaches to American Education: Does Either Make Much Sense?* Madison: Department of Political Science, University of Wisconsin, 1991.

# 8

# Employee Involvement in Industrial Decision Making: Lessons for Public Schools

**Clair Brown**

During the past two decades, productivity growth has slowed in the United States, while the productivity of our trading partners has continued to climb. As a result, Americans have experienced a relative decline in their standard of living. During this time, schoolchildren in the United States have lost ground in certain test scores to schoolchildren in other industrialized countries (Inkeles, 1977; Rothman, 1987; Walberg, 1983; Commission on the Skills of the American Workforce, 1990). These two trends have inspired educators and managers in the United States to search for ways to improve both the educational process and the work process, in order to improve educational performance and firm performance.

One idea that has been reconsidered by educators and managers alike is that of *employee involvement* (*EI*) in the decision-making process. This form of decentralization is not new, but in the past its application has largely been confined to managerial employees. Extending employee involvement in decision making to nonmanagerial employees has become popularized as part of the highly touted Japanese management system (Hashimoto, 1990;

*Note:* This chapter grew out of a joint research project with Michael Reich and David Stern. Our project has been supported by the Institute of Industrial Relations at the University of California, Berkeley; the U.S. Department of Labor, Bureau of Labor-Management Relations; the National Center for Research in Vocational Education at the University of California, Berkeley; and the Pacific Rim Foundation at the University of California, Berkeley. This chapter does not necessarily reflect the position of the sponsoring agencies.

Koike, 1988; Organisation for Economic Co-operation and Development, 1990).

This chapter addresses the following question: In what ways has decentralization been used in the private sector to improve the efficiency of decision making and increase the quality of labor input by drawing on employees' knowledge, and what can the public schools learn from these experiences?

The chapter organization is as follows. The first section develops a conceptual framework for analyzing decentralization. This is followed by a section discussing company practices in general. Then case studies of three companies in different sectors are presented. The three companies include a unionized manufacturing company (Company MU), a nonunionized manufacturing company (Company MN), and a unionized service company (Company SU). By contrast to the practices observed in U.S. companies, the role of employee involvement in the Japanese management system (JS) is discussed. The chapter concludes by asking what the policy implications of these experiences are for the public schools (PS).[1]

## Conceptual Framework

This chapter draws selectively on the large literature about organizational decision making, in order to construct a simple framework for comparing the processes of employee involvement in industry and education. The central issue of decentralization is whether managers should make decisions after collecting information from employees or whether employees should make those decisions themselves. The economist's conceptual framework identifies and compares the alternative decision-making processes with the attendant costs and returns.

Here, employee involvement is seen as a form of decentralized decision making undertaken by employees in nonmanagerial ranks. The EI process can be viewed as a subset of the larger organizational control process. The broader issue of decentralizing decision making among various levels of management will not be addressed here, however. In general, the literature has been concerned with the application of decentralization to managerial employees only. Extending the process to nonmanagerial employees affects the analysis in important ways and includes legal and other institutional constraints.[2]

Most economic models of organizational decision making emphasize the costs associated with collecting, transmitting, and assimilating information and the costs associated with coordinating various divisions (monitoring and transaction costs), the costs associated with divergence in the goals of the organizations and those of the employees involved in decision making (agency costs), and the difficulties involved in measuring outcomes resulting from the decisions made (moral hazards) (Anandalingam, Chatterjee, and Gangolly, 1987; Arrow, 1964; Clarke and Barrough, 1983; De Groot, 1988; Lazear, 1991; Williamson, 1985). Sociological theories of bureaucracy make an important contribution by delineating the unintended consequences associated with different control techniques.[3] These occur whenever the control mechanism affects the institutions (that is, rules and customs) that structure behavior within the organization.

Decentralization, then, includes these identifiable (although perhaps not measurable) costs and benefits, as well as the possible unknown risks of unintended consequences. Theoretically, an incentive structure exists for optimal decentralized decision making, or for the revealed knowledge required for centralized decision making. The costs associated with monitoring or gathering information usually make such an incentive scheme impractical, however. In addition, the agency costs associated with the discrepancy between the objectives of the organization and those of the employees are often unknown because of the problem of unintended consequences.

For an organization to know which decisions should be delegated to nonmanagerial employees, it needs information about the following areas.

### *The Objective or Production Function*

It is assumed that the goals or outcomes can be measured (the monitoring system) and that the system of control (usually either a system of performance-based compensation or a system of rules regulating procedures or outcomes) is well defined. It is further assumed that the impact of the decentralized decisions on the objectives, as well as the impact of the new system on behavior within the system (including unintended consequences), is known.

### *Information System*

It is assumed that the value of the employees' knowledge, and the transaction costs associated with acquiring, disseminating, and processing this information, are known. Specifically, we must know what type information is needed for what types of decisions.

### *The Decision-Making Structure*

The primary factor here is the presence or absence of a union. In a unionized organization, a cooperative union-management relationship at the centralized level is a necessary but not sufficient step in implementing decentralized decision making, which includes union-management cooperation at the site or shop-floor level. Whether the union-management relationship is adversarial or cooperative affects the decisions made, as well as the costs of decision making. In the absence of a union, the decentralization process lacks an important mechanism for gathering employees' input, voicing discontent, and ensuring trust in employers' commitments. The managers of a nonunion work force must find alternative ways to gather information, process grievances, and negotiate commitments.

Neither of the first two items is usually well known in the real world, and all three items involve a complex relationship of important underlying structural variables. The overall impact of decentralizing decision making depends in crucial ways on the objective function, the information system, and the decision-making structure, and so this triad is used to analyze decentralization in private organizations and to compare private organizations to public schools.

Decentralization in decision making is a complex economic and managerial process, and there are no simple rules for what decisions should be decentralized under what conditions. Enough experience has been gathered, however, to allow us to make some crude generalizations about the process and prospects of decentralizing decision making.

## Company Practices

Since employees have always been involved in decision making to some extent, we are concerned here with the innovations in employment systems that increase employees' input into decision making. In general, we can categorize three specific types of employee involvement: *traditional,* which includes the types of decisions traditionally made by employees in unionized firms; *innovative,* which includes the types of decisions made by employees when companies increase employee involvement on the shop floor; and *advanced,* which includes employee involvement in strategic decision-making and personnel activities. Operationally, these three types of decision-making categories can be described as follows:

*Traditional*

1. Solving routine (recurring) problems
2. Involvement in scheduling vacations, shifts, work assignments, and transfers (usually by seniority)
3. Resolving conflict among co-workers
4. Processing grievances against management for contract violations
5. Training co-workers

*Innovative*

6. Solving nonroutine problems
7. Suggesting improvements in the work or production processes
8. Suggesting improvements in the service or product
9. Involvement in the design and assignment of work
10. Monitoring one's own work

*Advanced*

11. Evaluating performance of co-workers
12. Selecting leaders or supervisors
13. Working without supervision
14. Involvement in strategic planning of output, investment, and budgeting

Each category builds on the previous category, so that a company introducing innovative EI will be adding activities 6–10 to activities 1–5.

Workers and their unions sometimes participate in nonproductive types of "decision making," such as absenteeism, nuisance grievances against an unpopular supervisor, and rigid enforcement of detailed job classifications. This behavior is matched by similar types of adversarial behavior on the part of supervisors, such as rigid enforcement of break procedures and policies regulating shop-floor behavior. In practice, decentralization of policy making often means changing the type of employee involvement at the shop-floor level, so that workers and supervisors work cooperatively to reach production and quality goals. These innovative EI activities require a basis of trust and a sense of shared interests between employees and employers.

In manufacturing, for example, the expansion from traditional EI to innovative EI for production workers often begins in an atmosphere where feedback is viewed by foremen as obstructionism and where working informally outside narrow job descriptions is viewed by union shop stewards as rate busting. Although there are exceptions to these stereotypical descriptions, workers generally believe that their input is not wanted (and may be punished), the union believes that strict work rules are required to constrain arbitrary (and undesirable) management actions, and managers believe that they have to protect their decision-making prerogatives in order to ensure control over production.

To implement innovative EI requires the company and the union to build an industrial relations structure that increases the trust between management and worker on the shop floor and between union and company at the bargaining table, and that enlarges the area of shared interests between these parties. Traditionally, the union has short-run power over production standards, job assignment, and layoff procedures, but it has no long-run power over size of the labor force, location of plants, automation, or any other strategic decisions. The company has little short-run control over who does what job, although it controls the size of the labor force through short-run layoffs. The company controls its long-run investments, and its ultimate power rests in its ability to determine plant locations and the size of its domestic work force.

In order to implement innovative EI, the company needs to share more of its long-run power with the union and the workers, in exchange for greater short-run power over production standards, use of the work force, and involvement of workers in making quality and productivity improvements. Even though the workers' long-run economic interests may lie in the financial success of their company, the traditional industrial relations structure prevents their trading the short-run benefits associated with exercising shop-floor power for the long-run benefits associated with guaranteed sharing in the company's success. With an excess of short-run power for the union and an excess of long-run power for the company, the area of shared interests is small indeed.

The innovations that companies desire involve having the union accept fewer job classifications with flexible assignment (that is, having the union give up control over job assignment) and encouraging workers' input into daily decision making (balancing of work loads, solving problems, suggesting improvements). In return, companies usually make a commitment to employment security. The issue that arises from a policy of job security, however, is the company's need to ensure that workers remain motivated once they have secure jobs. Motivation, which is a form of agency cost, is a problem under the alternative employment system, which does not have employment security but has seniority-based layoffs and transfers.

Since job titles do not usually change as workers become more involved in making suggestions and solving problems, workers usually are not paid for these skills except through an awards program and the commitment to job security. Long-run job security usually provides the motivation, as well as the reward, for employee involvement. Although the goals of the company, the union, and the workers do not change, the structure of power within which they function does change, and the area of shared interests is enlarged. Conflict has not been eradicated, since employees and the company still have areas of divergent interests. With more information exchanged, however, and with the shared goal of short-run improvements to ensure long-run success (without bargaining tit-for-tat), outcomes that might not ever have been considered previously can now be negotiated, to make both sides better off than under adversarial bargaining. Successful implementation of cooperative union-management relations will lower transaction and agency costs.

## Case Study: Company MU

Company MU is a unionized manufacturing company that has successfully implemented innovative EI for production workers. For this reason, a detailed description of the employment system at MU is useful. Production workers are formed into teams and are involved in daily decision making on the job through the process of standardizing work, which forms the basis for making improvements, problem solving, and ensuring that work is done safely and efficiently. The workers are also involved by inspecting their own work ("pass on no defects") and by participating in the voluntary suggestion program.

In the early stages of production, workers spent months standardizing work. Today, new hires receive one week of training in standardized work.[4] Analysis of jobs (basically performing time-and-motion studies) is done by the production workers themselves, although they can ask for help from industrial engineers (IEs). Workers break each job down into its component parts (including hand work, walking time, and machine time), with location and the time required (in seconds) for each part of each job to be completed in the allowed cycle time. Standardized work as it is applied at Company MU differs from Taylorism in that production workers are involved in both the conception and the execution of work. Company MU has at least partially replaced IEs with EI.

During the changeover to a new product model, the process of standardizing work and assigning it to teams had to be accomplished again. An assembly pilot team, which included both management and production workers, designed the line after "target times" were established by production control. The pilot team spent a year working on the changeover. During group meetings, team members reviewed new parts and equipment and safety. They reviewed pilot products in the pilot room, reviewed job-process sheets, and set up racks and equipment on the assembly line, where they tried out operations, checked ease of assembly, and made improvements.

Even so, the transition on the floor was a bumpy one, and many changes in allocation of work had to be made. For example, among the seven teams in one department, three had to redistribute work. They needed to add more members and to reallocate work within the group, but these problems were solved by the teams on the shop floor, instead of through the filing of product-standards grievances, which is the way the problems would have been handled before.

### *Suggestion Program*

In a formal suggestion program, employees can make suggestions either individually or with others, and these suggestions are reviewed and assigned points by the group leader, which are translated into merchandise certificates (valued at one dollar per point earned) for those making the suggestions. The number of points awarded depends on the costs and labor hours saved (on a monthly basis), with points added for improvements in safety, in the environment, and in quality. Most suggestions are awarded less than $100.

Some major cost savings have been realized through suggestions. For example, one suggestion on how to redesign the conveyor chain to reduce its breaking resulted in an annual savings of $80,298 and 1,429 labor hours. The suggestion was given 2,612 points, to be shared by the three team members (653 points each) and the group leader (326.5 points) making the suggestion. Other suggestions have included decreasing the shipping rack size (3,330 points; $251,424 saved), using sealant remnants (1,103 points; $35,124 saved, plus environmental improvement), and using a regulator on the paint line (2,018 points; $62,760 and 48 hours saved, plus quality and environmental improvement).

The number of suggestions has grown rapidly since implementation of the program in 1986. In 1987, 5,225 suggestions were made. In 1988, 10,671 suggestions were made by 71 percent of the employees, which exceeded the participation goal of 60 percent.

The average value of points awarded for implemented suggestions was 18.89.[5] Three out of four suggestions have been adopted. Over the twelve-month period from June 1987 through May 1988, suggestions were made that would save the company more than $1.2 million yearly.

### *Problem Solving*

Both individually and within teams, Company MU workers are expected to solve problems occurring on the job. A formal six-step problem-solving procedure is taught to all workers. The steps are to identify and select the problem and set the goal, to analyze the problem, to generate potential solutions, to select and plan the solution, to implement the solution, and to evaluate the solution. For most problems, however, workers apply a simpler approach: asking *why,* until one goes from the observed problem to the root cause. As one worker said, "We're not engineers, so we just look at the next step, rather than the whole problem."

### *Continuous Improvement*

The culture of making small but continuous improvements drives suggestion and problem-solving activities. Improvements cover all aspects of the production process, including efficiency, costs, safety, quality, and communications. The preconditions for improvements are trouble-free machines, tools, and parts; standardized work procedures; and good record keeping. These preconditions provide a functional baseline from which to make improvements. On the shop floor, improvements usually involve small changes in layout or in operation methods, and workers use their job knowledge to make improvements. As one worker said, "Every job has a secret shortcut or formula."

Numerous examples exist of how teams here have reorganized their work stations to eliminate some walking or other wasted motion. One supply team reorganized its system of supplying gloves to the workers. Instead of teams' sending a member to pick up gloves, a drop-off and pick-up system was instituted. This system decreased walking time. It also improved the planning and ordering of gloves so that more recycled gloves could be used, which reduced costs.

### *The Stop Cord*

Many small problems are solved daily, often by a worker's pulling the stop cord to get help. All workers are told that they have a duty as well as a right to pull the stop cord to fix a defect or solve a quality or safety problem. If the problem is solved before the cycle time is up, as is usually the case, the cord is pulled again, and the line is not stopped. Otherwise, the line stops at the end of that cycle time.

The stop cord allows problems to be solved on the shop floor as they occur. This procedure has replaced the earlier practice of letting problems pile up as grievances, until sometimes work stoppages occurred over production standards or safety. The stop cord also helps identify areas where job assignments may be unrealistic and where work may need to be redistributed, or where machinery or the production process may have problems that need to be corrected. Workers distinguish between making emergency repairs to equipment and making more extensive repairs to prevent the recurrence of problems.

### *Strategic Decision Making*

The company makes decisions about products, manufacturing methods, line speed, outsourcing, standards of conduct, and personnel decisions. The company is obligated by contract to inform the union about changes in top management; about company objectives (yearly), business plans (semiannually), and production schedules (quarterly); about major organizational changes; about long-range plans; about contemplated insourcing or outsourcing; and about technological changes. In practice, this means that management consults in advance with the union on production schedule changes, major investments, and possible layoffs. The company unilaterally decides the level of manpower and line speed.

The union's goal is to be more involved in decision making at every step of the way. As a union leader said, "We can't depend on management to always make the right decisions. Our people's jobs are on the line."

Overall, Company MU has expanded employee involvement in decision making to include both traditional and innovative activities (see Table 8.1). The union's role in advanced EI has been limited to one area; the selection of team leaders. Of the three case studies discussed here, Company MU has implemented the greatest degree of EI in decision making, both on the shop floor and at the centralized union-management level.

## Case Study: Company MN

Company MN is a large nonunion manufacturing company that has successfully introduced innovative EI at its new plants. The transition at the older plants has taken longer and encountered more problems.

In the mid 1980s, Company MN began a program for improving quality and productivity. Its new plants, with highly au-

**Table 8.1. Types of Employee Involvement in Decision Making.**

| | *MU* | *MN* | *SU* | *JS* | *PS* |
|---|---|---|---|---|---|
| Traditional | | | | | |
| 1. Solving routine problems | X | X | X | X | X |
| 2. Scheduling and transfers | X | — | X | — | X |
| 3. Resolving conflict among co-workers | X | — | X | X | X |
| 4. Processing grievances | X | — | X | X | X |
| 5. Training co-workers | X | X | X | X | X |
| Innovative | | | | | |
| 6. Solving nonroutine problems | X | X | X | X | X |
| 7. Improving work design | X | X | — | X | X |
| 8. Suggesting product improvements | X | X | — | X | X |
| 9. Design and assignment of work | X | — | — | X | X |
| 10. Monitoring own work | X | X | — | X | X |
| Advanced | | | | | |
| 11. Evaluating co-workers' performance | — | — | — | — | X |
| 12. Selection of leaders and supervisors | X | — | — | — | — |
| 13. Working without supervision | — | — | — | — | — |
| 14. Strategic planning | — | — | — | — | X |

tomated equipment, were the first to move to the innovative system, where employees work in teams, solve problems, cross-train for multiple job functions, receive pay for skill, inspect and correct their own work, and make suggestions for improvements. Jobs are rotated, usually on a weekly or monthly basis. Job assignments are made by supervisors according to production needs. Company MN workers have been told that eventually all workers, even those who do not change jobs, will be involved in teamwork and problem solving and that this arrangement will require basic math and English skills, teamwork skills, problem-solving skills, and cross-training.

The company has focused on goals of quality and cycle time to measure improvements as work is redesigned. Quality problems result in large numbers of expensive production-in-process becoming scrap and in dissatisfied customers if defective products are shipped. Cycle time indicates the efficiency of the production process, and it affects inventory costs. Cycle time also affects quality, since semifinished parts are often damaged or deteriorate while stacked up waiting for the next stage in the production process.

Workers can stop the line if three defects in a row are found. This usually happens when a new product is introduced, which is also when most of the problem solving occurs. New products are introduced often, since orders change frequently and the life cycle of products is short. After production of a new product is running smoothly, the production line looks similar to a traditional line, since work is seldom disrupted, and high-volume output is emphasized.

A manager emphasized that improvements in the production process are probably more important than innovations in the human resource system. At one factory, the new technology uses one-third as many parts as the old technology, and a dedicated manufacturing line with a pull system is used. Under a pull system, a work station does not begin to work on a new batch until the next work station signals that it is ready to receive another batch for processing. Since a pull system prevents partially built units from piling up, inventory is kept to a minimum, and problems in the production process are easily spotted as workers become idle. A pull line is often used in the absence of a machine-paced line to simulate an assembly line with a stop cord: the pull system forces workers to maintain the same pace in the absence of a machine-paced line; a pull line is similar to a machine-paced assembly line with a stop cord, since the stop cord idles workers until a problem is solved.

As Company MN has introduced innovative EI, it has also introduced an elaborate system of pay for skill and merit to motivate production workers. Pay for skill has six regular grades (entry level plus five upgrades). The difference in pay between skill levels is approximately 6 percent. Each job has its own point value, and a worker collects points after working on a job with zero defects for five days, as certified by the supervisor. Job assignment is an important part of the certification process, and this is controlled by the supervisor, who assign, trains, and certifies workers. One problem is that workers may be certified to do many jobs but may have only infrequent opportunities to do some of those jobs. Moreover, many workers do not have the opportunity for certification on some of the more popular tasks, such as working with programmable equipment. Each worker is given an annual minimum certification opportunity equivalent to two skill levels. In addition to being upgraded, workers can be downgraded because of inability or because a job has been changed or removed from the process. Workers who refuse to complete certification opportunities or who refuse to attempt certification can be terminated. This is seldom if ever a problem. From the company's viewpoint, the problem is that most workers become certified for the highest level within three or four years, and the company then has high labor costs, and workers face a plateau.

The performance review weighs perfect attendance heavily and relies on the supervisors' subjective evaluation of workers' behavior regarding assignments, extra effort, voluntary overtime, contributions to problem solving, and sharing of job knowledge with other workers. A worker's performance rating can move up or down with each evaluation. Contributions and problem solving measure the worker's effort to contribute to team problem solving and process improvement. Standard performance includes contributing ideas for problem solving, when the ideas do not end up as workable final solutions. Merit level 1 includes contributing ideas or suggestions that can be implemented directly (or with slight modifications by management.) Merit level 2 includes providing workable solutions and sharing experience with other workers, such as informal training of new operators or passing on tricks of the trade.

The company has a profit-sharing program in addition to the regular wage schedule at its U.S. plants. The profit-sharing (or bonus) program supposedly rewards employees for working in teams and participating with management in solving problems and improving the process, but few workers connect the bonus to changes in the employment system and in work design. The bonus program has generated controversy and some discontent, especially among workers who receive small bonuses. Needless to say, workers at the newer plants, where output is growing rapidly and bonuses tend to be high, favor the bonus plan, which has accounted for 20 to 35 percent of their pay for the past two years. Workers at the older, traditional plants, where bonuses tend to be low, perceive that their efforts are not rewarded and that they can do little to increase their bonuses, which they see as depending on the product market and on the state of technology used. Since the bonus program was supposed to have been carefully designed to overcome these problems, Company MN's experience points out the difficulties with any type of program that rewards workers differently within plants or across plants.

Introducing innovative EI in plants using old technology with redesigned work has been more difficult than transitions in factories with new technology. The basis of the problem seems to be that the production process using the old technology has inherent flaws that cannot easily be corrected by workers. For example, workers end up using defective parts, trying to find parts when they run out, and building products with outdated design instructions. Product design changes are often made without the workers' knowledge. Many tasks in the traditional factory eventually will be automated, but they have to be done by hand until then.

As the design of automated machines has improved, the skills needed by operators have declined. Earlier, technicians had to do more with the machines in setting them up for a job, and mistakes would occur in checking machine readings with levels allowed in the directions. The setup was not done correctly 60 percent of the time. Now diagnostics are checked, and troubleshooting is done internally by the machines. Production workers can operate the machines. Workers like these smart machines, since the internal setup takes away the need for judgment. They can produce more with fewer mistakes, and their jobs are less stressful. Operators can focus on goals of quality and cycle time. The former setup technicians now do preventive maintenance and design ways to improve the machines so that they are easier to support.

Since MN in not unionized, this company had less employee involvement in decision making before its efforts to increase EI (see column MN of Table 8.1). Workers solved routine problems and were involved in training co-workers, both formally and informally. In the absence of a union, supervisors were in charge of scheduling and transfers; they used a system to record employees' preferences, including posting and bidding for transfers. Without a union, workers had no mechanism for being involved in resolving conflicts and handling grievances.

When Company MN implemented innovative EI, workers became more involved in solving problems, making suggestions, and monitoring quality. Management continues to control the design and assignment of work and training, however. Workers are not involved in the standardization, equalization, and assignment of work or in the design of training as at Company MU.

### Case Study: Company SU

This company's centralized union-management cooperation was not extended to site-level employee involvement. In addition, the company eventually reduced its employee involvement at the centralized union-management level.

Company SU has focused more on downsizing the work force as new technology has been introduced than on implementing teams and employee involvement in problem solving. With surplus workers, a regulated pricing structure whereby costs could be recouped, and a commitment to employment security, the emphasis was on how to entice workers to quit or transfer to customer-contact jobs.

Company SU was able to accomplish this decrease in the size of the work force without disruption because it enlisted the help of the union in planning and implementing voluntary reductions through the use of union-management committees (UMCs). This is an example of the effective use of a joint committee to help a company through a major transition. Let us look in more detail at how the UMC system worked.

A memorandum of agreement attached to the 1986 contract empowered the UMCs "to enter into agreements, modify work rules, and resolve and/or make recommendations on issues of mutual concern" in the following areas (when the management and union members of the UMC could not agree, the contract prevailed):

- Employment security (including changes in the work force, adjustments, and reassignments as necessary to ensure employment security)
- Contract work (including review of all new significant contract proposals, review of all existing contracts having major work-force implications, the making of recommendations, and the discovery of creative ways to resolve contracting issues)
- Issue resolution (including informal resolution of problems)
- Flexible working arrangements
- Business partnerships
- New ventures

The fifteen UMCs were composed of company vice presidents and union local presidents.

The flexible and broad language opened the way for the UMCs to formulate various types of policies that would modify the contract in practice. Because of the number of committees, different types of practices could arise. Both the scope and the number of committees undercut the power of the human relations managers and the district union representatives, who had traditionally been the primary negotiators and administrators of the contract. In interviews, both sides cited incidents in which the UMCs devised new policies that were against existing company policy or inconsistent with the contract and that had to be modified or rescinded. These traditional keepers of the industrial relations system saw their role as having been changed from that of "primary instigators" to "clean-up crew." They believed that the role of the UMCs needed to be clarified and that the UMCs needed to work within a structure that prevented duplicate or competing policies from arising. By contrast, the vice presidents and local union presidents participating in the UMCs were generally pleased with the process of the committees and with what had been accomplished. This is not too surprising, since their power and status had been increased by the UMCs.

Over time, the UMCs became focused primarily on the employee surplus problem, and they developed their own plans for dealing with the surplus that replaced the work-force movement process in the contract. The 1986 contract included an employment security clause, which was conditional on no change materially altering achievement of the business plan and which required employees to meet performance standards and accept reassignment, retraining, and relocation. During the life of the contract, the company declared only one formal surplus with mandatory reassignment, which affected approximately fifty people. In practice, relocation of workers to new jobs or new sites was done only on a voluntary basis. This appeared to be the price paid by the company to engage the union's help in downsizing.

In general, local union presidents thought that the UMCs had done a good job of dealing with the problem of surplus while protecting members' rights and minimizing disruption to workers' lives. The union realized that the old "womb to tomb" philosophy of job security had to be modified, but it wanted to find a way other than displacing people. Even with the reduction in work force that was accomplished, management became dissatisfied with its inability to force surplus employees to relocate or change jobs. The company wanted to take away employment security; the district union wanted to take away the UMCs and emphasize training.

In the 1989 contract, new language indicated lowered expectations for the joint union-management efforts, and the number of UMCs, as well as their role, was reduced. For example, to a clause stating that the two sides would "endeavor to mutually plan and evaluate proposed actions" was added the condition "while management maintains the right and responsibility to make decisions." As another example, the language stating that when the union representative identified an issue or dispute, he or she would work with the manager "to jointly resolve the problem" was changed to "an effort should be made by both parties to resolve the problem." As still another example, language stating that "communication to the employees will be conducted jointly" with respect to operational changes was changed to "Where agreement is reached, communication to the employees will be conducted jointly." The broad language empowering the UMCs in 1986 was replaced by language constraining them to "service, productivity, and quality improvements and problem resolution involving operation issues." UMCs are restricted from any agreements that would modify the contract or company policy, and they cannot adjust or resolve grievances or administer the work-force qualification and movement process. Shortly after the contract's ratification, which had followed tough negotiations and a short strike, the union withdrew from participation in the UMCs.

Cooperation seemed to have outlived its usefulness for downsizing, and Company SU now wants to implement quality-improvement teams without active union involvement. These voluntary quality teams, some of which have been in existence for several years, would focus on quality improvements in their own work groups. Future company goals include linking compensation plans to individual, team, and company performance. Company SU already had a team award (4.5 percent of pay for production workers in 1990 and 5.0 percent in 1991), given if Company SU meets its net income and service goals. If the goals are exceeded, the award can be as much as 30 percent higher. If goals are not met, the award can be as low as zero.

Overall, Company SU has not moved much beyond the traditional types of EI. Some office workers have become more involved in nonroutine problem solving as a result of the computerization of their jobs; other craft workers had traditionally engaged in nonroutine problem solving as part of their jobs; still other entry-level workers view their jobs as requiring less problem solving as the jobs become more computerized.

The impact of the changes in Company SU's handling of job movements and reductions, which now are being carried out without the involvement of the union, remains to be seen. One sign of union resistance and of declining employee morale can already be perceived in the sharply increased grievance rate. Company SU serves as an example of a company that returned to an adversarial approach after a cooperative period, a company that intends to turn to employee involvement without union participation.

## The Japanese Management Style

Let us now look at the extent of EI in the Japanese management system. These observations are only general, since Japanese companies, like U.S. companies, vary widely in their practices. Overall, nonmanagerial employees in large Japanese companies, who are represented by enterprise unions, engage in traditional and innovative EI activities but do not engage in advanced EI. In contrast to the situation in the United States, one traditional EI activity is controlled by management: the scheduling and assigning of work (see column JS of Table 8.1). Although supervisors typically ask workers their preferences for work assignments, management sees the final decision as its own. We were told that managers often know better than the workers what job assignments will be best for them. Since job assignment and transfer appear to be crucial parts of the training process (Koike and Inoki, 1990), Japanese managers want to control job assignment in order to control training.

The other two areas of scheduling—vacations and shifts—are also performed differently in Japanese and unionized U.S. companies. Japanese workers often do not take personal holidays (that is, paid vacation days outside of national holidays), and the granting of such days seems to be on a personal basis. Since workers usually rotate shifts, there is no assignment of workers to different shifts.

Large Japanese companies provide employment security, and they motivate workers by basing pay and promotion on performance evaluations, as well as on tenure. Employees and their enterprise unions do not participate in performance evaluations, which are usually made once or twice yearly by immediate supervisors and the next level of management. These evaluations are often kept secret from employees, who know only their job classifications, grades, and monthly pay. In rare instances, the union will ask that a worker be reevaluated.

In general, Japanese companies seem less interested than their U.S. counterparts in the direct monitoring of individual output. Evaluations depend more on such subjective factors as perceptions of attitude and leadership ability. More objective criteria, such as skills and suggestions, are also included. This type of evaluation process is in keeping with the use of promotions to train workers to take on more skilled work and more responsibility. The same process eventually promotes some workers into management positions. One important characteristic of the Japanese performance-based pay system is that nonmanagerial workers cannot be downgraded. Workers can be transferred to another plant or even to another company during a downturn, however, and these decisions are made by management. Managerial employees can be downgraded after a certain age, in addition to being retired early or being transferred to another company.

EI in the Japanese management system is distinguished from its use in U.S. companies in one important way: in Japan, EI is mandatory. Workers must participate in quality-circle activities (termed "voluntary mandatory" activities), and they are required to make suggestions. The suggestion program is integrated into the work process, so that many of the suggestions reflect actions already taken by teams or quality circles. The suggestion program generates a large number of suggestions per employee per year, and few suggestions are rejected.

## Policy Implications

Do companies implementing innovative EI tend to fulfill the three criteria presented in the conceptual framework?[6] In general, the companies can monitor output and quality at a low marginal cost, since this information is automatically collected by the information technology that controls the production process. The system of control is less well defined, however. Pay for performance is not found in nonmanagerial jobs except in one nonunion company. Instead, companies rely on systems of rules, whose workings are often not well understood. Because of the large number of intervening variables (such as changes in orders, personnel, and product design), the relationship between the impact of decentralized decisions and measured outcomes is difficult to isolate. Even with pay for performance, pay is tied to potential more than to actual performance, so that the impact of decisions on outcomes is not clearly established. In addition, management often seems unable to predict consequences of the system for such variables as morale and attitudes toward supervisors.

Decentralized decision making clearly increases the input of employees' knowledge. The transaction costs associated with the collection and processing of workers' knowledge appear to be less than the gains from innovative EI. In general, the transaction costs are minimal when part of the information process is embedded in the production process (for example, team activities and job rotation). Some of the information process is formal, however (for example, team meetings), and so has a direct cost.

Agency costs increase with decentralization, and so monitoring and control costs also exist; these have a direct component (for example, awards for suggestions) and an indirect component (for example, supervision). In a unionized setting, the difference between the net increase in information or transaction costs and the net increase in agency costs depends to a large extent on the union-management relationship at the local level, which is influenced by the relationship at the central level. A cooperative union-management relationship at the plant level will greatly reduce agency costs. Union-management cooperation at the central level seems to be a necessary but not sufficient condition for such cooperation at the local level, in the long run. Innovative EI cannot be implemented without prior implementation of a cooperative union-management structure at both the central and the local levels.

Cooperation is often the product of adversity. This should not surprise us, since changing the structure of decision making in conditions of imperfect information implies taking risks. Both the union and management appear risk-averse; the two sides often experiment with innovations only when faced with a structure that is no longer economically viable. The fact that such changes are made during a period of economic crisis does not necessarily mean that they benefit management and harm the union or workers.

A cooperative relationship is often attempted by the union

and management, independently of the goal of increasing employee involvement on the shop floor. Cooperation is tried if the parties believe that cooperation will lower the net transaction costs of bargaining, without changing the size and division of the pie. Such a windfall gain, including possible increase in the size of the pie, can be split between the parties through negotiation, so that both sides gain (Fisher and Brown, 1988).

## Lessons for Public Schools

Let us now turn to the central question of this chapter: What are the similarities and differences between decentralization of decision making in public schools and in the private sector? Let us first consider the objective function, the information system, and the structure of decision making, moving on to a discussion of the types of decentralized decision making that could involve teachers in innovative or advanced EI in the public schools.

The economic, political, and social structure within which the public schools operate differs from the structure governing the private sector in important ways that affect the process of decentralizing decision making. Since market exchange does not provide a connection between demand for the product and cost of production in public education, output and unit costs cannot be used to evaluate the impact of changing inputs, including the employment system. As scholars of education are acutely aware, educational reforms are hard to evaluate on a large scale because the objective of "educated people" is hard to define and measure. Proxy measures (such as dropout rates, college-bound rates, absentee rates, and standardized test scores) are less than satisfactory because we do not know the relationship between these proxies and the broader goal. If these factors were defined as subgoals of the educational process, however, then they could be used to measure changes in inputs. Until measures of output can be designated, rational evaluation remains impossible.

Once we have agreed on a way to measure outputs, we must know how decentralized decisions will affect outputs. Here, the schools differ from the private sector in that the relationship between inputs and outputs is even less well established. The production process in education is vastly more complicated than in the private sector, because of the large number of intervening social, political, and economic variables that are outside the control of schools. Although researchers may assume the existence of a stable production function in manufacturing, in order to predict the impact of changes in inputs on outputs, such an assumption cannot be made in education with any confidence, since variations in the intervening variables will cause the assumed function to be in flux. We are left with the unsatisfactory prospect of evaluating the impact of EI by evaluating the decision-making process (for example, number of meetings or number of suggestions made) or the decisions themselves (for example, actual suggestions made). The former type of evaluation can offer incentives for wasteful meetings or useless suggestions; the latter type can easily collapse into a simple comparison of teachers' decisions with decisions that would have been made centrally by principals or superintendents, and such a comparison negates any potential gain from EI.

The involvement and treatment of production workers in the Japanese system has been characterized as the white-collarization of blue-collar workers. By contrast, the centralization of decision making has resulted in the blue-collarization of white-collar work in many occupations and industries, including education. Normally, we would expect professional workers to be involved in decision making, to have responsibility for their decisions, and to have performance standards and a pay system that reward experience and skill. The movement to increase EI in decision making is partially a response to the earlier centralization of decision making throughout the economy, and as such it allows us to experiment with forms of organization that may be more efficient. Increasing the decision making of teachers, however, is only one aspect of their employment system, which should be an integrated system that includes standards, accountability for decisions, and pay dependent on skills and experience. We must be cautious about applying any generalizations for nonprofessional workers in the private sector to teachers, since education differs in important ways from the private sector. Teachers are professionals who provide a public good within a politicized process, and so the agency costs and the monitoring problems are more complicated than in the private sector. Although the potential of advanced EI is greater for these professionals than for production workers, the difficulties of managing EI are much greater because of the difficulties of defining and measuring the objective goal in education. The agency costs are magnified by the provision of employment security in an employment system that does not relate workers' performance to the organization's long-run performance.

Security also functions differently in the schools and in private industry. Exchanging employment security for innovative EI in the private sector increases employees' stake in the company, since the promise of security and the ability to raise wages depend on the company's long-run performance. A school's costs and revenues are not affected by performance in the short or long run, however, and so security commitments do not increase the teachers' stake in the school. Budgets are formed in an unreliable political process and a changing economic environment. Teachers find that budgets can be lowered unexpectedly, with the result being a decline in the quantity and quality of education and in the quality of teachers' working conditions. Demand is formed primarily by demographics.

In this situation, where job security is granted and budgets are unrelated to long-run performance, we must ask how to provide motivation. The fate of the schools should not be tied to teachers' performance, but the pay of teachers (including pay for skills and experience, job assignments, and tasks undertaken) should be partially related to their performance.

This raises the question of what types of additional EI could be used in the schools to lower transaction costs more than monitoring or agency costs would be raised. Innovative EI at the site level requires a budget to pay for meeting time, training for communication and problem-solving skills, and the costs associated with the implementation of improvements. Over time, these costs should be offset by output (quality and quantity) improvements and by unit-cost reductions (or innovative EI is not efficient). As already mentioned, however, these costs and improvements may be impossible to measure accurately, and so perhaps the costs and returns of EI programs cannot be quantified.

Teachers know a vast amount about their students and classroom dynamics. This type of information cannot be economically transmitted and used in a centralized fashion. Teachers may or may not know as much about subject matter as the centralized authorities, however. For this reason, decision making has tended to be divided in that teachers make decisions about individual students and classroom dynamics, and districts make decisions about the curriculum. This approach precludes the possibility of using teachers' knowledge of subject matter and introduces the problem of monitoring teachers to ensure that subject matter is well taught. Decentralization that increases teachers' control over the curriculum addresses the first problem but worsens the second. Less ambitious types of EI, such as training programs for staff development, use teachers' knowledge in an efficient way without incurring monitoring costs. Perhaps for this reason, EI experiments have successfully focused on such topics as teacher development.

Teachers are already engaging in traditional EI activities (see column PS of Table 8.1). By the nature of their jobs, they are also already engaging in nonroutine problem solving, and they monitor the quality of their work because external monitoring is too difficult. Many California districts have been implementing innovative and advanced EI activities at the site level. Besides transforming the union-management relationship into a cooperative one at the district level, districts have experimented with programs to decentralize decision making so that principals have more decision-making power and accordingly can involve their teachers in the decision-making process. The types of decisions usually made are those that would be categorized as suggesting improvements or as design and assignment of work. Although there are discussions about how to monitor the quality of work, peer review has been limited to new teachers.

As Smith and O'Day (1991) argue, effective site-level restructuring (that is, innovative EI) must have a well-defined structure within which to function.[7] This is equivalent to having a well-designed production system in the private sector. Smith and O'Day believe that the state must provide the structure with an instructional guidance system, including a curriculum framework, student achievement goals, professional development of teachers, and student assessment.

In the current budget crisis, some California districts have used EI in the budget-cutting process. Several districts have reported that EI activities resulted in creative solutions, helping to minimize the impact of cuts. The use of EI appears to have increased teachers' willingness to take on larger burdens as budgets are cut. Although the use of teachers' knowledge to find creative solutions is valuable, the use of EI to impose additional burdens must be carefully evaluated in a labor market where some policy makers would like to increase the supply of highly qualified candidates. These increased burdens may not be sustainable for the affected teachers in the short run or for the labor market for teachers in the long run. In either case, the public, which pays for education, may be misled about the true impact of budget cuts on the quantity and quality of education being provided.

In summary, the impact of decentralized decision making on the performance of an organization may be viewed with cautious optimism. Nevertheless, decentralization as a sole strategy in education should not be expected to have any direct impact on learning, although it may have a direct impact on the working conditions of teachers.

Perhaps the most important lesson we have learned from the private sector is that EI is a complement to, not a substitute for, well-designed products and a well-functioning production system. EI cannot solve deeply rooted problems (inoperative communication systems, poorly designed products, defective or broken equipment). EI cannot solve the problems caused by poor macroeconomic performance. Decentralization of decision making appears to work effectively when it is part of an organization that is already functioning well. Innovative EI then allows marginal improvements to the overall system. Over time, the accumulation of many small decisions add up to a potentially large payoff for innovative EI.

A growing economy is important in supporting high-performing workplaces and schools. Without sufficient demand, companies are not able to honor employment security commitments, and workers are not motivated to make improvements in productivity. Without the promise of a job that uses a student's education, the student is not motivated to learn. Literacy, which includes mathematics, language, and analytical skils, prepares students to be trained on the job and to become productive workers who can increase their skills over a lifetime. For employers to hire and train new entrants and provide them with opportunities to improve their skills and be promoted, however, growing demand is required. Improvement in the education provided by high schools will not by itself strengthen the weak labor market or raise the returns on high school graduates' investment in schooling (Cutler and Katz, 1991).

Innovative EI can have a powerful impact, over time, on a well-functioning school, which includes cooperative industrial relations at the district and site levels, adequate and well-maintained physical facilities, adequate books and supplies, well-trained teachers, and healthy and eager students with grade-level skills. Innovative EI cannot be expected to overcome serious shortcomings. Once schools are at a functional baseline, however, innovative EI can be a powerful tool for making continual improvements and maintaining high performance.

## Notes

1. Brown, Reich, and Stern (1992) argue that EI must be analyzed as part of the broader employment system and that its success depends on the concerned training and security programs.
2. Some important court cases concerning the legal right, under the Fair Labor Standards Act, of nonexempt employees to make decisions that were previously made by exempt managers are pending final adjudication. Another legal issue concerns the possible use of teams or quality circles as (illegal) "company unions." This chapter does not address the legality of EI activities.
3. The theories of Merton, Sleznick, and Gouldner are discussed in March and Simon (1958).
4. The course includes material from Barnes (1968), as well as material on communications and problem solving. Members learn how to fill out work-standardization forms.
5. Seven out of ten team members are in the plant, and plant participation rate is below the participation rate in other departments (40 percent versus 50 to 55 percent in engineering,

human resources, and quality control, or 83 percent in production control for January through May 1988). Within the plant, the participation rate varied by department, from 37 percent to 82 percent.

6. These conclusions cannot be made concerning advanced EI, since these activities were seldom observed. Innovative EI is a type of decentralization that is an extension of multidivisional structure in which operating decisions are delegated to divisional managers and strategic decisions are made centrally.
7. Benson (1991) and others would emphasize that college-bound and non-college-bound students should be taught different materials in a different manner. Students planning to enter the labor market after high school would be better prepared by high schools that integrated academic and vocational learning, used cooperative (student team) learning and teacher collaboration, and created a school connection with a company (or companies).

## References

Anandalingam, G., Chatterjee, K., and Gangolly, J. S. "Information, Incentives, and Decentralized Decision-Making in a Bayesian Framework." *Journal of the Operational Research Society,* 1987, *38*(6), 499–508.

Arrow, K. J. "Control in Large Organizations." *Management Science,* 1964, *10*(3), 397–408.

Barnes, R. M. *Motion and Time Study.* (6th ed.) New York: Wiley, 1968.

Benson, C. S. *Current State of Occupational and Technical Training: The Need for Integration and High-Quality Programs.* Berkeley: National Center for Research in Vocational Education, University of California, 1991.

Brown, C., Reich, M., and Stern, D. "Becoming a High-Performance Organization: The Role of Security, Employee Involvement, and Training." Unpublished paper, 1992.

Clarke, F. H., and Barrough, M. N. "Optimal Employment Contracts in a Principal-Agent Relationship." *Journal of Economic Behavior and Organization,* 1983, *4,* 69–90.

Commission on the Skills of the American Workforce. *America's Choice: High Skills or Low Wages.* Rochester, N.Y.: National Center on Education and the Economy, 1990.

Cutler, D. M., and Katz, L. F. "Macroeconomic Performance and the Disadvantaged." *Brookings Papers on Economic Activity,* 1991, *2,* 1–74.

De Groot, H. "Decentralization Decisions in Bureaucracies as a Principal-Agent Problem." *Journal of Public Economics,* 1988, *36,* 323–337.

Fisher, R., and Brown, S. *Getting Together.* Boston: Houghton Mifflin, 1988.

Hashimoto, M. *The Japanese Labor Market.* Washington, D.C.: Upjohn, 1990.

Inkeles, A. "The International Evaluation of Educational Achievement: A Review of International Studies in Evaluation." *Proceedings of the National Academy of Education,* 1977, *4,* 139–200.

Koike, K. *Understanding Industrial Relations in Japan.* New York: Macmillan, 1988.

Koike, K., and Inoki, T. *Skill Formation in Japan and Southeast Asia.* Tokyo: University of Tokyo Press, 1990.

Lazear, E. "Labor Economics and the Psychology of Organizations." *Journal of Economic Perspectives,* 1991, *5,* 89–110.

March, J. G., and Simon, H. A. *Organizations.* New York: Wiley, 1958.

Organisation for Economic Co-operation and Development. *Labor Flexibility and Work Organization: Japan, 1990.* Paris: Organisation for Economic Co-operation and Development, 1990.

Rothman, R. "Foreigners Outpace American Students in Science." *Education Week,* Feb. 28, 1987, p. 1.

Smith, M. S., and O'Day, J. "Systemic School Reform." In S. Fuhrman and B. Malen (eds.), *The Politics of Curriculum and Testing.* New York: Falmer Press, 1991.

Walberg, H. J. "Science Literacy and Economic Productivity in International Perspective." *Daedalus,* 1983, *112,* 1–28.

Williamson, O. *The Economic Institution of Capitalism.* New York: Free Press, 1985.

# 9

# Epilogue: Reframing the Debate

Just about everyone, from educational reformers to politicians to the American public, has a fatal attraction to changing the governance of America's schools—despite the complete absence of evidence that governance reforms in and of themselves affect learning. In the late 1980s and early 1990s, the fatal attraction has reappeared. Schools are "in trouble"—or, rather, America is "in trouble"—and schools are allegedly a big part of the problem. School governance must be changed, it is argued, this time through school restructuring, decentralization, and even decentralization to the point of privatizing school management.

In these pages, we have grappled with the political and educational realities of the proposed reforms. We have asked whether decentralization is likely to improve American education and whether the reforms will produce the results promised by the reformers.

Our answer is measured. Many of us would like to believe that decentralization will help produce better education for America's children. As democrats, we find the concepts of local control and locally controlled management embedded in our ideals. We have observed that schools well run by principals and teachers with clear objectives do innovate educationally and do produce much better results. We have also observed the stultifying impact of bureaucracies on teachers, parents, and children. In theory, at least, we think that decentralization reforms could have a positive impact on learning.

Nevertheless, the chapters in this volume are generally skeptical. Education is a complex enterprise, and the current reform proposals are far more politically than educationally driven. Because of politics, the proposed governance reforms are highly contradictory, as both Weiler and Lewis make clear. At one extreme, some reformers push for choice and privatization, on the premise that decentralized management, unleashed in a free-market setting, can make schools significantly more efficient in producing achievement. At the other extreme, reformers want centrally controlled national examinations to make sure that teachers achieve centrally determined educational norms.

Tyack reminds us that educational change is "steady work" and that a key to improving schooling is to start with the classroom and attend to the teachers who do that steady work. The main point is that for any reform to improve instruction, it must ultimately be focused on instruction and must affect instruction.

The question is whether decentralization reforms can improve instruction and, if so, under what circumstances. When we met as a group, the first difficulty we encountered in responding to this question was to settle on what we meant by the term *decentralization.* In his chapter, Elmore is mainly concerned with the community control movement at the local level and with what decentralization means for instruction when the community and the teachers are in conflict. Hannaway and Brown focus on decentralization of management. Winkler and Weiler refer primarily to financial and managerial decentralization and Tyack to management decentralization and community control, all in the context of a wider view of educational reform. Carnoy and Lewis address the issue of decentralization as privatization—placing both the financing and the management of education in the private market, rather than in the domain of public choice. Lewis also poses the issue of community control, in ideological opposition to privatization.

Our group discussion concluded with the idea that both community control of education and financial decentralization can have indirect impacts on instruction by increasing the connection between clients (pupils and their families) and producers (teachers and administrators). Yet there is little evidence that such impacts are significant or positive, and most of the recent privatization discussion exaggerates any evidence that does exist. That clients' demands on school producers are apparently linked so loosely to pupils' educational performance is not good news, either for community control advocates or for free marketeers. The loose link does confirm that it takes more than ideologically based conceptions of how education should work to produce better instruction.

Potentially the most promising type of decentralization for improved instruction appears to be organizational, and this is indeed the focus of some of the current reform debate. But even here, we conclude, much care is needed in jumping to hopeful conclusions. A high degree of discretion in delivering instruction on the part of schools or school district personnel can be a positive force for instructional improvement, provided that local personnel and administrators have a clear picture of the instructional objectives and the skills to reach them. It also helps to have good relations with the community and to involve parents in the instructional project. Where these conditions have been met, schools and districts have seemed to do better.

This finding suggests that organizational decentralization has merits, and there is some empirical evidence for the potentially positive effects of teachers' and administrators' having control of instructional policy. Other elements must exist, however, for this potential to be realized. Indeed, it could be argued that unless organizational change springs organically from educational leadership at the local level, it will have only a minor impact on instruction and educational improvement.[1] And even if it does emerge locally, it may fail to improve educational outcomes if objectives are not clear and if the technical ability to implement the objectives is not there.

Such guarded conclusions should not be interpreted as cynicism or as a loss of faith in public education. To the contrary, one of these chapters' most interesting aspects is the implicit confidence that the authors show in public school leaders' ability to bring about meaningful educational improvement. From the point of view of these authors, the flight away from the "public" in public education reveals a misconception of America's educational problems and a misdirected belief in free-market solutions to social issues. The setting and realization of high performance standards in schools must ultimately come from public school personnel and government leaders as much as from the public itself. High standards and high performance are social choices with equally important implications for the amount of work that pupils take home and for what teachers organize for pupils in school.

Decentralizing decisions about what is to be learned and how learning is to take place in schools is only a small part of the larger issue of educational standards and performance. In that sense, the promise of decentralization must be couched in a much larger debate: What do Americans want their educational system to be, and how much time, energy, and money are they are willing to devote to it?

## Notes

1. Lockheed and Zhao (1992) question the effectiveness of centrally planned decentralization with evidence that shows that students in national government schools in the Philippines outperform students in local schools even after taking into account the socioeconomic status of the students.

## Reference

Lockheed, M., and Zhao, Q. "The Empty Opportunity: Local Control of Secondary Schools and Student Achievement in the Philippines." World Bank Working Paper PRE-WPS825, January 1992.

# Name Index

## W



## Y



## Z

# Subject Index